# HUMAN
# AGGRESSION

MAPPING SOCIAL PSYCHOLOGY SERIES
Series Editor: Tony Manstead

*Current titles:*

**Icek Ajzen:** Attitudes, Personality and Behavior
**Steve Duck:** Relating to Others
**Russell G. Geen:** Human Aggression
**Leslie A. Zebrowitz:** Social Perception

*Forthcoming titles:*

**Robert S. Baron, Norman Miller and Norbert L. Kerr:**
  Group Processes
**Marilyn B. Brewer and Norman Miller:** Intergroup Relations
**J. Richard Eiser:** Social Judgment
**Howard Giles:** Language in Social Interaction
**Richard Petty and John Cacioppo:** Attitude Change
**Dean G. Pruitt and Peter J. Carnevale:** Conflict and Bargaining
**Wolfgang Stroebe and Margaret Stroebe:** Social Psychology
  and Health
**John Turner:** Social Influence

# HUMAN AGGRESSION

**Russell G. Geen**

BROOKS/COLE PUBLISHING COMPANY
PACIFIC GROVE, CALIFORNIA

Open University Press
12 Cofferidge Close
Stony Stratford
Milton Keynes MK11 1BY

BF
575
· A3
G43
1990a

First Published 1990

This U.S. edition published by
Brooks/Cole Publishing Company,
A Division of Wadsworth, Inc.
511 Forest Lodge Road
Pacific Grove, CA 93950


**Library of Congress Cataloging-in-Publication Data**

Geen, Russell G., [date]
    Human aggression / Russell G. Geen.
        p.   cm. — (Mapping social psychology)
    Includes bibliographical references and indexes.
    ISBN 0-534-15630-4
    1.  Aggressiveness (Psychology)      I.  Title.      II.  Series.
BF575.A3   1990a                                          90-49644
155.5'32—dc20                                                CIP


Typeset by Rowland Phototypesetting Limited
Bury St Edmunds, Suffolk
Printed and bound in the United States by
Malloy Lithographing, Inc.
Ann Arbor, Michigan

Dedicated to the memory of my
Father and Mother

# CONTENTS

# FOREWORD

There has long been a need for a carefully tailored series of reasonably short and inexpensive books on major topics in social psychology, written primarily for students by authors who enjoy a reputation for the excellence of their research and their ability to communicate clearly and comprehensibly their knowledge of, and enthusiasm for, the discipline. My hope is that the *Mapping Social Psychology* series will meet that need.

The rationale for the series is twofold. First, conventional textbooks are too low-level and uninformative for use with senior undergraduates or graduate students. Books in this series address this problem partly by dealing with topics at book length, rather than chapter length, and partly by the excellence of the scholarship and the clarity of the writing. Each volume is written by an acknowledged authority on the topic in question, and offers the reader a concise and up-to-date overview of the principal concepts, theories, methods and findings relating to that topic. Although the intention has been to produce books that will be used by senior level undergraduates and graduate students, the fact that the books are written in a straightforward style should make them accessible to students who have relatively little previous experience of social psychology. At the same time, the books should be sufficiently informative to win the respect of researchers and instructors.

A second problem with traditional textbooks is that they are typically very dependent on research conducted in or examples drawn from North American society. This fosters the mistaken impression that social psychology is an exclusively North American discipline and can also be baffling for readers who are unfamiliar with North American culture. To combat this problem, authors of books in this series have been encouraged to adopt a broader perspective, giving examples or citing research from outside North America wherever this helps to make a point. Our aim has been to produce books for a world market, introducing readers to an international discipline.

This volume on *Human Aggression* by Russell Geen does a first-class job of introducing readers to a complex and often controversial research topic. Having conducted research on aggression over many years, Professor Geen is excellently placed to provide an overview of the social psychological and personality research on this topic. His focus is very much on the scientific research, rather than on methods for controlling or reducing aggression; his intention is to inform the reader about different theoretical approaches to the topic and to describe and evaluate classic and recent empirical studies. In reviewing this research the author provides a model of "affective" (or angry) aggression in which both individual and situational factors are regarded as determining aggressive behavior. The individual factors are those attributes a person brings to a situation, and can range from innately endowed temperament to more fleeting qualities of the individual that enhance his or her readiness to aggress. The situational factors are those which originate outside the individual, and which provoke him or her to behave aggressively; included under this heading are frustrations and provocations caused by other persons, environmental attributes such as heat, crowding and pollution, and the influence of the mass media.

Russell Geen is known for his care and professionalism in reviewing research findings, and his scholarship is evident throughout this volume. The book also benefits from a fluent and direct writing style, from a clear structure, and from comprehensive, balanced, and up-to-date coverage. As one reads the book, one has the sense of an author who is completely in command of his subject-matter, and who is therefore able to communicate it to his readers in a lucid way. It is a book that can be assigned for reading in the confident expectation that students at all levels should learn from it and enjoy it.

Tony Manstead
*Series Editor*

# PREFACE

Books about human aggression tend to be of two types. Some are organized around particular points of view. These books organize and explicate research findings from a perspective determined by the theory that underlies the approach. Other books are broader, more inclusive, and less theory-driven. They organize material along topical lines such as the development of aggression, the social and environmental determinants of aggressive behavior, and strategies for the control of aggression. This book falls somewhere between the two. As a volume in a series of short texts, it does not pretend to be exhaustive in its review. As a book intended for classroom use, it does not aspire to make any innovative contributions to theory. Instead, it reviews a body of literature that has accumulated in the study of one type of human aggression and it organizes the findings of the literature along the lines of a simple process model.

The book is characterized by two features that should be noted. First, it addresses only that type of human aggression which includes a strong affective and emotional component along with aggressive behavior. This variety of aggression — usually called affective — constitutes what most people tend mean by the word. Aggressive behavior that is not animated or accompanied by this strong affective component — usually called instrumental because it serves some other end or purpose — is important, but beyond the scope of this book. The reasons for this are twofold. In a short book the line must be drawn somewhere, and we simply know a great deal more about affective aggression than we do about the instrumental kind.

Second, the book is organized in terms of a simple model of the process of aggression. Affective aggression is defined as the joint product of one or more background variables and some eliciting condition in the immediate situation. Background variables are what predispose the person to aggress. They make aggression a possibility, provided that the required situational elicitors are present. They may be thought of as necessary, but not sufficient, conditions for aggression. They are, moreover, of two types. Some describe long-standing characteristics of the person which are more or less always present, such as genetic inheritance, biological make-up, sex, and personality. Others are momentary and determined by present conditions, such as stressors in the environment, stimulation from the mass media, and expectations and demands from the social environment.

Immediate elicitors of aggression are such provocations as frustration, attack, harassment, and other aversive stimuli arising in a context of interpersonal conflict. It is assumed that these elicitors of aggression either do or do not elicit aggression as a function of the degree to which background conditions are present, and that, furthermore, the background variables influence the intensity of aggression that does occur. Finally, the model provides for several intervening states that mediate the effects of both background and eliciting conditions. These are states having to do with cognitive processes, emotions, and affect.

Examination of research and theory on human aggression from the standpoint of this simple model reveals that most of the attention devoted to the problem has been on background conditions and antecedents of aggression. Four of the seven chapters to follow (Chapters 1, 3, 4, and 6) deal mainly with predisposing factors in human aggression. One chapter (Chapter 2) summarizes the eliciting conditions. Chapters 5 and 7 are addressed for the most part to intervening variables.

As I have indicated, this book was written for classroom use. It is addressed primarily to undergraduate students who have had at least an introductory course in psychology and are therefore acquainted with the fundamentals of the field. At the undergraduate level it could serve as the basic textbook for a course. Because of the general orientation of the book to basic research on aggression, it may also be useful for graduate students who desire an overview of that research. At the graduate level it will probably best serve the function of a primer used in connection with primary source materials. Students using the book as either a textbook or as a secondary sourcebook may find useful the annotated references listed as suggestions for further reading at the end of each chapter. It should also be noted that, although the major focus of the book is on a social psychological approach to human aggression, it also contains material of relevance for the areas of physiological, developmental, and personality psychology.

No attempt is made in this book to recommend strategies for the control or elimination of aggression. The book is intended only for purposes of introducing the reader to what is known about human aggression at the present time from research that has been conducted on the problem. Thus, there is extensive discussion of the results of studies but no chapter on public policy. My intention is to inform the reader. It is hoped that any decisions that are eventually made with respect to the problem of human aggression, and what can be done about it, will be based on the information that research has given us.

Russell G. Geen
Columbia, Missouri
USA

# 1 / APPROACHES TO THE STUDY OF AGGRESSION

Few people would deny that "aggression" is commonplace in contemporary society. For some, such as those living in South Africa, Northern Ireland, Central America, and the Middle East, aggression and violence are experienced daily and in intensely personal ways. For others the phenomenon is known, for the most part, in only indirect ways, such as through the mass media of communication. However, even those fortunate enough to have been spared the direct experience of lethal violence may occasionally encounter something perceived to be aggression in a less intense form, such as a verbal insult, rough physical contact, or hostile rejection. Aggression, whether harmful to life and limb or merely painful to the ego, seems to be a real and important part of the human condition. The broad and inclusive way in which the word has been used, however, makes the systematic study of aggression difficult. To put the matter simply: does it make sense to use the same word to refer to such dissimilar events as a gangland murder, the bombing of a restaurant, a fight at a football game, and a cutting remark at a cocktail party? Even if the term is used only in casual everyday speech, its usefulness is obviously limited by the numerous motives and forms of expression that characterize "aggressive" behavior. When we attempt to use that same word in scientific discourse, the problem becomes even more serious. Science depends on precision and clarity of definitions. From that standpoint, we might do well to forget about a unitary concept such as "aggression" and to search instead for functional relationships between specific acts and their equally specific causes. The various behaviors now subsumed by the word "aggression" could undoubtedly be studied as individual phenomena defined in terms of their own antecedent conditions, intervening processes, and out-comes. Nevertheless, such studies would obscure the possibility that the aggressive behaviors noted above, however different they may seem, possess some commonalities. If we are to make any sense of the whole idea of aggression, it is these commonalities that we must seek. We must therefore begin by defining our term.

## Definition of aggression

### Problems of definition

Seeking a definition of aggression raises some problems. One might think that people would be in substantial agreement on defining something so important and pervasive, but such is not the case. The term "aggression" is applied to a wide array of behaviors that often appear to be highly related, but that on closer analysis prove to be quite different from each other. Perhaps most people, including psychologists, would agree in general with the definition of aggression given by Buss (1961, p. 1): that aggression is "a response that delivers noxious stimuli to another organism". Certainly what we ordinarily call aggression does involve noxious stimulation of one person by another, in the form of a bullet in the body, a shattering bomb blast, a physical blow, or a more subtle stimulus such as an insult or verbal harangue. The problems of definition do not arise until we turn to definitions more elaborate than a basic behavioral one. Aggressive behavior is not as simple or unambiguous as a purely behavioral definition would indicate. Other elements must be added, and these elements create certain complexities.

### Intent to harm

One construct that most people would probably consider necessary in aggression is *intent* to harm another person. The notion of intentionality is explicit in the definition of aggression given by one influential group of psychologists: "Aggression is . . . an act whose goal-response is injury to an organism . . ." (Dollard *et al.* 1939, p. 11). Use of the term "goal-response" implies motivation and striving, so that aggression is regarded as the end result of a moti-vated series of acts. Dollard *et al.* (1939, p. 11) conclude, therefore, that the infliction of noxious stimuli must be intentional: "One person may injure another by sheer accident. Such acts are not aggression, because they are not goal-responses". The idea of intent has been considered unnecessary by some who follow a behavioral approach to aggression on the grounds that it is a mentalistic concept that defies rigorous analysis (e.g., Buss 1961). In theorizing about aggression, however, a concept of intent seems unavoidable despite the problems it raises. For example, a team of firefighters attempting to rescue a man who has been trapped in a burning building may cause the person pain, but they do it in order to spare him even greater suffering or even death. Their intentions are not to harm the man but to save him, and thus their behavior would not be labeled as aggression by most observers.

Intent to harm is, of course, not something that can be directly observed. It must be inferred from behavior, and such inferences are not always easily made. Nevertheless, some such inference must be drawn in labeling an observed act as one of aggression.

## Aggression and expectancy

Another element that should form part of a definition of most kinds of aggression is the expectation that a behavior will result in harm to the victim. This idea is consistent with that of intent: an attacker must judge that there is greater than zero probability that his or her attack will reach its target (Kaufmann 1970). For example, a boxer must think that he has some chance of landing a blow before he unleashes it, and a soldier firing his automatic weapon into the jungle must think that his bullets may hit an enemy. If either of these persons thinks that his behavior is futile and that there is no chance of delivering the intended aversive stimulus, we would not call his behavior aggressive. Expectancy is an intervening inferred variable that, like intent, allows a more detailed definition of at least most forms of aggression.

## A working definition of aggression

A definition of aggression that provides at least a working basis for further discussion can therefore be summarized in three points:

1 Aggression consists of the delivery of noxious stimuli by one organism to another.

2  The noxious stimuli are delivered with the intent to harm the victim.

3  The aggressor expects that the noxious stimuli will have their intended effect.

It is admitted that this definition can be attacked on several points and that the reader can undoubtedly, with a little thought, come up with examples of aggression that do not fit it. All of this merely underscores the difficulty of formulating a unitary definition. Nor does this simple definition begin to deal with many of the variables involved in aggression. It does not, for example, mention the possible role played by anger. It does not include consideration of complex cognitive judgments that may precede a decision to aggress. It does not consider the possible role of aggression in influencing the behavior of others or in providing a possible "safety valve" for high levels of emotional arousal. These, and many other such problems, all impinge upon a basic definition of aggression, yet they go beyond a simple one. They in fact comprise the many variables involved in aggressive behavior. As such, they constitute the matters discussed in the chapters of this book which are to follow. For now, however, we are seeking only to formulate a simple working definition. Having done that, we may then go on to study the behavior and to discover some of the antecedent conditions that produce it. We should bear in mind that the "aggression" studied by one researcher may not be the same as the "aggression" studied by another, and that each person is seeking the causes of the particular behavior that she or he is observing.

**Affective and instrumental aggression**

The examples given above exemplify what appear to be several different kinds of aggressive behavior inasmuch as they reveal varying antecedents and motives. It is customary in the study of aggression to identify such varieties of aggression on the basis of antecedents and intervening processes. Hence we discriminate among such behaviors as "angry aggression", "instrumental aggression", and "learned", "imitative", or "biogenic" aggression because these behaviors differ from each other in important ways with respect to what motivates them. However, in the interests of economy we should always strive to reduce the number of "types" of aggression to as few as possible, provided that some useful integrative model can be created. It is proposed here that the various types of aggression that are usually discussed can be reduced to two which subsume the others. These two will be labeled *affective* and *instrumental* aggression.

## Affective aggression

Aggression is often accompanied by strong negative emotional states. The emotion that we call "anger" is usually aroused by some provocation. Anger is most often thought of as an intervening condition which instigates, and then guides, aggressive behavior. This type of aggression is therefore called affective or angry aggression and its main goal is injury or harm to the provocateur (Feshbach 1964). It is accompanied by distinctive patterns of activity in the central and autonomic nervous systems, including activation of the hypothalamus, increased blood flow to the musculature, heightened blood pressure and pulse rate, pupillary dilation, and decreased flow of blood to the viscera (Johansson 1981).

It is important to note, however, that the emotional state of anger may be involved in affective aggression *without necessarily causing that aggression*. This idea may be difficult to grasp because in everyday thinking we tend to assume that anger always plays such a causal role in aggression. When I am provoked I become angry and I aggress; the close juxtaposition of the emotion and the action encourages the assumption of a cause–effect relationship. However, Berkowitz (1983) has argued that aggression which shows many of the hallmarks of affective violence need not be motivated by anger or strong emotion. To some extent aggressive behaviors may be part of larger associative networks in which cognitions, emotions, and dispositions to act aggressively may be set off by other elements with which they have been closely associated (cf. Bower 1981). Such aggression may be accompanied by strong anger without being caused by the anger. The anger may simply be a process that parallels the enactment of aggressive behaviors that are elicited by other stimuli. This matter is discussed further in Chapter 5.

## Instrumental aggression

Behavior need not have a strong emotional basis to be aggressive, however, nor does it have to be associated with aggressive cognitions or affective states. People often attack others with intent to harm without necessarily feeling any malice toward the victim. The primary goal of such aggression is not injury or harm to the victim; the aggression is simply a means to some other desired end. One such end is self-defense. Most courts of law recognize self-protection as a valid defense for acts of violence. Aggression that occurs in military contexts is also often instrumental to some larger end such as winning a war or defending territory. Another use of aggression that is instrumental is the attempt to establish social and coercive power over others (cf. Tedeschi 1983) through aggressive means. Finally, in one of the most widely-cited research studies of recent times, Milgram (1963) showed that people were capable of committing gross acts of violence against another human being simply in obedience to commands from a person with authority.

The chapters that follow will not be concerned with instrumental aggression. This emphasis is in no way intended to imply that instrumental aggression is unimportant. However, instrumental aggression has not been studied in nearly the same depth as has affective aggression. For example, there is no large body of literature on the variables involved when one person hurts another for money, nor do we have extensive data on the mediators of self-defense. On the other hand, we do have a great deal of information on affective aggression and the various processes that contribute to it.

## The two factors in affective aggression

In order to organize this broad body of findings a model of affective aggression will be presented. In this model a two-factor approach will be taken. As part of this approach, it is proposed that the concept of affective aggression subsumes such processes as learning, individual differences in genetics and temperament, and aggression that is a reaction to a broad range of situational conditions. In this section the rudiments of the approach are introduced. Elaboration of the approach into a more comprehensive model is carried out in Chapter 2.

The basic premise of the approach taken here is that aggression is the result of two variables. One is a *state of the person* in which the person is capable of aggressing, is ready to aggress, and has aggressive responses available. The other is a *situation* that elicits the actual aggressive behavior. The proposed state of the person can be thought of as a background condition that makes aggression possible, given the right situation. This state may be the result, for example, of past learning, or of a biologically inherited aggressive temperament, or of temporary reactions to certain stimuli that elicit readiness to aggress. Anything that creates in the person a potential for aggression is to be counted among these so-called "background" or "setting" variables. The situations that elicit aggression from a person who is in a state of readiness include a wide range of aversive conditions or provocations that cause the person to feel stressed and aroused. When one of these situations occurs for a person who is potentially aggressive, aggression is elicited.

This two-process approach is, admittedly, only a preliminary statement about affective aggression. It is, furthermore, simple to the point of triviality. However, we gain something by using such a simple framework in approaching the subject of aggression. One sometimes hears the argument that because aggression is part of "human nature" there is little that we can do about it. Hence, the argument goes, society should forget social reform and other ameliorative measures that are addressed, among other things, to the control and reduction of violence. We do not deny a basis in human nature for aggression, i.e., that the potential for aggression is present in the physical constitution of human beings. However, by defining aggression as a reaction to situations, we can have some reason for hope that proper social measures may at least limit, if not remove altogether, the likelihood of violence. In addition, we can seek to create social conditions that elicit behaviors that are incompatible with aggression.

On the other hand, one sometimes hears that all aggression is the result of bad social conditions, cultural deprivations, unhappy childhood experiences, and so on. Such arguments tend to remove all responsibility for violence from the perpetrators and to lay the blame entirely on others. Such arguments do not explain why many, if not most, people who experience the various conditions thought to be the sole causes of violence do not in fact manifest much aggression in their lives. We would argue that such people, though instigated to aggress as much as others, do not possess the background characteristics of aggressors. If this is the case, then society's task is to discover the conditions under which such relatively unaggressive tendencies are fostered and to seek to implement them more widely.

## Origins and development of aggression

Considerable controversy exists over the origins of aggression in humans. In this area of study we see repeated the old issue of nature versus nurture in psychology, with many of the old questions raised again. Is human behavior the result of genetically inherited biological drives and impulses or is it acquired through experience, learning, and conditioning? Is aggression a "normal" part of human behavior carried over from man's primate ancestors or is it an aberration of human nature that arises from social and environmental conditions? Does belief in a biological basis for aggression preclude attempts at social control or even elimination of human violence? Are conflict and war inevitable? Evidence can be adduced for both the biological and the behavioristic explanations of aggression. Undoubtedly much human aggressive behavior is learned. Behavioral biologists do not deny this. However, neither is there any denying that humans share with lower animals certain dispositions to aggress which are transmitted genetically. In the following two sections we will review some of the evidence that bears on both of these viewpoints.

*Evidence from genetic studies*

*Hereditary aggressiveness*
The possibility that some human aggression may be attributable to hereditary factors has been suggested by a growing number of investigators in recent years. At one time, especially in the United States when behaviorism was dominant, few psychologists believed that human behavior had hereditary origins. At that time it was practically a truism that all behavior is learned. Nowadays this premise is not as widely held, and some students of aggression believe that human aggressiveness may be founded, at least in part, on innate mechanisms. Evidence for such effects in lower animals is unquestioned. For example, Lagerspetz (1979) has shown that mice can be selectively bred for aggressiveness, with inherited aggressive tendencies emerging as early as the second generation. The question we must ask is whether similar evidence has been found for human beings.

One obvious problem that arises in the study of genetic bases of human behavior is methodological. Human reproduction cannot be controlled through selective breeding in the same way as that of lower animals. However, one method of study that can be used among humans involves comparisons between pairs of twins. Twin studies analyze similarities between members of identical (monozygotic) and non-identical (dizygotic) twin pairs. The method rests on the fact that, whereas dizygotic twins share a common environment but are not identical in genetic make-up, monozygotic twins share a common environment and are also identical in heredity. If a trait has some hereditary basis, therefore, it should be shared by monozygotic twins to a greater extent than by dizygotic pairs. Correlations between pairs of twins of each type are compared, and evidence of higher correlations among monozygotics is taken as evidence for some heritability associated with the trait.

In one such investigation, Rushton *et al.* (1986) have presented evidence that aggressiveness is partially hereditary in humans. More than 500 pairs of monozygotic and dizygotic twins responded to questionnaires that assessed five personality variables: altruism, empathy, nurturance, assertiveness, and aggressiveness. Rushton *et al.* reported higher correlations for monozygotic twins in the case of each personality variable, as Table 1.1 shows. Additional analyses indicated that approximately 50 per cent of the variance for each personality variable was due to hereditary causes. These data therefore indicate a role for genetic determination in the case of several traits related to aggression in either a positive (aggressiveness and assertiveness) or a negative (altruism, empathy, nurturance) way.

### The XYY karyotype

In recent years some attention has been paid to certain anomalies in human behavior that are associated with deficiencies or excesses in chromosomal material. One behavior that biologists have sought to link to genetics in this way is aggression in males. The normal male possesses 46 chromosomes arranged in 23 pairs, but some men have been found to have an extra Y chromosome and are therefore

*Table 1.1*    Intraclass correlations for personality variables

| Scale | Monozygotic twins | Dizygotic twins |
|---|---|---|
| Altruism | .53 | .25 |
| Empathy | .54 | .20 |
| Nurturance | .49 | .14 |
| Aggressiveness | .40 | .04 |
| Assertiveness | .52 | .20 |

*Source:* Rushton *et al.* (1986)

referred to as XYYs. Evidence of a possible role of this anomaly in aggression comes from several studies. Some data show that presence of the extra Y chromosome is associated with anti-social aggressive behavior even among males raised in family environments that manifest no more than average aggressiveness (Price and Whatmore 1967). In addition, the ratio of XYY males to normals in prisons and other security institutions ranges roughly from 1:35 to 1:100, whereas the ratio of XYYs to normals in the population at large has been estimated to be approximately 1:550 (Court-Brown 1968; Shah 1970). Findings such as these have led some investigators to conclude that XYY males have defects in the nervous system that are genetically determined (e.g., Jacobs *et al.* 1965).

The Y chromosome in the normal XY pair affects hormonal distribution, which in turn determines the masculine character of the sex organs and suppression of female characteristics. It is possible, therefore, that XYY males possess male sex hormones in greater than average amounts (Selmanoff and Ginsburg 1981). This could account for their aggressiveness as well as the unusual height that characterizes men of this genetic type (Daly 1969). On the other hand, the correlational nature of the data suggest the possible influence of other variables. For example, boys who are above average in height may find that aggression against smaller peers is frequently rewarded by success. Aggressive tendencies could be shaped through instrumental learning. We are not sure, therefore, of the reason for the correlation between the possession of the extra Y chromosome and unusual aggressiveness.

The notion that XYY males are more aggressive than normal males is based on studies in which aggressiveness has been inferred from evidence of criminal or anti-social behavior. Evidence linking the genetic type to more direct measures of aggressiveness is lacking. In one study addressed to this problem, Witkin *et al.* (1976) found that the XYY karyotype was related to both criminal behavior and low intelligence, but not to overall aggressiveness. Absence of findings that show a clear association between the XYY type and aggression, as conventionally defined, leaves the status of this concept in doubt.

*The physiology of aggression*

The role of the central nervous system in aggression among lower animals has been well documented. Numerous sites within the cerebral cortex and subcortical areas have been shown to be involved in such behaviors as predation, maternal aggression for protection of the young, fighting between males of the same species, and other manifestations of aggressive behavior. This body of data on animal aggression is the result of numerous experiments involving such techniques as lesioning and ablation of neural tissue and direct electrical stimulation of brain sites associated with aggression. Obviously, such techniques cannot be used systematically on humans. Our knowledge of the neural basis of human aggression is therefore based upon extrapolations from animal data and upon case studies of individuals who show both an unusual level of aggressiveness and some neurological anomaly or problem.

*A model of physiology of aggression*
Moyer (1976) has presented a scheme of physiological processes in aggression that applies to both humans and lower animals, and which subsumes a large amount of the evidence that we have on both. Moyer assumes that the word "aggression" refers to a number of related, but functionally different, behaviors. The main elements of the scheme are: (1) a number of innate systems of neural organization in the brain, with one such pattern for each kind of aggression; (2) activation of the innate systems by appropriate stimuli; and (3) a system for the generation of arousal which affects both the organism's reactivity to the aforesaid stimuli and the intensity of the aggression animated by the innate neural system. The general features of the scheme are shown in Table 1.2.

The precise neural substrate of each different kind of animal aggression (e.g., predatory, maternal, fear-induced) has been established through the methods, such as lesioning and direct electrical stimulation, described above. Although we may assume that human aggression also manifests itself in different ways (as noted earlier in the chapter), we have no idea exactly what neural process is involved in each. Nevertheless, it is helpful to assume that specific processes do underlie the varieties of human aggression. Specific stimulus situations elicit each type of aggression. In humans, for example, insults are likely to evoke angry aggression and promises of rewards for fighting are likely to generate aggression of the instrumental kind. The innate system for the given type of aggression is also linked to specific patterns of motor behavior by which the aggression is acted out. This gives each type of aggression its peculiar form. Finally, each of the innate neural organizations connects with another system in

*Table 1.2*   Some types of aggression

| Type | Stimulus | Biological process or mechanism | Form |
|---|---|---|---|
| Predatory | Natural prey | Lateral Hypothalamus Amygdala Hippocampus | Efficient Little affective display |
| Intermale | Male of species | Septal region Anterior Hypothalamus | Ritualized responses |
| Fear-induced | Threat | Amygdala Hypothalamus | Autonomic reactions Defensive behaviors |
| Maternal | Distress calls Threat to young | Pregnancy Parturition Lactation | Attempts to avoid conflict |
| Irritable | Frustration deprivation Pain | Hypothalamus reticular system | General, diffuse reaction Affective display |

*Source*: Moyer (1976)

the brain, the reticular activating system, in which general arousal is generated. Arousal enhances both responsiveness to the environment and intensity of responses. Thus the aroused person is both more attentive to stimuli that elicit aggression and more aggressive than is the less aroused person. Finally, the sensitivity of the innate neural pattern to stimuli is influenced by other systems in the body. Some of these systems increase sensitivity and others reduce it. Certain hormones, for example, tend to facilitate aggressiveness. On the other hand, emotional reactions such as euphoria and sadness arise from systems that have an inhibiting effect on aggressiveness.

*Brain mechanisms in aggression*
In Moyer's (1976) scheme, each of the various types of aggression in lower animals arises from activity in various centers in the brain.

Two such centers that appear to be critical for irritable aggression are the amygdala and the hippocampus. Both of these are part of that region of the brain called the limbic system, which is generally thought to be the part of the brain that controls emotion. Electrical stimulation of the amygdala of a cat creates a condition of readiness to react in the animal's sensori-motor system when certain other stimuli, such as a mouse, are also present (Flynn et al. 1971). Brain activity may therefore be associated with not only the intensity of aggression but also with its direction, by guiding perceptual and attentional processes. However, actual attacking and biting by the cat require also tactile stimulation of the region around the cat's mouth. When the trigeminal nerve, which connects the cat's whiskers to the brain, is severed, biting is eliminated in most cats, even during direct stimulation of the attack centers in the brain (Flynn et al. 1971). This suggests that stimulation from the environment (which innervates the oral region) interacts with ongoing neural activity inside the animal to determine aggressive behavior.

The exact nature of the amygdala's involvement in aggression is not simple, however. Moyer (1976) points out that while some of the amygdaloid nuclei do seem to create conditions for aggression, others seem to inhibit aggression. We must be careful, therefore, in drawing conclusions about the functions of brain structures as if they worked on an all-or-nothing basis. The same is true of the hippocampus. Although the general function of the intact hippocampus seems to be the inhibition of aggression, too little is known about the precise role of this organ in aggression to draw firm conclusions.

A well-known case of aggressive behavior coinciding with brain pathology is that of Charles Whitman, who, after murdering his mother, his wife, and a receptionist at the University of Texas administration building, took a rifle and several hundred rounds of ammunition to the building's tower and began shooting people at random. In 90 minutes he killed another 14 persons and wounded an additional 24. He was stopped only when police killed him. Analysis of letters and other notes written by Whitman reveal that he had been an introspective young man who was at pains to understand the violent emotions and motives that he experienced. He also suffered from severe headaches. An autopsy showed that Whitman had suffered from a malignant tumor in the temporal lobe of the cerebral cortex and that brain damage caused by the malignancy was extensive. We cannot conclude from this that the tumor caused the aggressive behavior. However, other cases in which aggressive behavior has been diminished through removal of brain tumors suggests that a cause-and-effect link may exist (Moyer 1976).

### The psychotic trigger reaction

Another investigation that suggests involvement of brain pathology in aggression has been reported by Pontius (1984), who based her conclusions on the intensive study of eight violent male patients. In each case a life history involving discontent and various psychological traumas was followed by the occurrence of some event associated with past negative experiences. In each case the event set off a "seizure-like" rage reaction that culminated in an outburst of violence. The event is therefore referred to as a *trigger* for the violent episode.

Pontius (1984) has hypothesized that the origins of the problem lie in an imbalance between the activity of the frontal lobe of the cortex and the limbic system, so that the cortex fails to exert normal cognitive controls over emotions (including rage and anger) arising in the limbic structures. At this point some event occurs to trigger the emotional response that the person is disposed to make. One reason why this may happen is that the person is especially likely to associate the triggering event with some event from the past that has been an occasion for rage. Why this heightened recall of past traumas occurs is not clear. It may arise from further brain dysfunctions involving the amygdala and the hippocampus.

Additional evidence suggests that aggressive behavior is associated with a combination of neural disorder and some event that precipitates an aggressive reaction. In a study by Lewis *et al.* (1985), nine men, all of whom had been arrested for murder, were evaluated on the basis of neuropsychiatric data that had been gathered several years before, when all of them had been adolescents. The data revealed that seven of the nine showed some major neurological impairment (e.g., epileptic symptoms, lapses of consciousness, or other seizure-like activity) and that the other two had suffered damage to the head in accidents. All nine had showed some signs of psychotic symptoms (e.g., paranoid thinking, hallucinations), and seven had been abused by their parents. All came from families with a history of psychotic disorder, and all nine had been extremely violent before they committed murder.

In these descriptions we can again observe that neurological disorder appears to serve as a background or setting condition for aggression, making the person more likely to aggress, given some threat or provocation, than a more normal person would be. Lewis *et al.* (1985, p. 1165) concluded:

> It seems that severe [central nervous system] dysfunction, coupled with a vulnerability to paranoid psychotic thinking, created a tendency for the nine homicidal subjects to act quickly and brutally when they felt threatened. Living within psychotic households, they were frequently the victims of and witnesses to psychotic parental rages, experiences that undoubtedly further exacerbated their tendencies toward the physical expression of violence.

*Body chemistry and aggression*

Neurochemical systems in the body may sensitize the person to various conditions for aggression and make such behavior more likely (Moyer, 1976). The sex hormones are especially implicated in this. Several studies have reported positive links between secretion of the sex hormone testosterone and some measures of aggressive and criminal behavior in men. Testosterone appears to be related to some indicators of aggression, but not others. Dabbs *et al.* (1987) found that testosterone level was not correlated with rated violence of prison inmates, but that it covaried closely with the violence of the crime for which the inmate had been sentenced. Olweus *et al.* (1980) have reported data indicating that testosterone level may be related primarily to a *disposition* to aggress, and that other stimuli must be present before the disposition is manifested in aggressive behavior. In a sample of adolescent Swedish boys, testosterone level was positively related to measures of both physical and verbal aggression. However, the correlations were of the greatest magnitude for questionnaire items that assessed aggressive responsiveness to provocation or threat. In addition, testosterone level was positively correlated with lack of tolerance for frustration.

Evidence bearing on the role of sex hormones in aggression among women is less clear cut than it is in the case of men. Some studies have reported increased irritability and hostility in women prior to menstruation, along with evidence that such feelings often generate aggressive behavior. Incarcerated women are more likely to get into trouble with other prisoners during menstruation (Dalton 1964). These symptoms may be related to a drop in progesterone level during menstruation, along with a rise in the ratio between estrogen and progesterone. Dalton (1977) has reported data indicating that administration of progesterone, to offset the normal decrease, alleviates the feelings of irritability and hostility and also decreases the likelihood of aggression. However, the findings of several other studies have shown no such treatment effect associated with administration of progesterone. In addition, the link between premenstrual mood changes and levels of progesterone is difficult to explain and is probably not a direct cause–effect relationship (see Bancroft and Backstrom 1985, for a review of this research).

Certain biochemical agents other than sex hormones are related to aggression. Low metabolism of the fatty acid serotonin in the brain has been found more among habitually violent persons than among normal persons (Brown and Goodwin 1984), and Virkkunen (1986) has reported a lower than normal level of blood sugar in a sample of violent and impulsive offenders. These findings exemplify the role played by biochemical processes in aggression. It should be emphasized once again, however, that these body chemicals may not in and of themselves be causes of aggression. They may, as Moyer (1976) has proposed, make the person more sensitive to external stimuli that elicit the aggressive reaction and also, possibly, exacerbate the intensity of the aggressive response.

*Human ethology*

Another biological approach to human aggression is that of human ethology. This approach emphasizes the membership of human beings in the animal kingdom and attempts to define at least some part of human behavior in terms of its primate origins. Ethology, or behavioral biology, grew out of the systematic study of animals in natural settings. It rests on several premises. Perhaps the most important of these is the idea that behavior is "pre-programmed" into members of a species to serve adaptive purposes. Aggression is one such behavior. Aggression has evolved as a natural element in the behavioral repertoire of some species because it facilitates survival and adaptation to the environment. Inter-male fighting may, for example, be purposive and adaptive because it assures an optimal spacing of animals within a given amount of territory (Eibl-Eibesfeldt 1977). Aggression also allows the formation of dominance structures and thereby serves to enhance natural selection through mating of the strongest members of the species.

*Features of aggression*

Aggression in animals is characterized by certain features. It is, first of all, founded on an innate *aggressive drive*, or need to aggress. Ethologists most commonly define this drive in terms of energy that accumulates in certain hypothetical centers within the nervous system. It has been compared to water confined to a closed system and building up in pressure over time (Lorenz 1966): as this *action-specific energy*, as it is called, builds up, the motivation to behave in the appropriate way (e.g., with aggression) becomes progressively stronger. This energy is manifested in behavior when some specific stimulus, called a *releaser*, is made available to the animal. An example of a releaser is the bright coloration (along with other body signs) presented to each other by male members of the species *Betta splendens*, or Siamese fighting fish. These stimuli elicit reflexive attack behavior in conspecific males. In addition, species behave with certain innate *expressive motor patterns*. In the case of aggression, members of species may react to releasers with head butting, clawing, biting, menacing gestures, or other such acts. Each species has its own innate response pattern.

Aggression in infra-human species has one other common characteristic: it seldom produces the death of the vanquished party. Animal aggression appears to possess an innate inhibition against killing. Once dominance has been established through fighting, the loser assumes a subordinate position to the dominant animal. This may involve baring the throat, or laying on the back in a helpless posture. At this point the dominant animal forgoes further attack and breaks off the combat. It may even make a nurturant or friendly approach to the subordinate animal at this point. The adaptive significance of this inhibition against killing is obvious.

The ethological analysis of aggression in animals is well established (see, for example, Brain and Benton 1981). Whether ethology can explain human aggression is a question that engenders considerable debate, however. Some observers reject the idea that aggression in humans has any basis in innate mechanisms (e.g., Montagu 1973), whereas others argue for a continuity in the behavior of humans and lower organisms (e.g., Lorenz, 1966). Opponents of the ethological approach insist that aggression in humans is the product of environmental demands and is acquired through the customary laws of learning. Proponents of the ethological viewpoint do not deny the importance of learning in human aggression, yet they insist that this does not rule out the operation of native mechanisms. Given the evolutionary history of the human species, it is difficult to believe that human violence is free of all innate determinants.

## Homology and analogy

We must admit, however, that claims for an ethological analysis of human aggression do not rest on as solid a data base as do those for animal ethology. We do not have, as yet, empirical evidence for innate aggression in humans derived from patient and systematic observation of naturally occurring behavior. What evidence we do have is to a large extent circumstantial. In order to evaluate this evidence we must understand two concepts from biology that are critical to the drawing of comparisons between humans and lower animals. The first of these is *homology*, a term referring to genetically-based resemblances between members of different species that can be traced to some common ancestor. For example, humans, apes, and monkeys have several common features that are homologous. The second is *analogy*, which refers to resemblances across unrelated species that are due to common evolutionary histories. Humans and rodents are not closely related homologously, yet they share certain physical features that are the result of common evolutionary pressures.

What we must seek are analogies and homologies as explanations for similarities in the behavior, including aggressive behavior, of humans and lower forms. We do have some data that enlighten us to some extent on the matter of behavioral homologies. Rajecki (1983) reviewed data from a wide array of studies of monkeys, apes, and humans, and was able, as a result, to compare similarities across a number of behaviors. For many of these behaviors (e.g., details of threatening facial expressions, establishment of dominant–subordinate behaviors, intensification of dominance–subordination under conditions of threat and stress) a high degree of similarity was shown across the three species. Evidence of behavioral analogies tends not to be as clear-cut, but is still suggestive. For example, humans show a tendency to claim a certain zone of personal space around themselves and to experience displeasure if this space is entered by another person (see Chapter 3 for a discussion of this). Perceptions of personal space may reveal a vestige of territoriality in human behavior which, in lower species, manifests itself in attack behavior aimed at establishing a more optimal spacing. Consider also the fear and rejection of strangers, or *xenophobia*, a phenomenon found in many species, including humans. It has been suggested that xenophobia may have evolved out of a need to be able to predict the behaviors of those within the society. Strangers, by being unknown and unpredictable, may represent a source of potential threat to the social order (Rajecki 1983). Xenophobia would therefore be the result of evolutionary demands and would be shared by all species that had evolved under roughly similar conditions.

## The problem of lethal violence

We are left with one final question. If human and animal aggression share some common bases in innate mechanisms, why is violence among humans so much more lethal than it is among lower animals? Recall that one feature of animal aggression is a general inhibition against killing. Certainly human aggression shows little such inhibition by comparison. In fact, human aggression in some forms kills not only the loser of the combat but large numbers of innocent bystanders as well. The reason for this may be that as humans have developed the use of weapons, the usual animal restraints on violence have become less effective. We may still possess the same aggressive drive that motivated our primate ancestors and which to this day activates the aggression of the great apes. Unlike them, however, we have firearms, explosives, chemical weapons, and thermonuclear bombs. Lack of inhibitions against killing in human violence need not, therefore, be taken as evidence against an innate and animal basis. The drive may be similar, with only the means of expression altered.

## Social learning and aggression

Psychologists who take a social-psychological approach to behavior usually tend to treat aggression as a set of acquired behaviors and to attach less emphasis to innate and biological determinants. Advocates of this approach apply to aggression the principles of social learning theory (e.g., Bandura 1973), in which aggressive behavior is usually dealt with in terms of (1) features of the environment which foster the initial learning or *acquisition* of the behavior; (2) environmental influences that facilitate the *performance* of aggressive acts, once learned; and (3) conditions that *maintain* aggressive behavior.

## Modeling and imitative learning

Much of what children learn from adults or other children is learned through observation and imitation. It is not necessary in such instances that the child act out the behavior; images of the behavior of the actor, or model, become encoded in memory for later retrieval by the child when he or she is given the opportunity to perform the same acts. In training a child to tie shoelaces, unlock a door, dial a telephone number, throw a ball, or many other such behaviors, we usually show the child first and then ask the child to practice what has been observed. Aggressive behaviors can be acquired through the same process.

Several experiments carried out by Bandura and his associates established the validity of observational learning of aggression. A study by Bandura *et al.* (1963) serves as the prototype of this research. Nursery school children of both sexes observed an adult female model enter a room containing several toys, among which was a large inflated plastic clown doll. After playing with the toys for a time, the model began to assault the doll while uttering a particular aggressive verbalization. Several of the model's aggressive behaviors were fairly unique and novel. It was expected that the child would be unlikely to perform such a precise pattern of physical and verbal responses under ordinary conditions. Other children observed the same model play with the toys in a non-aggressive way. It is to be noted that in both conditions the child simply sat passively and watched. Later children from both conditions were let into the toy room and allowed to play. Those who had observed the aggressive model performed more of the specific verbal and assaultive behaviors than did children who had seen and heard the non-violent model. Even though the children had not acted out the observed responses and had not, for that reason, received any reinforcement for aggressing, they nevertheless learned the modeled behavior.

## Performance of the aggressive response

### Role of incentive

Whether or not aggression that is learned through observation will actually be performed by the subject depends on the perceived consequences of both the model's and the child's behavior. If the model is punished for aggressing, the child may learn the aggression yet be afraid to act it out. In addition, even in the absence of fear, the child may not carry out the observed aggression unless she or he has some motive for doing so. Both of these contingencies were shown in a study by Bandura (1965). Children saw films in which a male model acted aggressively. In some films the model was rewarded for aggressing; in others he was punished; and in still others he was neither rewarded nor punished. Children who had seen the model punished emitted fewer acts of imitative aggression than those who had seen the model in either of the other two conditions. Later, however, the experimenter offered an attractive reward to the children for imitating the model. In this condition, all previous differences disappeared, and children who had seen the punished model imitated him as much as those who had seen him being rewarded or experiencing no outcome.

*Presence of others*
Modeling of observed violence may also be affected by the presence of others in the viewing situation, as well as by actions taken by those others. The presence of an adult may influence imitative aggression in children. In a study by Eisenberg (1980), an adult either approved or disapproved of the violent actions of a televised character being watched by children. Children who had observed an adult make approving statements later expressed more verbal aggressiveness than did children in whose presence adults had made disapproving statements. The children were no less aggressive when attended by a disapproving adult than when they watched alone. The presence of an approving adult therefore enhanced the expression of aggression, but the presence of a disapproving one did not inhibit it.

Other studies have shown that the presence of other children may influence modeled aggression. Imitative aggression is greater when the observer is accompanied by another child who also imitates (O'Neal *et al.* 1979; Leyens *et al.* 1982). Collectively, these studies indicate that the presence of others may provide incentives to the child to act out aggressive responses previously learned through observation, or it may threaten disapproval and thereby suppress such acting out. These findings are therefore an extension of Bandura's conclusion that imitative aggression requires both an occasion for learning and a sufficient incentive to carry out the learned behavior.

## Maintenance of aggression

### Reward for aggression

As is true of any learned response, aggression is maintained by positive reinforcement. The aggressive response that is learned by imitation must be rewarded from time to time or it will extinguish. In experimental settings, positive reinforcement of aggressive behavior produces a gradual increase in the level of aggression. For example, Geen and Stonner (1971) found that subjects who were given verbal approval by the experimenter for delivering aversive stimuli to another person increased the intensity of those stimuli across a long series of trials (Figure 1.1). In everyday life, of course, the reinforcement of aggression comes about mainly through its consequences.

*Figure 1.1*   Average intensities of shocks given during reinforcement or non-reinforcement of shock responses

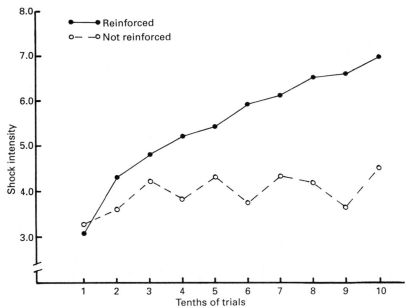

*Source:* Geen & Stonner (1971)

*Note:* Intensity of a shock is defined as the number of a button (from 1–10) on a Buss aggression apparatus (see Buss 1961 for details). Because all subjects did not deliver same number of shocks, subject data are given as average intensities of each one-tenth (of all shocks) given by subject (see original article for more complete description)

The playground bully whose threats coerce weaker children to do his bidding, or the criminal whose practice of armed extortion enriches his income, are both likely to become ever more aggressive in their behavior as the rich rewards roll in. The American mobster, Al Capone, is supposed to have remarked at one time that one gets more with a kind word and a gun than with a kind word alone.

*Generalization of aggression*
Reinforced aggression tends to generalize in accordance with the principles of response generalization. Increasing the likelihood of one aggressive response through reinforcement increases also the probability of occurrence of other aggression. Loew (1967) has shown that subjects who are given the experimenter's approval for making hostile verbal statements are more likely than non-reinforced subjects to attack another person with physical violence. Geen and Pigg (1970) found the reverse of that effect. In their study, subjects who were reinforced for attacking another person were subsequently more likely to emit hostile verbalizations than were non-reinforced subjects. Giving rewards to a person for aggression may therefore have the ultimate effect of making that person more violent in general.

*Nature and nurture in aggression*
The general approach to aggression that is being followed in this book, which was introduced earlier, helps us to reconcile the issue of whether aggressive behavior is biologically determined or socially learned. The distinction, which reflects the old "nature versus nurture" debate of years ago, is actually not a meaningful one. It should be obvious from the studies reviewed here that both one's biological inheritance and one's repertoire of learned aggressive behaviors are elements in the general background state that predisposes a person to react aggressively to certain situations. We cannot say, therefore, that either learning or biological make-up explains aggressive behavior; both play important roles in creating the conditions for aggression.

## Social and cultural antecedents of aggression

The predisposing variables in aggression are many and diverse. Biological inheritance and social learning history are important ones. In addition, the origins of human aggression can also be found to a considerable extent in the social and cultural context. This being a book about the psychology of aggression, it is not meant to provide an exhaustive treatment of the sociological literature on the subject. However, unless we at least recognize the importance of culture and social values, we miss an important interpersonal antecedent of aggression.

### Aggression in cultural values

Most societies sanction violence to some degree. Down through the centuries some have been in fact "warrior states" whereas others, though relatively more peaceful, have maintained that some violence is necessary for social order and defense against external threats. The espousal of violence within the norms and cultural values of a society serves as still another background variable that renders aggression more or less probable when suitable provocations occur. An extensive study of violence in the culture of one country – the United States – has shown that aggressive values form an important part of the overall value system in that society (Mulvihill and Tumin 1969).

This study assessed various attitudes toward aggression and violence in a large sample of people. It showed, for example, that 78 per cent of all respondents agreed with the statement: "Some people don't understand anything but force", and that 70 per cent agreed with the item: "When a boy is growing up, it is important for him to have a few fist fights". Fully 65 per cent believed that police use no more force than necessary in carrying out their duties, and 56 per cent endorsed the view that "any man who insults a policeman has no complaint if he gets roughed up in return". These attitudes also generalized to beliefs about international conflict: for example, 62 per cent believed that in "dealing with other countries in the world we are frequently justified in using military force".

### The subculture of violence

Given the prevalence of such beliefs in American society, it is not surprising that aggressive attitudes also enter into everyday social interactions. After reviewing the case histories of several individuals who manifested high degrees of violent behavior in their lives, Toch

(1969) concluded that much of the behavior he had studied was guided by "violence-prone premises" or assumptions. Social encounters that might for some people lead to innocuous outcomes often erupt into aggression in the case of violent men. Toch (1969, p. 189) observed that "persons who tend to interpret situations as threatening, or goading, or challenging, or overpowering can turn harmless encounters into duels, purges, struggles for survival, or violent escapes". From where do these violence-prone ways of interpreting situations come? Toch suggests that in certain segments of American society such premises are widely held and accepted, and are therefore available for adoption as beliefs by individuals.

This idea – that certain "subcultures of violence" exist – was proposed by Wolfgang and Ferracuti (1967) on the basis of their findings that some groups are more likely than others to use violence in solving their problems. This is not a phenomenon restricted to any one society or nation. In many societies we may observe such practices as the vendetta, the blood feud, and the practice of stereotyped masculinity seen in the familiar *machismo* syndrome. The origins of the various subcultures of violence depend on the history and circumstances of the society, but regardless of origins, the subculture mandates the values, beliefs, and attitudes of its members. As such, it forms part of what we have been calling the background variables in aggression.

*Aggression in gangs*

The concept of the subculture of violence helps to explain a part of the aggressive behavior of juvenile gangs. To a certain extent the violence of gangs reflects the prevailing standards of aggression in a society. In addition, however, gang violence has more precise origins. Klein (1969) has argued that its ultimate origins lie in the social change found in societies in transition (such as the city center or the urban neighborhood). Such changes produce a breakdown in traditional norms and a consequent loss in communal control over the aggression of individuals and small groups. In such a setting, aggression eventually becomes part of the new normative structure that emerges to replace the old one. The gang serves as a focus for young people in so far as it provides a means of immediate gratification, a strong peer group, social status, and an opportunity to assert masculinity and toughness. In turn the gang legitimizes aggression. It also promotes aggressive behavior through what Klein (1969) has called a "shared misunderstanding": each member of the gang assumes that the norms of the peer group demand more aggression than the individual would prefer to undertake. In this way the gang implicitly compels a certain level of violence from each of its members.

## A note on methods of study

Before going on to a review of studies of human aggression, a word on methodology is in order. Most of the research that will be reviewed in the chapters to follow comes from experimental laboratories. The laboratory study in aggression usually involves a simple two-person interaction in which one person is led to believe that he or she is the victim of a willful infliction of an aversive treatment by the other. Eventually the first person is allowed to retaliate in some way. Aggression is operationally defined in terms of the overall magnitude of the retaliation. Most often the provocateur is an experimental accomplice playing a well-rehearsed role. Three variations of the method involving provocation and retaliation are most commonly used. In one (see, for example, Berkowitz and Geen 1966), an experimental confederate and the subject each perform some task and rate each other's product. The confederate, judging first, provokes the subject by giving him or her a bad rating, usually accompanied by aversive punishments such as electric shocks or loud noises. The confederate may also make gratuitously insulting remarks during the proceedings. The subject then has the opportunity to rate the confederate's work in a similar manner. Aggression is usually defined in terms of the number and/or duration of aversive stimuli delivered by the subject.

In a second method (Buss 1961), the subject is designated as the teacher and the confederate the learner in a learning situation. The confederate may then frustrate the subject by showing an apparent inability to learn, or may insult the subject in some way during the course of the procedure. The subject is instructed to deliver shocks or other aversive stimuli as punishments for errors. The subject is free to choose the intensity of each aversive stimulus from one of ten different intensities and to carry out this choice by pressing one of ten buttons on a panel. Aggression is defined in terms of the intensity of aversive stimuli chosen.

A third method involves two subjects who compete with each other in a reaction-time task (see, for example, Epstein and Taylor

1967). Each ostensibly chooses the intensity of an aversive stimulus to be received by the other on trials in which one subject wins and the other loses. The experimenter actually controls all outcomes and arranges to convey to each subject the idea that the other has chosen intense punishments. Aggression is defined by the actual level of aversiveness chosen by the subjects after receiving this bogus information.

Several methods other than the ones described here have been used in aggression research, and we will note these as they arise in the review. However, these three, and variations on them, constitute the most popular methods. One question we must ask, therefore, is whether these methods are valid for the study of aggression. Does a highly contrived laboratory setting really provide insight into the dynamics of human violence? Or would we be better off to eliminate aggression experiments and to study actual violence in real-life settings?

These questions are not easily answered. The aggression experiment has one advantage over other methods in that it allows a high degree of control, precision, and operational definition. It is, therefore, ideally suited to testing causal hypotheses (Berkowitz and Donnerstein 1982). For this reason, experiments have a high degree of what is called "internal validity". External validity, i.e. the degree to which the experimental findings describe what happens outside the precise conditions of the laboratory, may be another matter. Some investigators have found that counterparts of laboratory procedures can be used in natural settings with results fairly similar to those found in the more contrived setting (e.g., Turner *et al.* 1975). Others have found that such generalization does not occur (e.g., Milgram and Shotland 1973). Whether specific findings generalize from the laboratory to the world is not the point, however. Few people would doubt that the best source of information of violence in society comes from studies of real-life behavior. How, then, may the laboratory experiment be reconciled with the naturalistic study of aggression? Probably the best way is by fulfilling the function it serves best: generating causal hypotheses. The experiment is best suited to clarifying the theoretical issues in aggression, by defining the independent variables and the intervening processes, and by linking both to aggressive outcomes in theoretically meaningful ways. Research in natural settings may then be guided by the conclusions from the laboratory, which assume the status of hypotheses in the real world.

## Summary

1 Aggression is defined as the delivery of a noxious stimulus to another person with the intent of harming that person, and in the expectation that the aversive stimulus will reach its destination.

2 Several different kinds of behavior fit the definition of aggression, leading us to conclude that we should recognize more than one type of aggression. Each type is characterized by different antecedent conditions, by varying motives in the aggressor and, often, by various patterns of behavior. Aggression in human beings takes one of two general forms: (a) angry, or affective; and (b) instrumental.

3 Controversy surrounds the origins of human aggression. The biological viewpoint is that humans share with lower animals certain genetically determined tendencies toward aggressive behavior. The behaviorist position is that aggression is acquired through experience, conditioning and learning. The two views are not mutually exclusive. Some aggressive behaviors in humans have biological origins just as some are learned through observation of other people. Furthermore, aggressive behavior, once it is part of a person's repertoire, is shaped and developed through learning processes. Both biological inheritance and learned tendencies serve as background conditions for aggression, which is a response to certain features of the situation.

4 Evidence for a genetic basis of human aggression is not plentiful. To a large extent the study of genetics in humans is slowed by ethical constraints against control of breeding patterns. Research on twins has barely begun, but at least one study indicates evidence for heritability of both aggressiveness and other traits related to aggressiveness.

5 The quest for heritability of aggressiveness in the XYY karyotype has so far been generally unsuccessful. Some studies have shown greater than normal levels of criminal and anti-social behaviors among XYY males, but no evidence has linked the gene type to broader and more inclusive measures of aggressiveness. The connection between the XYY genotype and aggressiveness may also be explained in terms of mediating variables involving learning and instrumental aggression.

6 Neural mechanisms are involved in aggression. The various types of aggression in lower animals are associated with specific patterns of brain activity and the same may be true of humans,

although so far convincing evidence of the latter has not been reported. The neural bases for aggression involve complex inter-relationships among several centers in the brain. The overall result of this activity is to dispose the person to behave aggressively and to energize certain patterns of aggressive motor expression. Given this, aggression is a response to environmental stimuli. This pattern of disposition followed by aggressive action in response to stimuli is seen, for example, in the psychotic trigger response, in which some past violent association engenders a seizure-like rage response.

7 Biochemical systems may also contribute to the person's disposition to aggress. Sex hormones play an important role in aggression in this regard for men. The potential role played by sex hormones in aggression by women is less well established. Other biochemical systems may also be involved in aggression.

8 The ethological explanation of aggression also involves premises of a physiologically determined disposition to aggress and a stimulus situation that elicits aggressive behavior. Although the ethological approach to aggression has been formulated with animal subjects, it may have some extensions to humans through the use of arguments from homology and analogy. Evidence for behavioral homologies pertaining to aggression between humans and related species has been presented. An argument from analogy can be founded on evidence of territorial aggression and xenophobia in humans.

9 The social learning theory of aggression pertains to the acquisition, performance, and maintenance of aggressive behavior through principles of learning. Novel aggressive responses may be acquired through observation. Provision of incentives is generally necessary to bring about performance of the acquired response, and the presence of others may either facilitate or retard this performance depending on how the others are perceived.

10 Reward maintains aggressive behavior. Instrumental aggression, therefore, tends to become habitual. One such reward for aggressing is the removal or attenuation of aversive conditions that elicited the aggressive response. Successful aggression may lead to increased aggressiveness in this way. Rewarding one type of aggressive response may also generalize to related responses, producing an overall increase in aggressiveness.

11 To some extent the origins of aggression can be traced to social

and cultural roots. Every society promotes aggressive beliefs and values to some extent. These values help to form various "subcultures of violence" within the society. Such subcultures also develop out of the breakdown of traditional social norms and the emergence of new norms that contain a heavy emphasis on aggression.

## Suggestions for further reading

Bandura, A. (1973). *Aggression: A Social Learning Analysis*. Englewood Cliffs, NJ: Prentice-Hall. This book provides a good overview of the social learning theory of the acquisition and maintenance of aggressive behaviors.

Bertilson, H. (1983). Methodology in the study of aggression. In R. G. Geen and E. I. Donnerstein (eds), *Aggression: Theoretical and Empirical Reviews, Vol. 1: Theoretical and Methodological Issues*. New York: Academic Press, pp. 213–45. An overview of methods used in research on human aggression, including laboratory and non-laboratory approaches.

Brain, P. F. and Benton, D. (eds) (1981). *Multidisciplinary Approaches to Aggression Research*. Amsterdam: Elsevier/North Holland. This collection of 34 papers reviews theory and research on aggression from a wide range of perspectives, with both human and infrahuman emphases.

Eibl-Eibesfeldt, I. (1972). *Love and Hate*. New York: Holt, Rinehart and Winston. A review of studies of animal aggression from the ethological viewpoint is combined with an argument for a human ethology of aggression.

# 2 / INTERPERSONAL ANTECEDENTS

A person's biological constitution and repertoire of learned behaviors may make that person disposed or not disposed to behave
aggressively, but neither guarantees or necessitates aggression. In
both cases something must happen to evoke the potential aggressive
response. Those who consider aggression to be learned, for example,
consider it to be one of several possible behaviors that may be elicited
by situational conditions. The strength of the aggressive response,
relative to the strengths of other possible responses, determines
whether it in fact occurs. Furthermore, as Moyer (1976) has
observed, even though aggression may arise from certain neural
structures in the brain, aggressive behavior is elicited by some
appropriate stimuli that set off activity in these centers. To account
for aggression we must know not only how people become potential
aggressors, but also what conditions *elicit* the aggressive response.

In this chapter some conditions that elicit aggressive reactions in
human beings will be considered. The first is frustration, which was
one of the first variables to be studied systematically in research on
human aggression. Another is interpersonal provocation, including
such acts as physical attacks, verbal insults, and blows to the victim's
self-esteem. Still another is a context of violence in the immediate
social environment, which may act as a source of aversive stimulation for the individual. Each of these conditions can be placed within
the theoretical scheme introduced in Chapter 1.

## Frustration and aggression

### The frustration–aggression hypothesis

An early attempt to formulate a unitary theory of aggression was represented by the frustration–aggression hypothesis first put forward by Dollard *et al.* (1939). This work was important because it brought to bear on the study of aggression a set of concepts derived from contemporary research in learning and motivation. Moreover, the hypothesis that it offered has led, either directly or indirectly, to a large number of investigations extending to the present time. The frustration–aggression hypothesis as formulated by Dollard *et al.*, and in a subsequent paper by Miller (1941), states that frustration produces a state of readiness or *instigation* to aggress, and that aggression is always preceded by some form of frustration. Frustration, defined as the blocking of a sequence of goal-directed behaviors, is therefore directly linked to aggression, which is defined as a response having the goal of injuring an organism or object (cf. Chapter 1).

The frustration–aggression hypothesis has usually been interpreted as a statement of the role of *aggressive drive* in behavior. By this is meant that frustration creates a drive state which motivates behaviors in the same way as do such primary drives as hunger and thirst. Just as hunger animates food-seeking and eating, so does the aggressive drive engendered by frustration motivate fighting. As will be shown later, this idea has been criticized and largely rejected in favor of other interpretations of the outcomes of frustration.

The hypothesis also spells out certain intervening variables that mediate the relationship between frustration and aggression. If an individual fears that direct aggression will meet with punishment, such aggression will be inhibited. When this happens, the person may turn to substitutes for direct aggression, such as indirect acts of violence. Someone who is motivated to aggress against another person but who fears punishment may, for example, secretly destroy some object belonging to the latter. Aggression may also be displaced to targets that serve as substitutes for the desired one. The phenomenon of scapegoating, whereby convenient persons are targeted as "enemies" on whom pent-up resentments and angers may be vented, is an example of displacement. Finally, the hypothesis holds that aggression of any sort produces a reduction of tension or drive which makes further aggression less likely. This hypothesized "draining off" or *catharsis* of aggressive drive is a matter of some controversy, which will be discussed in greater detail later (Chapter 7).

The heart of the hypothesis, however, is its statement of a *causal* relationship between frustration and aggression. Probably no psychologists still adhere to the hypothesis in its original form as the *single* explanatory mechanism for *all* aggression. As was noted in Chapter 1, people aggress against each other for many reasons. They may do so in order to gain some valued end such as money or power. Aggression may also be a response to speeches, rousing music, and a display of weapons of war. Sometimes, as we noted earlier, especially horrible acts of violence are carried out simply in obedience to higher authority.

Although it is now recognized that aggression may be caused by many conditions besides frustration, the other assertion of the hypothesis – that frustration creates an instigation to aggression and ultimately to aggressive behavior – rests on somewhat firmer ground. Certainly anecdotal evidence for this idea is abundant. Most people can think of times when they became so exasperated by persistent failure to accomplish some task, or by the interference of others, that they felt like blowing up and expressing aggression against some person or object. Results of experimental studies do not provide clear confirmation of this common experience, however. Several investigations have concluded that frustration is not a reliable antecedent of aggression (e.g., Buss 1966). Others have proposed that although frustration is perhaps not the strongest instigator of aggression, it does, under some conditions, lead to aggression. For example, both Buss (1963) and Rule and Percival (1971) have shown that subjects give more intense electric shocks to another person, presumably as punishments for errors on a learning task, after having been told that the person should learn the task easily than they do after having been informed that learning would be difficult. Presumably the subject was more frustrated by the learner's inability to master an easy task than by inability to handle a difficult one.

Frustration does not always arise, of course, from the actions of others. Sometimes people become frustrated through their own inability to accomplish a desired end and the repeated failure that such inability produces. Geen (1968) compared the extent of aggression following interpersonal frustration with that caused only by inability to perform a task. In one condition subjects were prevented from completing a block design puzzle by the well-intentioned but intrusive efforts of an experimental accomplice whereas in another they were hindered by the fact that the task, while appearing to be easily solvable, had been rendered impossible by slight distortions of some of the pieces. During this period of task-induced frustration the accomplice sat nearby without being involved in any way. In a control condition subjects easily completed the puzzle as the confederate observed. When subjects later delivered shocks to the accomplice, ostensibly in connection with another phase of the study, those who had been frustrated, either by the accomplice's actions or by the difficulty of the puzzle, gave more intense shocks than did those who had succeeded at the task. In fact, frustration caused by inability to do the task led to as much aggression as did frustration caused by the other person's behavior.

Why should frustration lead to aggression even against a person who is only an innocent bystander? One possibility is that aggression is a reflexive and innate reaction to being thwarted. Studies of lower animals have shown that abrupt termination of a reward is often followed by attack on a cagemate (Azrin *et al.* 1967) or, if another animal is not present, on an available inanimate object (Azrin 1970). Evidence of such a reflexive response to frustration in humans is difficult to obtain, however, because learned behaviors may overshadow and obscure innate ones. It has been suggested, however, that very young children may have a reflexive tendency to "hit" when frustrated, though not necessarily to "hurt" (Feshbach 1964), i.e., to show an aggression-like reaction devoid of the element of intent that we have considered necessary to true aggression.

A study which suggests a possible innate aggressive response to frustration has been reported by Kelly and Hake (1970). In this experiment subjects were rewarded with money for pulling a knob. Concurrent with this, subjects had to terminate an aversive noise by performing either of two responses: an easy one consisting of merely pressing a button, or the more difficult one of punching a cushion with some expenditure of effort. As long as the knob-pulling was rewarded with money subjects showed a strong preference for the easy response in the concurrent task. However, when delivery of money was abruptly stopped, subjects' preferences in the noise-escape task shifted to the harder, but more obviously "aggressive" one of hitting the cushion. If frustration brought about only an increase in overall arousal, the more likely outcome should have been enhancement of the more probable of the two responses (i.e., subjects should have pressed the button more vigorously). The fact that they changed to the punching reaction suggests some possibly innate connection between frustration and hitting.

The argument for a fundamental connection between frustration and aggression is undermined somewhat by studies showing that frustration may elicit behaviors other than aggressive ones. People may respond to frustration with instrumental actions designed to remove the block to goal-directed behavior (Buss 1961). Frustration may also produce useless, maladaptive, or regressive behavior (see, for example, Barker et al. 1941). Furthermore, Mandler (1972) has argued that a person's response to being frustrated in a sequence of behaviors depends on his or her understanding of the responses that are available. If no alternative responses to the frustrated one are considered viable, the person will react with helplessness and anxiety, not aggression. Thus, although the point may appear trivial, we would conclude that for aggression to be a reaction to frustration, it must first be a part of the person's repertoire of responses. In addition, it must be a more likely response in the given frustrating situation than other responses which would interfere with aggression. The importance of this becomes clear when we consider the possibility that frustration may serve primarily to elevate the person's level of arousal.

*Frustration and arousal*

Berkowitz (1969), in a major reinterpretation of the frustration–aggression hypothesis, proposed that the power of frustration to serve as a cause of aggression lies in the extent to which it generates increased arousal. A study by Vasta and Copitch (1981) demonstrates the power of frustration to raise levels of arousal. In their experiment each adult subject believed that he or she was interacting with a child and was required to present to the child a body of material to be memorized. The job of "teaching" was presumably to be done through the use of feedback to the learner. A pre-programmed set of responses was given to each subject by the experimenter to simulate the child's performance (no child was actually involved). These responses were such that the child's performance appeared to deteriorate over time due to lack of effort and motivation. The subject was also required to throw a switch every time the child gave an answer, whether the answer was correct or incorrect. The actual purpose of the study was to measure the amount of force which the subject used in making this response. It was reasoned that frustration would be experienced each time the child made an error, and that this frustration would produce increased arousal. The latter would, in turn, be manifested in force applied to the switch. The results bore out this prediction. Even though the response of pressing the switch had no bearing on the alleged performance of the child, subjects made this response more intensely after errors than after correct responses.

Arousal may also energize any responses that a person is predisposed to make. The critical concept here is that of "predisposition". People may be disposed to aggress for a number of reasons. Their biological constitutions may make them potentially aggressive, as we noted in Chapter 1. Aggressive behavior may have become habitual through previous reinforcement and learning. Furthermore, preexisting favorable attitudes toward aggression and violence may make a person likely to aggress when aroused. A finding by Briere (1987) is interesting in this connection. Briere found that male subjects' ratings of how likely they were to beat their wives were positively correlated with generally favorable attitudes toward wife abuse and also with overall acceptance of violence. Wife-beating may represent a behavior that occurs when men who are highly disposed to attack their wives become emotionally aroused for some reason. Frustration could be one such reason.

If we consider frustration to be mainly a source of increased arousal, many of the problems discussed earlier appear to be resolved. To answer the question of whether frustration may lead to behaviors other than aggression, such as instrumental action or regression, the answer would be that it does when these responses have a higher probability of occurrence than does aggression, i.e., when the person is disposed to do something other than to aggress. However, when the person is disposed to aggress more strongly than to commit some other response, frustration will probably elicit aggression. As for Mandler's (1972) proposal that frustration will elicit anxiety and feelings of helplessness when no alternative response is available, we would suggest that the person will experience those states when aggression cannot, for whatever reason, be a response.

Furthermore, frustration can, according to the viewpoint expressed here, be a source of aggression any time it raises arousal to the level at which it can activate responses. This line of reasoning can therefore be used to explain the findings of an interesting study by Haskins (1985) in which aggression in school children was found to be a result of their experiences in day-care centers several years previously. The subjects of the study were in their first two or three years of public schooling. Before that time all of the children had attended day-care facilities. Some had spent a lengthy period of time (an average of five days per week for 49 weeks per year over several years) in a center that stressed a high level of cognitive development as well as fulfilment of the child's social-emotional needs. Children from several comparison groups had received day care that differed from this in terms of both quantity and quality. The average time spent in day care for the control children was 27.9 months and the overall quality of care did not match that received by the other children.

Teacher ratings of aggressiveness in the children after they had begun school showed that children who had received the extended day care in the cognitively-oriented program were more aggressive during their first year in school than those who had received less day care in more traditional centers. Moreover, their aggressiveness was general and pervasive: they were more likely than the control children to engage in physical violence, as well as to swear, threaten, and argue. They were more aggressive than controls in all settings: playground, hallway, lunchroom, and classroom. By the end of the third year in school the difference between the two groups disappeared, mainly because the aggressive children who had received extended day care became less aggressive over time whereas the control children did not vary in aggressiveness over the years.

Haskins (1985) explained these findings in terms consistent with a revised frustration–aggression hypothesis. He points out that the children who had received extended day care were a highly homogeneous group of average intelligence. Exposure to a more heterogeneous group of children in school may have forced these children into competition, often with classmates superior to themselves in ability. They may, therefore, have experienced some frustration over failure in the new setting. In addition, the school setting afforded these children less individualized attention from teachers than they had become accustomed to receiving in day care. With drawal of attention may also have been frustrating. Thus, if Haskins's reasoning is correct, frustration may represent part of a response to a major change in the school environment. Furthermore,

increasing exposure to the new environment led to adaptation and a
consequent reduction in aggression.

## Stress, arousal, and aggression

Explaining the findings of the Haskins (1985) study in terms of
frustration following a change in environments raises the possibility
that the frustration–arousal–aggression relationship may be a special case of a more general phenomenon. Investigators of problems
other than aggression have pointed out that both major life changes
and smaller "daily hassles" tend to place people under stress
(Holmes and Rahe 1967; Kanner *et al.* 1981). What we have been
calling frustration, i.e., the blocking of progress toward a goal, may
be just one event in a larger family of events. What makes frustration
in pursuit of a goal aversive and arousing may be the fact that such a
condition represents a change from a state to which the person has
become adjusted and which the person finds acceptable. Thus we
might speculate that the frustration–aggression relationship may be
expandable into a more general hypothesis. Such a hypothesis would
assert that any significant change for the worse in a person's situation
may be sufficiently aversive to cause increased stress and arousal, and
that the arousal thus engendered may activate and energize aggressive responses if these responses are highly probable in the situation.

One advantage of broadening the hypothesis in this way is that it
can, in its revised form, account for aggression caused by a wider
range of antecedents, such as environmental conditions or physical
pain (see Chapter 3), or situations involving interpersonal attack and
provocation. To put the argument in the terms of the model of
affective aggression introduced in Chapter 1, any situation in which
the person experiences a significant change for the worse from a level
of stimulation to which he or she has become accustomed and finds
acceptable may be an occasion for aggression.

## Frustration and negative affect

In recent theoretical writings, Berkowitz (1983; 1989) has argued
that frustration leads to aggression by initiating *negative affect*
which, in turn, is linked to aggression through an associative network. Negative affect is the unpleasant feeling elicited by aversive

conditions. This unpleasant experience is linked associatively to a variety of cognitions, emotions, and expressive-motor responses which produce immediate tendencies both to aggress and to flee from the situation. If the latter tendency is stronger than the former, the result will be inhibition of aggressive behavior and the so-called "anger-in" response (see Chapter 7). If the tendency to aggress is stronger than the flight tendency, the person will be likely eventually to aggress. Thus the initial reaction to frustration is an affective one leading to a simple associative process. However, Berkowitz also points out that higher cognitive processes such as attributions and judgments (see Chapter 5) may intervene to facilitate or inhibit aggression after the initial associative reaction has taken place.

Berkowitz's cognitive-associational model of affective aggression has wide utility in the study of human aggression. In Chapter 4 it will be cited in connection with the relationship between televised violence and aggressive behavior. For now, however, it need only be noted that this model provides an explanation of the frustration–aggression relationship.

*Frustration and coping*

Frustration does not always lead to aggression, and one reason for that is that sometimes people have available responses that allow them to cope with the stress of frustration. If people can make responses that lead to instrumentally useful ends instead of aggressing, they may not react to frustration with aggression regardless how predisposed to aggress they may be. This point is illustrated in a study by Moser and Levy-Leboyer (1985). Persons were observed as they attempted to use a coin-operated telephone that was not functioning. In one condition of the study a set of instructions was posted on the wall of the telephone booth giving information about the location of nearby phones and procedures to follow for recovery of lost money. In the other condition no such information was given. The authors observed that the amount of aggression shown by participants (e.g., hitting, kicking, or butting the telephone) was greater among those who had not been given the additional information than among those who had. Possibly the latter group, by possessing specific information about how to proceed, were better able to cope constructively with the frustration than were those who had no such accessible coping response.

The role of coping in stress reduction has been well documented. Lazarus and Folkman (1984) have proposed that when persons are subjected to stressful events they respond by making an appraisal of the means open to them to manage the stress. Having adequate resources for coping may enable people to escape the worst effects of stressful situations. In terms of the approach that we have taken, it may make aggression a less probable reaction to frustration than it would otherwise be.

## Frustration and social conflict

The frustration–aggression hypothesis has attracted some interest as a general model of social and political unrest. Application of the hypothesis to such large-scale matters requires, of course, that the terms "frustration" and "aggression" be defined in ways appropriate to the problems being studied. The former is generally inferred from evidence of dissatisfaction over unfulfilled desires and expectations within a society. The latter is often linked to riots, insurrections, civil wars, and other such acts of collective violence. In this section two such lines of investigation will be described.

### Aggression as a response to political instability

Feierabend and Feierabend (1972) have invoked the frustration–aggression hypothesis as an explanation of socio-political violence within a society. Such violence is taken as evidence of political instability. Furthermore, they have linked this social violence to systemic frustration, which is the level of discontent within a society over unsatisfied wants, needs, and expectations. If such discontent exists, political aggression and instability constitute a possible outcome, provided that political means for expression of the public will are not available. Furthermore, even when such political options are available, instability can be expected unless these means can provide constructive solutions to the problems of social discontent.

To test their hypothesis, Feierabend and Feierabend studied events occurring in 84 countries between 1948 and 1962. Using statistics from each country on the incidence of such events as civil wars, assassinations of public figures, overthrow of governments, and mass arrests, judges rated the countries for their levels of political instability along seven-point rating scales. Next, the relative level of systemic frustration in each country was inferred from data on

(1) how modern and literate the country was, and (2) how well developed it was in terms of provision of basic services such as radios, newspapers, medical care, and daily caloric intake. It was assumed that a wide discrepancy between literacy/modernity and the delivery of basic services will manifest itself in social dissatisfaction and frustration. The comparisons of levels of social frustration with ratings of political instability supported the authors' major hypothesis. Politically stable countries were found to deliver a greater proportion of desired and expected services than were politically unstable ones. The results were also influenced by the coerciveness of the governments in the countries studied. Despite systemic frustration, political stability tended to be higher in coercive states than in less coercive ones. This finding is consistent with the statement in the original frustration–aggression hypothesis that fear of punishment may inhibit aggression even when instigation to aggress is strong (Dollard *et al.* 1939).

### Relative deprivation and political violence

Following a line of reasoning similar to that outlined above, Gurr (1970) has linked political violence to the level of *relative deprivation* in a society. Gurr defines the latter in terms of the extent to which people realize desired standards of material welfare, self-determination, decisional freedom, and satisfactory social relationships. If the realization of such outcomes falls short of expectations, a potential for political violence exists within the society. Political violence is defined by Gurr in terms similar to those used by Feierabend and Feierabend. If frustrated people do not blame their problems on the social-political system, the likelihood of *political* violence is diminished. It is possible, for example, that a convenient scapegoat may be found, such as a disliked racial or ethnic group, and that frustrations may be taken out on that group rather than on the system. If frustrations are attributed to the political system, however, some form of political violence should be expected. Gurr lists three general types of such violence: turmoil, which is relatively popular, spontaneous, and unorganized; conspiracy, which is smaller in scope but more highly organized; and internal war, which is both popular, organized, and larger in scope.

Whether the potential for political violence actually produces any of the above classes of event depends in part on two antagonistic forces. The first, already noted, is the level of coercive control that the political system possesses. A highly coercive government can, of course, hold down political violence to some extent. However, Gurr proposes that dissident elements within a society also possess some power to coerce, and that if this dissident coercive control exceeds the control exerted by the government, political violence will occur. In recent times we have observed that revolutionary guerilla armies do appear to have some degree of coercive control over people living within territory controlled by them.

Analyses such as those of Gurr and of Feierabend and Feierabend represent interesting speculative extensions of the frustration–aggression hypothesis to large social phenomena. They show that the hypothesis can be invoked to explain certain social and political changes. However, it should also be noted that such analyses have been seriously criticized by social theorists who believe that such extensions from experimental psychology are overly simplistic. For example, Billig (1976) has argued that such explanations emphasize emotional and affective reactions to social conditions at the expense of cognitive and ideological ones.

Gurr's analysis of relative deprivation has also been criticized on theoretical grounds. Walker and Pettigrew (1984) have argued that in defining the condition in terms of an individual's feelings of being deprived relative to other individuals, Gurr has described what others (e.g., Crosby 1976) have called *egoistic* relative deprivation. This condition is different from *fraternal* relative deprivation, which is a result of the person's believing that his or her social group is deprived relative to other groups. Walker and Pettigrew propose that collective action such as rioting is a result of this latter condition and not of egoistic relative deprivation. The results of a study conducted in Australia by Walker and Mann (1987) support this hypothesis. In this study, reported feelings of fraternal relative deprivation were positively correlated with expressions of approval for acts of social and political protest. Feelings of egoistic relative deprivation were not correlated with expressions of protest, but were instead related to experiences of physical and psychological stress. Criticisms such as these point out some of the problems that arise in using a concept like frustration, which grew out of individual psychology, in explaining collective aggression. To a certain extent, groups may behave in ways that suggest an analog of the behaviors of frustrated individuals, but a thorough analysis of collective violence requires the invocation of other principles that better describe strictly social phenomena.

## Interpersonal attack and aggression

### Comparison of frustration and attack

There can be little doubt that one of the most powerful motivators of aggressive behavior is the desire or need to retaliate following an attack from another person. Attack may take the form of physical assault or it may be verbal, such as an insult, a harangue, or badgering. Some investigators have compared frustration with attack as antecedents of aggression and concluded that attack is by far the more clear-cut of the two (Buss 1963; Geen 1968; Geen & Berkowitz 1967). Attack has also been described as a more powerful source of arousal than is frustration (Diamond et al. 1984). Such comparisons may be misleading, however, in the absence of evidence that the two treatments – frustration and attack – have been manipulated in such a way as to produce comparable outcomes. For example, some frustrations may be extremely intense and some attacks relatively inoffensive. Lacking further knowledge of the subjective effects of each on the person, we cannot simply assume that the attack is more likely to elicit aggression than the frustration.

In addition, the relationship between interpersonal attack and aggression is not a simple one. One does not always lead to the other. One important variable that mediates the connection between an attack and subsequent aggression is the victim's interpretation of the meaning and intent of the attack. If an attack is judged in such a way that it seems justified or if it does not reveal maliciousness or intent to harm on the part of the attacker, retaliation is less likely than if such intent is clearly inferred.

### Intent of the aggressor

As was noted in Chapter 1, definitions of aggression almost always include the idea of intent to harm. When such intent is lacking, behavior is generally not considered to be aggressive regardless how aversive its consequences may be to the victim. Attacks upon oneself are judged in the same way: an attack is probably not considered to be aggressive unless the attacker is thought to be motivated by intentions that are malicious and hurtful. Intent to harm is in fact a more powerful determinant of retaliation than is the absolute intensity of an attack. For example, Epstein and Taylor (1967) showed that subjects who knew that another subject planned to attack them with a highly intense shock were more aggressive in retaliating against this person than when they had no such knowledge, even when the shock was not actually delivered. Furthermore, subjects engage in aggression against a provoking party to the extent that they perceive the latter to be acting out of hostile intention, whether or not he or she is actually hostile (Dodge *et al.* 1984).

One question that we must ask in noting the importance of intent in retaliatory aggression is why the absence of malice in the attacker constrains victims not to retaliate. One obvious possibility is that when an attack can be explained by mitigating circumstances, it is not regarded as a stressful event and thus it does not arouse the person. Another way of putting this is to say that an unintentional attack (e.g., being bumped into accidentally by someone) is not upsetting, whereas an intentional act (e.g., being bumped into by someone who deliberately makes contact) causes one to become highly upset. An alternative explanation is that an attack is upsetting and that it disposes the victim to strike back regardless of the intent behind it. However, because people generally do not regard an accidental attack as grounds for retaliation, most people inhibit such dispositions and desires out of a need to behave in a socially correct way.

A study by Zillmann and Cantor (1976) was addressed to this problem, and its results bore out the conclusion that when people believe that an attack is not malicious they do not become as aroused as they would if the attack were regarded as intentional. Subjects in this experiment were verbally provoked by an experimenter either before or after having been told that the experimenter was upset because of unusual pressures and stress. This explanation was found to have a mitigating effect on arousal, as measured by heart rate and systolic blood pressure. When the mitigating information was given before the provocation, assaulted subjects showed no increase in arousal as a function of the attack. When such information was given after the attack, subjects showed increased arousal as a result of the attack, but they became less aroused after the information was given. The data therefore show that when people believe that an attack made upon them can be attributed to extenuating circumstances and is not necessarily malicious, they tend not to become aroused by it (cf. Johnson and Rule 1986).

*Personality as a moderator variable*
The role of perceived intentionality in attack-elicited aggression is

influenced by personality. The importance of personality is seen in an experimental study by Dodge (1980). Boys who had previously been classified by teachers and peers as being customarily either aggressive or non-aggressive were prevented from completing a puzzle by the intrusion of another boy. For some subjects the other boy acted out of a hostile intent, verbalizing his wish to destroy deliberately the other boy's work. For others, the destruction of the unfinished puzzle was an accidental blunder which the other child, who verbalized a wish to help the subject, committed. In a third condition the situation was arranged so that the intention of the boy who destroyed the subject's work was ambiguous. All subjects were then given a chance to retaliate against the other boy, by destroying a puzzle which the latter was doing as well as by expressions of verbal hostility. Dodge found, as expected, that the hostile boy invited greater retaliation than did the ambiguous or the benign one. In addition, subjects classified as aggressive were more aggressive toward the other boy than were non-aggressive subjects only when the other boy acted out of ambiguous motives. Therefore, when the intent of an attacker is clearly understood, people retaliate or not depending on the nature of that intent. However, when the attacker's motives are not clear, individual differences in aggressiveness predict the victim's behavior.

The tendency shown by aggressive boys to attribute hostile intent to another even when the latter's actions are really ambiguous has been called the *hostile attribution bias* (Nasby et al. 1979). It is a result of a generally aggressive disposition. Recently, Dodge and Coie (1987) have further refined the definition of this aggressive disposition by proposing that people differ in their tendencies to engage in both affective and instrumental aggression. The personality variable related to the former they call *reactive* aggressiveness and the one related to the latter they call *proactive* aggressiveness. Reactive aggressiveness is defined by such behaviors as striking back when provoked and overreacting angrily to accidental annoyances. Proactive aggressiveness is revealed by such behaviors as using force to dominate others and engaging in bullying behavior. Dodge and Coie have developed scales to measure each personality variable. In a study involving use of their scales, Dodge and Coie found that subjects who scored high in reactive aggression showed the hostile attribution bias more than did subjects scoring low in this type of aggressiveness. Individual differences in proactive aggressiveness were not related to differences in commission of the attribution bias, however. Thus, the personality variable involved in this manner of perceiving the intentions of others is related to individual differences in tendencies toward affective aggression.

## Violation of norms

An interesting question is when, and under what conditions, malicious intent is attributed to an attacker. To answer this question, we must remind ourselves that interpersonal aggression takes place in an interactive setting involving two people. Aggression is not an isolated act in most cases. It arises in the context of an ongoing relationship. Each party to the relationship has a perspective on the situation, including a set of expectations regarding what is the proper behavior of the two people involved. In other words, a certain set of norms exists for behavior in that setting. Concepts like "attack", "maliciousness", and "aggression" must be defined with reference to these norms.

Such an approach to aggression has been defined by DaGloria and DeRidder (1977; 1979). These investigators discuss aggression as one possible outcome within a situation in which both parties strive for some goal and each party attempts to prevent the other from attaining that goal. In the course of this process it is assumed that each party must deliver some level of aversive stimulation to the other. The norm that is implicit in such a setting is that participants will deliver such stimulation only in the amount and degree necessary to attain their goals. Should the participants exceed that normative level, their behavior will be judged by the other to be excessive and motivated by intent to hurt, i.e., it will be regarded as a malicious attack.

For example, consider two teams engaged in a rough physical sport, such as American football or ice hockey. Each attempts to score points and to prevent the other team from scoring. Out of necessity each team must occasionally attempt to inhibit the progress of the other by making hard physical contact. As long as the level of contact is normative, i.e., no more than is required for scoring or defending one's goal, play usually proceeds without incident. Only when a player hits another with a force that the recipient considers excessive does the latter regard the behavior as malicious. The other is therefore labeled a "dirty player" or an "aggressor". The response to such a judgment of intent is the delivery of an aversive stimulus back to the other person at a level that exceeds the level needed by the victim to attain his goals, i.e. an exact retaliation in kind. (An interesting analysis of two actual cases of sports violence which illustrate some of the matters discussed here has been published by Mummendey and Mummendey 1983.)

DaGloria and DeRidder (1977; 1979) reported evidence supporting this line of reasoning. In each study, two subjects responded alternately to a series of signals by making a particular motor response. Each subject attempted to disrupt the other's commission of the response by delivering an electric shock precisely at the time of the other person's act. The shock could be delivered at one of three levels of intensity. Both subjects were told that shocks at either the highest or the intermediate level would be sufficient to disrupt the other person's response 100 per cent of the time. The experimenter manipulated the proceedings so that the subject received shocks of either an intermediate level or the highest level. Subjects retaliated with shocks of the highest intensity to a greater extent in the latter condition than in the former. In other words, subjects believed that highly intense shocks were unnecessary and uncalled for, and that they indicated malice on the part of the other person. The subject reacted to this belief by giving intense shocks in return. Along these same lines of reasoning, DeRidder (1985) has shown that people who observe others engaged in interpersonal attacks take the normative nature of the attacks into account in judging how malevolent the attacks are. DeRidder found that harmful attacks are labeled as being more aggressive and malicious than are non-harmful ones only when the attack is considered to be in violation of what is normative behavior in the situation.

A recent study by Ohbuchi (1982) may also be taken as evidence that judgments of what is normative enter into perceptions of malicious intent in others. Ohbuchi found that when one subject attacked another with electric shocks of widely varying intensity (some extremely high and some extremely low), retaliation by the victim was greater than it was when the range of shocks given was relatively narrow, even though the average intensity was equal in the two conditions. Giving shocks of widely varying intensity may serve to remind the victim that some of the shocks seem excessive in contrast with the ones surrounding them.

To answer the question that was raised at the beginning of this section: malicious intent will be attributed to an attacker by a victim when the level of aversiveness delivered is considered to be inappropriately high, given the norms for the situation. This judgment serves to justify retaliation. In addition, there is some evidence that the victim of aggression considers the attack to be more inappropriate to

the situation than does the attacker. A study by Mummendey *et al.*
(1984) has shown that not only does the attacker tend to regard his
or her acts as less aggressive and inappropriate than does the victim,
but also that the two persons reverse their perspectives when, at a
later time, the tables are turned and the former victim is given the
chance to retaliate. The overall conclusion of the study is that
"irrespective of the position in an aggressive interaction sequence,
one's own behaviour is evaluated as more appropriate and less
aggressive than [another's] behaviour" (Mummendey *et al.* 1984,
p. 307). Such an egocentric judgment on the part of the attacker
reinforces aggressive tendencies within a situation that allows bi-
lateral opportunities for attack. People can always conclude that
norms have been violated when they are attacked, but that aggressive
behavior is justified when they are the ones attacking others.

Justification of one's aggression may also involve certain strategies
used by persons who violate psychological equity in interpersonal
relationships. One such strategy is blaming the victim for the harm
that has been done to him or her. Harmdoers often attempt to restore
equity by concluding that the victim deserves to be harmed (Walster
*et al.* 1978). This strategy can also involve devaluating the victim. In
wartime, for example, it is common for propaganda to depict the
enemies of one's country as monsters or animals. Acts of aggression
against other people that would be considered excessive under
normal circumstances often become routine when perpetrated upon
those who have been dismissed as less than human.

### Violence in the family setting

The family is a particularly important source of aggression, especially for children (Green 1980). Research on family violence indicates
that the nuclear family influences aggression in children in two ways.
It first provides training in aggression and, hence, the acquisition of
aggressive responses and dispositions. This is done in several ways.
Parents who use physical punishment to discipline a child are, by so
doing, teaching the child that physical force is an acceptable means of
dealing with conflict. Often the training is more explicit, taking the
form of directives from parent to child to use aggression in standing
up for their rights and responding to provocations. In addition to
providing background conditions that make children potential
aggressors, the family setting may also provide numerous situations

that elicit aggressive responses. The close proximity of family members to each other assures that the members will occasionally irritate and upset each other. Parents can also make children upset by their own conflicts and problems with discipline.

That children learn aggressive habits as a result of the way they are raised is a well-documented finding (see, for example, Patterson 1980). In addition, children who come from families that are marked by discord, lack of affection, and inconsistent discipline are usually more at risk of developing aggressive behavior styles than are children reared in families that do not show these characteristics. Furthermore, training parents in effective methods of child-raising often leads to a reduction in anti-social behavior in the child (see, for example, Patterson *et al.* 1982). A recent study by Loeber and Dishion (1984) has shown a link between parental child-rearing practices and the extent to which aggressiveness is shown by children across different settings. The findings of this study suggest that certain child-rearing practices are associated not only with level of aggressiveness but also with the generality with which aggressiveness is manifested in a child's behavior.

The study involved a number of boys ranging in age from 9 to 16 years. The aggressiveness of each boy in the school setting was first rated by teachers and classmates. Aggressiveness in the home setting was assessed through ratings made by the boy's mother. From these data, four groups of boys were classified for further study: those who aggressed in school but not at home, those who aggressed at home but not in school, those who fought both at home and in school, and those who were not aggressive either in school or at home. From interviews with parents as well as direct observation of several of the families involved, the investigators discovered that the family settings of boys who were aggressive both at home and in school differed from those of boys in the other three groups in several ways. They were marked by greater discord between the parents, less affection and more rejection of the children, fewer consistencies in discipline of the children, and greater deficiencies in problem-solving skills. Families that showed the best family-management practices (in general, the opposite of the characteristics listed above) were those most likely to have boys that were non-fighters both at home and in school.

Conflict and discord in the home can be a powerful source of stress to young children. Cummings *et al.* (1981) have reported that children aged 12–30 months who witnessed expressions of anger among family members experienced high levels of distress and arousal. Moreover, ambient anger in the family had a cumulative effect: the more fighting that went on between parents, the more distressed the children became. These findings suggest that observation of the expression of anger may be a source of stress that can serve as an antecedent of aggression in young children. This possibility was tested in a subsequent experiment by Cummings *et al.* (1985).

In this experiment children aged two played together in pairs and were exposed during the play period to a sequence of interactions between two adult women. These women, who played roles assigned by the experimenter, began by being friendly but eventually got into an argument that became heated and included loud voices and the slamming of a door. The reactions of the children were videotaped and later analyzed for evidence of emotional reactions and aggressiveness toward the other child in the pair. Children in a control condition did not observe the two women. Children who saw the angry interaction were more distressed than those who did not and were also more aggressive toward the other child in the pair immediately after observing the outburst. A cumulative effect was also found. One group of children repeated the experimental procedure a month later and showed even higher levels of emotional distress and aggression on that occasion than they had shown the first time. The overall conclusion to be drawn from the research by Cummings *et al.* is that a climate of anger and aggression in the immediate social surrounding is stressful to young children, and that such stress can serve as a provocation to aggression.

The work of Straus and his associates (e.g., Straus 1980) further highlights the effects of the family on violence and aggression in children. Straus has identified several specific predictors of aggression in the family setting. These include such practices as physical punishment, child-abuse, spouse-beating, and encouragement of aggression as "normal" behavior. Straus (1980) has concluded that family violence is an interactive function of three conditions: the high level of stress and conflict in families; training in violence; and an implicit cultural norm which allows family violence to be regarded without disapproval. Stress is a particularly powerful antecedent of child abuse, for example (Straus *et al.* 1980). This stress may arise from a number of factors, such as problems at work, marital separation or divorce, and sexual or financial difficulties. Examination of the factors identified by Straus shows that they can be grouped into two classes. Some provide a background setting for aggression by making such behavior likely (e.g., explicit training in aggression, upholding of norms that countenance and encourage aggression). Others make the environment aversive and stressful (e.g., wife-abuse, conflict among siblings). These categories serve as examples of the two conditions for aggression (background conditions and specific stressors) spelled out in the model of affective aggression being proposed in this chapter.

## Affective aggression: the complete model

We have now reviewed several lines of research that can be subsumed by our model of affective aggression and the time has come to consider the model in greater detail. Once again, we note that aggression is a function of background variables that make aggression a likely response to stress-inducing conditions. We have reviewed evidence that biological inheritance, learning history, and social norms may all work to predispose people to behave aggressively. In a subsequent chapter we will review another contributor to the increased probability of aggression when we consider the effects of violent stimuli in the mass communications media. Second, we note that some change in the situation must create a condition of stress, arousal, and anger to which aggression is a reaction. Frustrations, attacks, and family conflicts are instances of such situations. In the next chapter two other classes of aversive conditions that may contribute to aggression will be described: environmental stressors, and physical pain. We have noted that even when situational stressors are present, however, people make judgments and interpretations of them (e.g., whether they were intentional or malicious, whether they violate the implicit norm for behavior in the situation) that may reduce their stress potential. Following Lazarus and Folkman (1984) we will label these judgments of situations as *primary appraisals* of the event. When the primary appraisal of a situation is one that makes the aversive condition appear to be relatively justifiable or normal, relatively little stress will be the result. When the primary appraisal makes the situation seem to be the result of actions that are arbitrary, malicious, or intentional, relatively high levels of stress will follow.

The state of stress that ensues will contain elements of arousal, observable in bodily reactions, and emotion, primarily anger. The status of anger in affective aggression is a matter of some interest. As we have already observed, we tend to think of anger as a cause of aggression, but not all investigators believe this. Some regard anger as essentially a process that parallels arousal and aggression but is not absolutely necessary to either. We will go into this matter in Chapter 5.

Whatever the role of anger, however, we expect that when stress and a state of disposition of readiness to aggress occur together aggression is highly likely. However, as was noted in this chapter, aggression may be lessened somewhat when the person is able to make other responses that allow him or her to cope with the situation in a more constructive and adaptive way. Again following Lazarus and Folkman, we will refer to the perception of such alternatives as a *secondary appraisal* process by which the person assesses the availability of such means for coping. We are being more than rhetorical when we say that much more research is necessary in order to understand more fully this important phase of affective aggression.

When aggression does occur, it has several possible outcomes or effects. It may lead to a reduction in arousal, a phenomenon sometimes referred to as *catharsis* of hostility. It may under some circumstances make the aggressor feel guilty or anxious. It may serve useful instrumental functions, such as terminating the aversive condition that first produced the stress, or increasing the aggressor's

*Figure 2.1*    Model of variables and processes in affective aggression

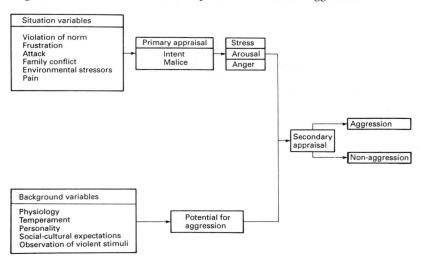

status and power. The various outcomes of aggression are the subject of a later chapter. Given all that we have covered in this section, the model for affective aggression is described in Figure 2.1.

## Summary

1 Even when a person is disposed to aggress and capable of behaving aggressively, specific situations must elicit the aggression.
2 Frustration may under some conditions elicit aggressive reactions. The older view of frustration as a necessary condition for aggression is no longer tenable, but assigning a role to frustration in some kinds of aggressive behavior is still considered valid. Frustration establishes an instigation to aggression, which leads to aggression if the person is not inhibited by other conditions, such as fear or anxiety.
3 Frustration may arise from being thwarted in pursuit of a goal by the acts of other people or from a person's own inability to carry out the goal-directed behavior.
4 The relation of frustration to aggression may be in part innate, but it is also shaped to some extent by experience and learning. If other reactions to frustration are dominant over aggressive ones, they may overshadow the latter.
5 Another way in which frustration may be linked to aggression is through general arousal. Arousal may motivate aggression by being an aversive condition to which people react by striking out. It may also serve primarily to energize dominant responses, including aggressive ones in some situations.
6 Although the frustration–aggression hypothesis was developed to explain the aggressive behavior of individuals, it has also been applied to larger collectives such as nation-states and revolutionary movements. Such extensions have, however, been criticized by social theorists who consider the emphasis on emotionality inherent in the frustration–aggression hypothesis to be inappropriate to larger collectives.
7 Attack by another person is a powerful instigator of aggression, especially when the attack is thought to be deliberate and motivated by an intent to do harm. When such intent is not clearly perceived, individual aggressiveness (i.e. tendencies to engage in affective aggression) becomes a factor in retaliatory aggression. In general, retaliatory aggression is regarded as an appropriate

response whenever force is applied in interpersonal relations in excessive and non-normative ways.

8 The family setting may promote aggressive behavior in two ways. One is by teaching children aggressive behaviors through observation and instrumental learning. The other is by creating a stressful and aversive situation which may elicit aggressive outbursts.

## Suggestions for further reading

Berkowitz, L. (1989). The frustration–aggression hypothesis: An examination and reformulation. *Psychological Bulletin*, 106, 59–73. The frustration–aggression hypothesis is analyzed and redefined with frustration described as a cause of negative affect.

Feshbach, S. (1964). The function of aggression and the regulation of aggressive drive. *Psychological Review*, 71, 257–72. In this important paper, Feshbach outlined the nature of angry (affective) aggression and distinguished it from instrumental aggression.

# 3 / ENVIRONMENTAL ANTECEDENTS

Interpersonal events such as interpersonal conflict and attack are not the only antecedents of aggression in humans. A number of conditions in the physical environment have also been shown to elicit aggressive reactions. It has long been recognized that some immediate environmental situations can be irritating and stressful, especially when the individual feels powerless to control or influence them (see, for example, Glass and Singer 1972). It is not unusual, therefore, that such situations should under some conditions lead to aggression.

An organizing scheme of relating environmental stressors to affective aggression has been proposed by Mueller (1983); in some respects this scheme is similar to the model that we proposed in the previous chapter and may, in a sense, be considered to represent a part of that more general model. Mueller (1983) proposes that environmental stressors produce four effects that have links with affective aggression: arousal; stimulus overload; interference with ongoing behavior; and negative affect. This scheme is shown in Figure 3.1. *Arousal* serves mainly to energize dominant responses; when aggressive responses are likely to be dominant, as is the case when a person is angry, aggression becomes likely. We have already noted how this same idea has been used to explain the effects of frustration on aggression (Berkowitz 1969). *Stimulus overload* develops when the environment becomes too exciting or irritating, and its main effect is to disrupt the person's normal processing of information about the environment. Inability to process information in a normal way annoys and frustrates the person, and thus leads to aggression. Likewise, *interference with behavior* is annoying and

*Figure 3.1* Hypothetical processes in environmental sources of aggression

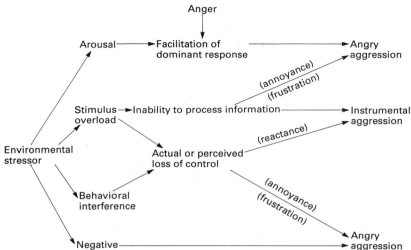

*Source:* Mueller (1983)

frustrating when this interference leads to a feeling of helplessness or loss of control. *Negative affect* (see Chapter 2) is aversive and unpleasant and may therefore serve as a stimulus for aggression, as will be shown later in this chapter. Each of the effects of environmental stressors identified by Mueller is an example of what we would call a significant change in the person's surroundings (see Chapter 2). Each, therefore, can be a cause of aggression provided that the person is capable of aggression and "ready" for aggressive behavior.

In several following sections of this chapter evidence of the effects of certain aversive environmental conditions on aggression will be reviewed. The conditions discussed are heat; noise; population density; air pollution; and ionization in the atmosphere. The final section will describe a hypothesis that ties these conditions together by indicating that the variable common to all five is *negative affect.*

### Heat

The belief that aggression is more likely in hot weather than in cool weather is a common one. It was expressed in the nineteenth-century "thermic law of delinquency", proposed by Quetelet in 1833 (Cohen 1941), a sophisticated version of the popular idea that crimes of violence are more likely in the summer months than during colder times of the year. Today we can observe the same principle expressed in the *Uniform Crime Reports* of the Federal Bureau of Investigation in the United States, which has shown that peak occurrences of common crimes of violence (such as assault, rape, and murder) occur in the hottest summer months. In recent years several attempts have been made to determine whether ambient temperature is a reliable antecedent of aggression and violence. Some of these investigations have been carried out under controlled laboratory conditions whereas others have consisted of analyses of archival data pertaining to temperature, crime, and riots. The conclusions of the two types of study have not been in agreement. The results of controlled laboratory experiments have usually been reported as showing that temperature and aggression are sometimes related in a curvilinear, inverted-U relationship, with high levels of temperature leading to *less* aggression than more moderate temperatures. Analyses of real-life data have shown that temperature and social indicators of aggression such as crime are directly related: the higher the temperature, the higher the incidence of violence. Some possible reasons for the discrepancy between laboratory and field studies will be reviewed below.

## Laboratory findings

Baron (1972) reported one of the first experimental studies of temperature and aggression. His procedure became the prototype for several succeeding studies: subjects were first either attacked with several electric shocks by an experimental confederate or given only a single shock; this treatment was shown to make subjects in the former conditions more angry than those in the latter. A short time later all subjects were given an opportunity to give shocks to the person who had shocked them. The ambient temperature in the laboratory at this time was either cool (around 21°C (70°F)) or hot (around 35°C (95°F)). Baron predicted that heat would intensify subject's motives to retaliate, so that more aggression was expected from subjects who had first been attacked and who then were exposed to the hot laboratory than from subjects in any other condition. The results did not support his prediction. Subjects gave shocks that were both weaker in intensity and shorter in duration when the laboratory was hot than when it was cool, regardless of whether or not they had previously been angered. A subsequent experiment by Baron and Bell (1975) yielded additional findings that were at odds with the original hypothesis. Using a methodology similar to that of Baron (1972), these investigators found once again that high temperature inhibited aggression in subjects who had been angered. However, they also found that high temperature, relative to cool, increased aggression in those who had *not* been angered. Baron and Bell (1975) explained these findings by proposing that negative affect is an intervening variable linking heat to aggression. Being attacked by another person creates negative affect, and so does being subjected to intensely high temperature. Moreover, these two sources of affect are additive, so that the person's overall level of displeasure results from a combination of the two. When negative affect is experienced to a moderate degree, the person is stimulated to behave with aggression toward an available target. However, extremely high levels of negative affect lead only to a desire to escape from the unpleasant situation. Subjects in the Baron and Bell experiment who were both attacked and exposed to excessive heat were therefore more highly motivated to get the experiment over with and leave than they were to retaliate against their attacker (see Figure 3.2). The strongest support for the Baron–Bell hypothesis has been provided by Palamarek and Rule (1979). After having been either insulted or not insulted by a confederate of the experimenter, subjects in this study were given a choice of task for the next part of the experiment. One task allowed subjects to deliver an aversive stimulus to the confederate whereas the other, which did not include such an opportunity for aggression, permitted subjects to leave the laboratory sooner. These tasks were carried out in either a hot room or a normally cool room. Under cool conditions, insulted men chose the aggressive task more than did non-insulted ones, but under hot conditions the insulted men chose the shorter non-aggressive task more than did non-insulted ones.

The results of studies such as those reviewed here indicate that under laboratory conditions the relationship of heat to aggression is a complex one that involves also the presence or absence of other sources of negative affect and the perception on the subject's part that escape from the situation is an available option. Another experiment suggests that high temperature may also have an effect on cognitions. Rule *et al.* (1987) found that high heat increases the

*Figure* 3.2  Hypothetical processes involved in relationship of heat and anger to aggression

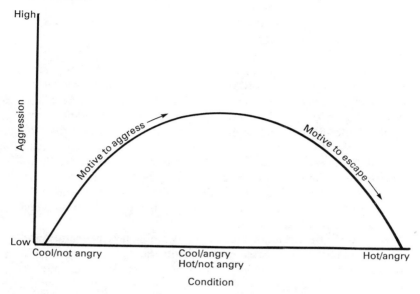

*Source:* Material reported by Baron and Bell (1975)

probability that subjects will have aggressive thoughts when suitable aggression-related stimuli are presented. Subjects provided endings for simple story items while working under either hot (33°C) or cool (21°C) surroundings. Some of the story items had the potential for aggressive endings whereas others did not. When aggression-relevant story items were given, a higher proportion of subjects' endings were aggressive under hot conditions than under cool conditions. No effects of temperature on story endings were found when neutral story items were used. Rule *et al.* interpreted these findings by suggesting that heat "primes" aggressive thoughts. They also proposed that a person who is primed to think aggressively may subsequently be more likely to aggress in the presence of suitable provocations than one who has not been so primed. The reason for this is that activation of a network of thoughts, emotions, and expressive-motor responses linked to negative affect (and elicited by provocation) is enhanced by the priming process (see Chapter 2). This could provide an explanation for the relationship of heat to aggression, although Rule *et al.* did not present evidence of aggressive behavior.

## Findings from archival data

In an investigation designed to find the relationship between heat and aggression under non-laboratory conditions, Carlsmith and Anderson (1979) studied the incidence of urban riots in several American cities between 1967 and 1971 along with average daily temperatures in the same cities over that period of time. They found that the relationship of riots to temperature was direct and linear, a conclusion more in keeping with the conventional wisdom about the "long, hot summer" and its association with aggression than that drawn from laboratory studies. The likelihood of a riot was found to be greatest when the temperature was extremely high and lowest when temperature was extremely low.

A similar direct relationship between ambient temperature and aggression has been reported by Anderson and Anderson (1984). In the first of two studies, these investigators analyzed the incidence of criminal assaults reported in Chicago on each of 90 days during the summer months of 1967. A clear and strong linear relationship was found: the number of assaults increased as temperature increased. In a second study Anderson and Anderson noted the number of murders and rapes reported in Houston over a two-year period and compared these data with the maximum ambient temperature on each day studied. Two significant findings emerged from this analysis. The first was a direct and linear relationship between temperature and incidence of the two types of crime. The second finding concerned a ratio between the assaultive crimes of murder and rape and the relatively non-assaultive ones of robbery and arson. This ratio indicates the proportion of crimes reported each day that are highly violent; it also varied with temperature in a direct way. The hotter the day, the greater the proportion of crime that was assaultive in nature.

In still another study, Anderson (1987) has shown that ambient temperature has a direct and linear effect on incidence of violent crimes (murder, rape, aggravated assault, and armed robbery) and a slight, but less potent, effect on incidence of non-violent crime (burglary, larceny, automobile theft). Anderson analyzed statistics on crime for the entire United States over the decade from 1971 to

1980, and found the incidence of violent crime to be significantly greater during the third quarters of the years (the months of July, August, and September) than in any other quarter. In the United States, these three months are typically the hottest of the year. Incidence of non-violent crime also peaked during the third quarters of the years surveyed, but not to the same extent as violent crime. The direct relationship of temperature to violent crime was found even when a large number of other variables known to contribute to crime (e.g., per capita income, age, education level) were controlled.

Taken together, therefore, the data from the studies by Carlsmith and Anderson (1979), Anderson and Anderson (1984), and Anderson (1987) indicate that, across a range of aggressive acts from riots to assaultive crimes, temperature is related to aggression in a direct way. Other studies tend to corroborate these findings. Harries and Stadler (1983) studied the relationship between the incidence of aggravated assault and a "discomfort index" in the city of Dallas between March and October 1980. The discomfort index is a composite measure that accounts for both heat and humidity. A modest but significant linear relationship between the two variables was found. A direct relationship between homicide and temperature has also been reported by DeFronzo (1984) on the basis of statistics from the 142 largest metropolitan areas in the United States. The magnitude of the relationship was relatively weak, however, and heat was found to have less of an impact on aggression than certain socio-economic variables. It should also be noted that DeFronzo's findings have been challenged, primarily on methodological grounds (Rotton 1986).

*Laboratory versus archival findings*

In a recent review of studies on temperature and aggression, Anderson (1989) observed that the only conclusion that can be drawn with confidence is that hot temperatures produce increases in aggressive motives and tendencies. This conclusion comes entirely from archival studies. Hotter regions of the world have more aggression than cooler regions. Hotter years, seasons, months and days are more likely than cooler ones to yield such behaviors as murders, rapes, assaults, riots, and wife-beatings. The evidence for this conclusion is quite strong. In contrast, the evidence from laboratory studies, such as those of Baron and his colleagues, fails to show an unambiguous positive heat–aggression relationship. This discrepancy in the findings from laboratory and archival data requires some comment.

First, it should be noted that nowhere do Baron and his colleagues argue for a curvilinear relationship between heat and aggression. What they do claim is that heat is one contributor to negative affect, and that this affective state will, if it becomes strong enough, elicit escape responses that interfere with aggression. The analysis of archival data such as that reviewed in this section does not allow us to make any judgments of whether or not people will choose to escape from heat rather than to riot or commit crimes. Furthermore, it is possible that heat and aggression *are* related in a curvilinear way and that if it were ever possible to observe behavior under hot enough experimental conditions such a result might be found. Furthermore, it is also possible that, if ambient temperature ever got high enough, crimes of violence might show a decrease.

Another possibility is that laboratory settings magnify a person's freedom to escape from hot situations. In the typical experimental laboratory, this option is usually quite salient. In fact, experimental procedures in effect in most American universities (where a large number of the experiments on aggression are carried out) require that subjects be explicitly reminded that they are under no constraints to stay. It is not surprising, therefore, that experimental research should show that the desire to escape conflicts with the motive to retaliate. In real life, however, people can be extremely uncomfortable in hot settings without believing that escape is a realistic choice. Under such conditions, heat and aggression may be more directly related.

Among several directions for future research on temperature and aggression, Anderson (1989) has suggested a greater use of field studies in which some measure of experimental control can be exercised while subjects still function in naturalistic settings. Such studies obviously have some of the advantages of laboratory experiments while retaining a high degree of realism. One such study has been reported, and it is described below.

*Heat and aggression: a field experiment*

Kenrick and MacFarlane (1986) have reported an experimental study carried out in a natural setting that lends further support to the conclusion that ambient temperature is directly related to aggressive behavior. An assistant of the experimenters contrived to get her automobile ahead of another automobile at a stop light, and then to remain motionless for the entire time that the green light was on. A record was made of the number of times the driver behind the assistant sounded his or her horn, the duration of the horn blasts, and the amount of time between the onset of the green light and the first horn sounding. A composite measure based on number of horn blasts and time until onset was taken to indicate frustration and irritation on the part of the blocked driver. This criterion measure was found to correlate highly with outdoor temperature, but only for drivers whose automobile windows were open. Those with closed windows, who presumably were operating air-conditioning units, showed no connection between horn sounding and temperature.

Kenrick and MacFarlane also found no evidence that the relationship between heat and horn-sounding was curvilinear. It was instead a direct and linear one. It should be noted, however, that this experiment was not designed to provide an alternative way out of the detainment for the driver. Thus, Baron's hypothesis that high temperature will motivate escape responses rather than aggression could not really be tested. It is also possible that horn-sounding was in fact an attempt at an escape response, since the blocked drivers may have perceived this to be the only way to dislodge the vehicle ahead of them.

## Noise

The stressful effects of noise have been well documented. Urban settings are usually characterized by high levels of noise which are usually variable, unpredictable, and uncontrollable by the average person. The harmful effects of noise include loss of hearing, hypertension, stress, and decreased efficiency in problem-solving. We might expect that because of its stressful nature intense noise might also be related to aggression. It is, but only under certain conditions. The major role of noise in aggression is that of an *intensifier of ongoing behavior*. If the behavior is for some reason aggressive, then the introduction of noise facilitates the expression of aggression. Noise may also contribute to aggression by reducing the individual's ability to withstand and tolerate frustration.

## Noise and frustration tolerance

In a series of studies, Glass and Singer (1972) investigated the reactions of people to frustrating circumstances after having been stimulated with noise under different conditions. These conditions involved manipulation of the intensity, predictability, and controllability of noise. Their findings led to some general conclusions. One is that the stress potential in noise is more a function of the "psychological" variables of predictability and controllability than of the physical intensity of the noise. Another is that the effects of noise are both physiological and behavioral. A third is that people are capable of adapting to noise and of functioning effectively in spite of its stressful effects.

Regardless of a person's ability to adapt, however, noise has a cumulative effect that can subsequently exert harmful influences on the person. One such delayed effect is a decrease in frustration tolerance. In one study, Glass and Singer (1972) stimulated subjects with bursts of noise as they attempted to solve problems. The bursts were either loud or soft in intensity and were delivered either on a regular and predictable schedule or completely at random. After this phase of the study, subjects attempted to solve puzzles that were in fact insoluble. Because it was assumed that people who become extremely frustrated with repeated failure would tend to give up at the hopeless task, persistence was taken as an indicator of tolerance for frustration. The results showed that loudness of the noise had only a small effect on the outcome: frustration tolerance was somewhat greater following soft noise than after loud noise, but only when the noise was also delivered on a random (i.e., unpredictable) schedule. The overall effect of predictability was strong. Exposure to unpredictable noise was followed by lower levels of frustration tolerance than prior exposure to predictable noise, regardless of the intensity of the noise.

In another study, Glass and Singer (1972) varied the extent to which subjects could control a series of loud and unpredictable bursts of noise. Some subjects were given access to a switch by which the noise bursts could be terminated whereas others were not. Despite the fact that none of the subjects who could turn off the noise exercised this option, they nevertheless manifested higher tolerance for frustration later on than did subjects for whom the offset switch was not available. Even when noise was intense and unpredictable, then, belief in control over the noise reduced the stress-related after-effect. From this study and the one discussed above we may conclude that controllability and predictability are important variables in reducing the stress potential of noise.

If the stress potential of noise is not mitigated through means such as those discussed here, it has a residual effect of reduced frustration tolerance after the stressor has been terminated. Why is this? At first, Glass and Singer suspected that the hard work involved in coping with, and adapting to, the noise stressor exhausted subjects, who then had little energy left to deal with frustration. This explanation was ruled out in later studies, however, leading Glass and Singer to conclude that the negative after-effects of noise are the result of an accumulation of stress that builds up even as the person is managing to adapt to the situation. Eventually a point is reached at which this stress has a harmful effect on the person even after the immediate stimulus is removed. The principal mechanism in this accumulation of stress is probably high arousal. Glass and Singer (1972) showed that unpredictable noise, for example, is more physiologically arousing than predictable noise.

## Noise and aggression

If we recall that frustration is often an antecedent of aggression, then any condition that reduces frustration tolerance becomes relevant for aggression: frustration may lead to aggression only when people lose their ability to live with it with equanimity. The less capable people are of living with frustrations, the more likely they are to react to them with aggression. This may represent one way in which noise contributes to aggression. A few studies have shown in a more direct way that noise can be an antecedent of aggressive behavior. The reason is each case appears to be that noise *intensifies* aggression that is elicited by other features of the situation. An example is provided by a study by Geen and O'Neal (1969). In this experiment male subjects were shown a scene from a motion picture – either a brutal prize fight or an exciting but non-hostile athletic competition – and then instructed to deliver electric shocks to another person as punishment for errors on a task. As will be shown in Chapter 4, observation of symbolic portrayals of violence frequently predisposes the observer to become aggressive. During delivery of the shocks half the subjects heard a tape recording of moderately loud noise whereas the other half heard no noise. The noise was not sufficiently loud to be painful to the subjects. The intensities of shocks delivered in the four conditions of the study are shown in Table 3.1. Subjects who were stimulated with loud noise after having seen a violent movie were more aggressive than subjects in any other condition of the experiment. Arousal elicited by noise apparently energized the aggressive reaction of the violent movie that subjects in that condition were disposed to make. The significance of this study is that it shows that arousal can energize aggression in a person who is disposed to aggress (in this case because of seeing a violent film) even though the person presumably has no reason to feel anger or hostility toward the victim.

Sometimes, however, people are angry with others and do have a clear motive to aggress. Under these circumstances, noise energizes and intensifies the anger-driven behavior. In addition, we might expect that certain features of the noise, such as its controllability or predictability, might influence the amount of arousal that it produces. Thus, in situations involving both noise and provocation, we would expect that aggression would be most intense when the noise is unpredictable and not under the control of the aggressor. Evidence supporting part of this hypothesis has been presented by Donnerstein and Wilson (1976), who found that subjects who had been attacked by an experimental confederate and then exposed to aversive and uncontrollable noise later retaliated more intensely against that person than did subjects who had received controllable noise.

Other studies show that predictability is not as important a factor in mediating noise-induced aggression as is controllability. Geen (1978) carried out a study in which these two variables were

*Table 3.1*   Total shock intensity given by subjects

| Arousal treatment | Film condition | |
| --- | --- | --- |
| | Violent | Non-violent |
| Noise | $22.25^{a*}$ | $10.33^{b}$ |
| No noise | $12.75^{b}$ | $14.75^{ab}$ |

* Cells with common superscripts (a and b) are not significantly different from each other

Source: Geen and O'Neal (1969)

Note: Intensity of a shock is defined as the number of a button (from 1–10) on a Buss aggression apparatus (see Buss 1961 for details).

Total shock intensity in the experiment described here is equal to the summed intensities of all shocks given manipulated separately. Some subjects in this study were first given a large number of moderately intense electric shocks by a confederate whereas others were given only a few mild shocks. Later all subjects were allowed to shock the confederate. During this period the subject heard moderately loud noise. In one condition the subjects were free to turn off the noise at any time, and most of them did in fact terminate the noise before the end of the period. In another condition the subjects were told ahead of time exactly when the noise would be turned off, but were also informed that this would be done by the experimenter; these subjects therefore could predict the duration of the noise but lacked control over it. In another condition subjects were not given control nor were they informed about the time of termination of the noise: the noise simply ended at the arranged time. A comparison group of subjects were given no noise at all.

The results of the study are shown in Table 3.2. Among subjects who had been provoked by being given strong shocks, possession of control over the noise had a mitigating effect on the intensity of their retaliation. Subjects who could control the noise were less aggressive than those who could only predict the time of offset and also less aggressive than those who could neither predict nor control the noise. Subjects who had control were, in fact, no more aggressive than those who heard no noise. Control over the noise, therefore, appears to be the single most important variable mediating the influence of noise-induced aggression.

Geen and McCown (1984) sought to replicate the findings of the Geen (1978) study and, in addition, to clarify the reason why control over noise led to reduced aggression. In an experiment similar to the

*Table 3.2*  Average duration of shocks given by subjects (in seconds)

|                   | Treatment | |
| Arousal condition | Provocation | No provocation |
| --- | --- | --- |
| No noise | $2.33^{b*}$ | $2.10^{c}$ |
| Control | $2.41^{b}$ | $2.07^{c}$ |
| Predict | $2.74^{a}$ | $2.11^{c}$ |
| No control | $2.83^{a}$ | $2.15^{c}$ |

* Cells having common superscripts are not significantly different from each other
Source: Geen (1978)

one just described, subjects who had first been given either two or ten shocks were allowed to shock the confederate while hearing noise. Only three conditions were used. In one the subject controlled the noise, in another the experimenter terminated the noise at an announced time, and in a third no noise was given. As in the earlier study, durations of shocks given to the confederate were less among subjects who had control than among those who could only predict the time of termination of the noise.

In addition, Geen and McCown (1984) found that possession of control over the noise led to less physiological arousal than did predictability alone. Blood pressure was measured three times: before the subject received shocks, after shocks were given, and during the administration of noise. Figure 3.3 shows the levels of arterial pressure at each of these three periods. Subjects who received ten shocks showed a greater increase than those who received two. During the period in which noise was administered, subjects who could control the noise revealed a small increase in arterial pressure, but no greater than that shown by subjects who did not receive noise. Subjects who could predict, but not control, the termination of noise showed a relatively large increase in pressure.

In general, then, arousal that is the result of aversive and uncontrollable noise intensifies aggression that is elicited by a provocation such as an attack. This may represent a special case of a phenomenon well known to stress researchers – the accumulation of stress across specific instances of irritation. A person who has been provoked to retaliate against another may aggress at one level. Add the further irritation of noise and the result may be a considerable exacerbation of the aggressive behavior.


## Population density

In recent years considerable attention has been given to problems arising from overpopulation. Although concern over population is usually animated by consideration of availability of food and natural resources, or of secondary effects such as pollution and industrial waste, part of the problem is now regarded as psychological. Population density may cause stress in more direct ways, inasmuch as the very bulk of humanity in a circumscribed space may be highly aversive to the individuals involved, and may also lead to social and behavioral disorders such as aggression.

*Figure 3.3*  Average arterial pressure over baseline, post-provocation, and noise-on periods

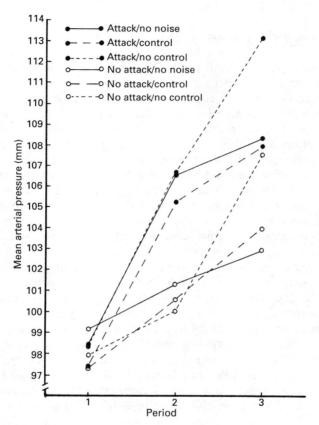

*Source:* Geen and McCown (1984)

Considerable controversy surrounds the issue, however. Much of the thinking on human crowding originated in studies of lower animals, and extrapolation from these findings to humans has been challenged. Furthermore, human culture and social norms may intervene to affect the extent to which high population density is aversive or undesirable. We do know that high density can produce increased physiological arousal in humans (see, for example, Aiello *et al.* 1975; Evans 1979), and that this arousal can be highly resistant to habituation (Epstein *et al.* 1981). All of this may suggest that density is at least somewhat aversive. However, research on behavioral and emotional responses to density is not conclusive.

## Crowding and aggression

However, some research studies do suggest a relationship between population density, on the one hand, and aggression and hostility, on the other. Griffitt and Veitch (1971) showed that ratings of another person were more negative and rejecting when the raters were run in groups of 12–16 people in a room measuring 7 ft (2.1 m) by 9 ft (2.7 m) than when they participated in groups of three to five people in the same space. In another study, men in a mock jury experiment were harsher in their judgments of defendants and in their recommendations for punishment when they made their decisions in cramped spaces than when they deliberated in more spacious rooms (Freedman et al. 1972). This finding is inconclusive, however, because in the same experiment high density led to *less* punitiveness than low density among women jurors.

Other studies have shown that density has little *direct* influence on frustration tolerance or feelings of aggressiveness compared to other variables that are linked to density, such as scarcity of available resources (e.g., Lange et al. 1979; Schopler and Stockdale 1977). However, an experiment by Matthews et al. (1979) shows that the aversive effects of crowding may summate with those of other stressful stimuli to influence aggression in much the same way as does heat. In this study, subjects who aggressed against another person shortly after having competed with three other people in a crowded setting were *less* aggressive than those who had competed in an uncrowded setting. Following co-operation at the task the degree of population density did not affect aggression. In addition, subjects in the crowded and competitive condition reported the highest levels of negative affect. Matthews et al. reasoned that an environment which is both competitive and crowded is sufficiently aversive to motivate subjects to escape rather than to remain and aggress.

## Density and crowding
We can better understand the relationship of population density to aggression if we first consider some principles that have emerged from the study of density in general. One is the distinction between *density* and *crowding*. The former refers to an objective condition of

the situation and the latter to a subjective state of the person. Density is operationally definable in terms of the number of people per unit of space. Crowding, however, cannot be defined with precision: people either feel crowded or they do not. Many variables – situational, cultural, personal – help to determine whether crowding will be experienced under given conditions of density. This distinction is important for the study of crowding and aggression. If population density influences aggressiveness, it probably does so by creating feelings of crowding and negative affect associated with those feelings. This is shown in a study by Welch and Booth (1975) in which aggression within family units was studied as a function of the amount of space in which the families lived. Density, as an objective condition, was found to be unrelated to family aggression. However, subjective perceptions of being crowded were significantly related to family fighting. Families that reported feeling crowded manifested more aggression than those which did not.

*Effects of control*
A second principle to consider is the extent to which people believe that they are either helpless or in control of situations in which there is high population density. Belief in control may reduce feelings of crowding and attendant negative affect even when objective conditions of density are relatively high (Schmidt and Keating 1979). At least one study has shown that belief in control can affect frustration tolerance, which in turn may be a moderator of frustration-induced aggression. In this experiment, exposure to high population density reduced subsequent frustration tolerance. This effect was weaker, however, in subjects who believed that they could terminate the treatment than in those who did not (Sherrod and Downs 1974).

*Spatial and social density*
A third principle to consider in studying population density and aggression is that increased density can result from either of two circumstances. In one the number of people remains the same while the amount of space available is decreased, producing a condition of *spatial density*. In the other the amount of space remains the same while the number of people is increased, leading to an augmentation of *social density*. In each case the number of people per unit of space is the same, but the subjective effects may differ. This distinction may explain some of the discrepancies in findings related to the effects of population density on aggression. Hutt and Vaizey (1966), for

example, found that normal children engaged in more aggression and destructive behavior during a free play period when they were formed into large groups (12 or more) than when they played in small groups of six or fewer. All groups played in a space that measured 27 ft (8.2 m) by 17.5 ft (5.3 m). Thus, in this study the manipulation involved increased social density. A study by Loo (1972), however, found that when groups of six children (three boys and three girls) played in a space measuring 90 square feet (8.4 square meters) they did not play any more aggressively than they did in a space measuring 265 square feet (24.6 square meters). Girls were unaffected by the size of the room, whereas boys were *less* aggressive in the small space than in the larger one. This experiment involved a manipulation of spatial rather than social density. Why was increased social density in one study associated with heightened aggressiveness while increased spatial density in the other was not? The answer is not obvious, but one possibility suggested by Loo (1972) is that when increased density is caused by the addition of more people to a fixed space people maybe blame their discomfort on those others. The loss of available space, on the other hand, may be attributed by members of the group to forces beyond their control. This "common fate" may serve to increase attraction within the group and inhibit aggression.


*Violation of personal space*

A matter that is related to population density is that of *personal space*. This term refers to an invisible "envelope" of space around each person that is felt to be off-limits to other people. When someone violates another's personal space, the result is discomfort, arousal, and a desire to re-establish an acceptable distance between the two people. We have little evidence associating violation of personal space with aggression or hostility. Worchel and Teddlie (1976) reported one finding that suggests such an association. Subjects who were seated close to each other were harsher and more punitive in their decisions about what should be done to a fictitious juvenile offender than were subjects who were seated farther apart from each other.

Personality may play a part in the relationship between personal space and aggression. Some studies have indicated that people who are characteristically aggressive maintain relatively large areas of personal space around themselves. Kinzel (1970) found that among inmates in a prison those diagnosed as violent preferred to maintain larger distances between themselves and others than did less violent prisoners. Similar findings have been reported by Hildreth *et al.* (1971). These findings suggest that violent people may look upon close physical proximity of another person as a potential threat or source of danger. Violent people may thus be more prone than others to be suspicious of other people and to mistrust their motives. Their establishment of a large area of personal space may therefore reflect a paranoid-like way of looking at other people which could also explain some of their aggressiveness and hostility. It is interesting to note, in this connection, that McGurk *et al.* (1981), in a study similar to Kinzel's, found that among violent inmates the only ones who maintained extended personal space were those who had scored high on the variable of psychoticism (cf. Eysenck and Eysenck 1972). This finding has been qualified somewhat in a study by Eastwood (1985), who found that violent prisoners maintained larger personal space than non-violent ones only if they were both high in psychoticism and low in intelligence. Obviously, the relationship between aggressiveness and need for personal space is moderated by several individual difference variables (cf. Gilmour and Walkey 1981).

It is also possible, of course, that an aggressive disposition causes a person to require more personal space than is needed by someone who is less aggressive. Possibly the need for more space is adaptive for the angry or hostile person in that the larger area reduces the probability of an encounter that could lead to fighting. A causal relationship of the type discussed here is indicated by an experiment by O'Neal *et al.* (1980). In this experiment some subjects were first either insulted or not insulted by the experimenter, and then approached by either the experimenter or an assistant. Subjects were asked to request that the approaching person stop whenever that person was close enough to cause discomfort. Subjects who had been insulted maintained a greater personal space in this way than did non-insulted subjects, especially when the experimenter approached.

### Air pollution

Pollution of the air with smoke, solid wastes, and noxious gas has become a major problem in industrialized societies. Air pollution is most often considered undesirable because it promotes various physiological disorders or because it upsets the ecological balance in nature. However, some recent studies indicate another potentially serious problem by showing that pollution can engender psychological problems as well, such as depressed mood, diminished liking for others, and dissatisfaction with one's surroundings (Rotton *et al.* 1978). In addition, air pollution has also been related to aggression in several studies.

### Noxious odors

Sometimes the atmosphere can become aversive not because it presents any danger to health but merely because it produces aversive sensations. One such sensation is produced by obnoxious smells, such as those emitted by stockyards, pulp mills, and oil refineries. An experiment by Rotton *et al.* (1979) shows that exposure to foul and noxious odors can dispose people to act aggressively provided that they have been provoked to aggress beforehand. In this study, subjects who had been insulted by an experimental confederate later had the opportunity to deliver shocks to that person. At this time the air in the laboratory was befouled by either a moderately offensive odor or an extremely offensive one. Subjects who breathed the moderately noxious air gave more intense shocks than either those who breathed very foul air or those to whom no odor was presented. The authors suggested that the extremely bad odor elicited such strong desires to escape that these responses interfered with aggression.

### Smoke

Another source of irritation to many people in public places is secondary cigarette smoke. In addition to being considered dangerous to physical health, the breathing of smoke generated by others is also a source of irritation that can under some conditions lead to aggression. Jones and Bogat (1978) found that subjects who were exposed to cigarette smoke in a laboratory while giving shocks to another person gave significantly more intense shocks than did others who breathed smokeless air. Furthermore, the intensity of shocks given to a person who had insulted the subject were no more intense than those given to someone who had not provoked the subject. Apparently exposure to smoke was aversive enough to elicit aggression even against an innocent person.

Additional evidence of the aversiveness of smoke comes from a study by Zillmann *et al.* (1981) in which subjects were asked to express verbal ratings of an experimenter who had either harassed and badgered them or treated them in a more friendly way. For some subjects the room was filled with cigarette smoke whereas for others it was free of smoke. For subjects exposed to the smoke, some were led to believe that it was produced by the experimenter and others to believe that it came from the experimenter's assistant. Verbal hostility towards the experimenter was influenced by the presence of smoke. Subjects who were compelled to breathe secondary smoke were more hostile toward the experimenter, regardless of his behavior, than were subjects who breathed clean air. Moreover, it made no difference whether the experimenter was responsible for the smoke or not; subjects were as hostile toward him when breathing the assistant's smoke as they were when breathing the experimenter's. Both this study, and the one by Jones and Bogat (1978) cited above, suggest that the mere presence of smoke can be a stimulus for aggression. The subject need not be angry with the victim of the aggression, nor need the latter be identified as the one responsible for the pollution.

*Atmospheric pollution*

Rotton and Frey (1985) have reported some findings that suggest a connection between airborne chemical pollutants and two types of aggression: family fights and interpersonal assaults. Using data from police sources and a local environmental protection agency in a moderate-sized American city over a two-year period, Rotton and Frey found a connection between the level of atmospheric ozone and the incidence of family fighting. The presence of high levels of ozone is an indicator of other photochemical oxidants (or smog). In addition, they found that ozone level was also related to incidence of assaults. This relationship was mediated by other polluting variables (i.e., ozone fostered the action of other pollutants, which in turn affected the assault rate). Furthermore, Rotton and Frey concluded that air pollution is associated with some of the other effects that they found. For example, wind speed was found to be negatively correlated with incidence of family fighting, a finding that is not readily explained until we recall that wind disperses airborne pollutants and thus diminishes their concentration.

## Atmospheric electricity

Variations in the weather often seem to have effects on the ways that people feel and act. We are all familiar, for example, with being depressed on gloomy days and with the relative elation that sunshine brings. Such swings in mood can also lead to outbursts of irritation. On a less anecdotal level, we also have evidence that changes in weather patterns may be associated with both affective processes and behavior. For example, in many parts of the world the seasonal onset of warm dry winds, such as the Santa Ana in California, the Chinook in northwest North America, and the Sharav in Israel, are associated with increases in suicides, accidents, and certain kinds of crime (Muecher and Ungeheuer 1961). Why these winds have such apparent effects is not clear. They do not produce intense heat, and they are low in humidity. However, they have a high concentration of electrically charged molecules, or *ions*, and recent research suggests that these ions may influence the emotions, behavior, and physiological states of people who are subjected to them.

Studies carried out in natural settings have suggested that high concentrations of positively charged ions are associated with unpleasant and negative emotions, but that high concentrations of negative ions are related to more positive feelings. The results of such studies are generally mixed, however, and some researchers have turned to experimental investigations in hopes of discovering the precise nature of ionic effects. In one such study, Charry and Hawkinshire (1981) manipulated the concentration of positive ions in the air by means of an electrical generator. Some subjects were exposed to ionic concentrations no higher than those normally found in the atmosphere whereas others were exposed to higher levels. Subjects exposed to a high concentration of positive ions showed several effects. Relative to those exposed to a normal level, they were less involved in the experiment and less attentive. They also reported more tension, less elation, and less sociability. All of these findings supported the idea that a concentration of positive ions produces a generally negative mood state.

The clearest findings of the study, however, emerged when the authors compared those subjects who were high in autonomic lability with those low in this characteristic. This measure indicates how quickly a person reacts and adapts to a change in stimulation; it is assessed through measures of physiological reactions (such as change in skin conductance) following exposure to a stressor (such as extreme cold). Charry and Hawkinshire found that whereas people who were highly labile and adaptive were not greatly affected by high concentrations of positive ions, those who were low in lability were influenced in a generally undesirable way. Relative to people exposed to normal ion levels, they showed slower reactions, a decreased physiological activity, more bodily symptoms, and more fatigue. The effects of high concentrations of positive ions on mood are therefore moderated by the individual's sensitivity and adaptability to environmental change.

These findings suggest that ionic concentration, by being involved in negative moods, may have some influence on aggression. To study this possibility, Baron et al. (1985) carried out an experiment in which subjects interacted with another person while the concentration of *negative* ions was manipulated so as to produce one of three different concentrations: in one condition the concentration level was normal, in another it was moderately high, and in a third it was extremely high. In addition, subjects had previously been classified according to the Type A/Type B classification (see Chapter 7; cf. Glass 1977). Previous research has shown that the Type A person is often more aggressive, irritable, and stress-prone than is the Type B person. The behavior of the person with whom the subject interacted (an associate of the experimenter) was manipulated such that this person insulted some subjects while treating others with indifference. Finally, the subject was given an opportunity to aggress against the confederate by delivering heat stimuli of varying intensity.

The level of concentration of negative ions was found to have an effect on emotions only for subjects who had been insulted by the experimental confederate. Subjects who had been provoked in this way expressed more depression, anger, and fatigue under conditions of high ion density than under normal density. By contrast, subjects who had not been insulted reported feeling *less* depression and fatigue under conditions of high ionic density than under conditions of low density. Aggression, defined as the intensity of heat that the subject administered to the confederate, varied with ionic density, but only among subjects classified as showing the Type A personality: Type As delivered more intense heat when being exposed to moderate or high levels on negative ions than under normal conditions, but no such difference was found for Type Bs.

The results of the Baron *et al.* (1985) study thus show several interesting findings. High concentrations of negative ions lead to a more positive mood than low concentrations, as expected from previous studies, but only when subjects have not first been provoked. When subjects have been insulted, negative ionic concentration produces the same sort of negative affect shown previously to be elicited by concentration of positive ions. Furthermore, among persons who have a disposition to be aggressive, i.e. Type A persons, increased density of negative ions leads to high levels of aggression. What conclusions may we draw from all this? Baron *et al.* propose that the effect of high density of negative ions is an increase in overall activation and arousal levels. If increased arousal occurs against a background of anger over an insult, or a propensity for aggressiveness rooted in personality, then it will be associated with aggressiveness, anger, and generally negative affect. In other words, arousal created by ionic density intensifies whatever behavior happens to be in progress or whatever mood the person happens to be experiencing. In support of this hypothesis, Baron (1987) has reported that high concentrations of negative ions produce an increase in both systolic and diastolic blood pressure in persons working at tasks.

In terms of the model proposed in Chapter 2, ionic concentration can be thought of as a stressor and a potential antecedent of aggression. Several background variables appear to moderate the effects of this stressor on mood and behavior. Among those identified so far are adaptability to the environment, anger, and the Type A personality pattern.

### Pain and negative affect

Most people are familiar with the experience of pain. Usually, the strongest motive aroused by pain is a desire to escape the cause of the suffering. We seldom think of pain as a cause of aggression. Research with animals has shown that pain sometimes leads to a highly stylized fighting behavior. Azrin (1970), for example, has shown that rats which are housed together attack each other in a reflexive way when painful shock is delivered to the animals' feet. The fighting consists of the two animals assuming upright postures, striking each other with forepaws, and simultaneously vocalizing. This behavior has therefore been described as "pain-elicited aggression". Many students of animal behavior now argue, however, that this behavior pattern lacks the more typical components of attack (such as biting, erection of body hair, and the full aggressive posture) and is therefore more a defensive reaction than an aggressive one (see, for example, Blanchard et al. 1977). On the other hand, there is no reason to think of physical pain as being essentially different from the other classes of stressor that we have reviewed in this chapter. Berkowitz (1983) has proposed that pain generates negative affect (in much the same way as intense heat and noise do), and that negative affect is the immediate precursor of aggressive reactions to aversive stimulation.

Furthermore, pain is a complex experience that includes the physical stimulus responsible for the aversiveness, the person's understanding of the cause of his or her experience, and the overall state of unpleasant negative affect that is the consequence. Berkowitz (1983) has reported an experiment in which subjects were required to immerse their hands in painfully cold water (the "cold pressor" task). Some were specifically told that this experience might be painful whereas others were not. Those who were warned of the painfulness of the cold pressor later expressed stronger feelings of irritation, annoyance, and anger than did those who were not so informed. In addition subjects in the former condition were also verbally harsher and more critical toward another person than were those in the latter. Thus, when the cold pressor was labeled as painful, more negative affect was elicited than when this labeling did not take place, as well as greater aggressiveness.

Pain may therefore serve as a condition for aggression. However, as we noted in Chapter 1, aggression is an act of delivering noxious stimulation to another person with intent to cause discomfort. People may experience negative affect and even strike out at someone when they are in pain, but does this mean that they intend to hurt the other person? The findings of a study by Berkowitz et al. (1981) indicate that they may. Subjects in this study gave rewards and punishments to another person in connection with a task performed by the latter; during this time subjects kept one of their hands immersed in water that was either extremely cold or comfortably tepid. In addition, some of the subjects were told that administration of punishments to the other person would hurt that person's performance whereas others were told that punishment would facilitate performance and therefore help the other. Overall, subjects gave more rewards than punishments. However, the proportion of rewards given, relative to punishments, was lowest among subjects who were exposed to the cold pressor and also told that punishment would hurt the other person. In other words, the combination of cold-induced pain and the knowledge that punishing the other person would hurt that person led to the highest relative degree of punishment. In addition, subjects who were given the cold-pressor treatment described themselves as feeling more tense, irritable, and annoyed than those exposed to warmer water.

Berkowitz's analysis of the affective consequences of aversive stimulation and consequent pain provides a general principle for explaining the effects of environmental stressors. Heat, noise, unpleasant crowding, and ambient pollution may facilitate aggression by producing high levels of negative affect and irritation. The same may be true for such interpersonal antecedents of aggression as frustration and attack. All of these events may elicit aggression to the extent that they engender strong negative affect.

## Summary

1 Changes in the physical environment may under some conditions elicit aggressive behavior. At least four reasons have been suggested. Environmental change may (a) raise the person's arousal level and thereby energize ongoing responses, including aggressive ones; (b) threaten the person with stimulus overload, which may render him or her unable to carry out necessary actions and thereby feel frustrated; (c) frustrate the person by interfering with ongoing behavior; and (d) elicit an aversive state of negative affect.

2 The relationship between heat and aggression is complex. Laboratory evidence indicates a curvilinear relationship between negative affect and aggression, with heat and the effects of other stressors summating to produce the total level of such affect. High levels of negative affect elicit motivation to escape from very hot environments which exceed motivation to aggress.

3 In contrast to laboratory studies, research on aggression in natural settings shows that aggression, in the form of riots and criminal behavior, increases as a direct function of increases in heat. Considerably more evidence supports the findings from natural settings than has been marshalled by laboratory studies. Direct comparisons of laboratory and naturalistic investigations are

difficult because conditions in the two situations (e.g., opportunity to escape from heat) are different. The two sources of data may therefore not necessarily be in conflict.

4 Noise influences aggression in two ways. It produces stress, which in turn brings about reduced tolerance for frustration. In addition, stress arising from noise intensifies behavior that is ongoing or highly probable. If a person is disposed to aggress, increases in noise may activate the aggressive response. Noise has the greatest effect on aggression when it is uncontrollable; noise that is controllable produces only somewhat more arousal than no noise, and no more aggression.

5 Population density is also related to aggression under some conditions. When density creates feelings of being crowded, aggression is more likely than when density does not translate into such feelings. Having a sense of being in control under highly dense conditions may also serve to reduce the aggression that a person will show. A distinction must also be made between social density (i.e. a large number of people in a given space) and spatial density (a small amount of space for a given number of people). Increases in social density may be more related to aggression than increases in spatial density.

6 Intrusions into the area of personal space that surrounds an individual may also evoke an aggressive response, especially if the person is highly aggressive to begin with. Highly aggressive people perhaps require greater personal space because of a general mistrust of others and/or because of a wish to avoid potentially violent contacts with other people.

7 Air pollution, in the form of noxious chemical odors, tobacco smoke, and ozone-related smog may also serve as an antecedent of aggression, by generating a state of negative affect.

8 A high density of positive ions in the atmosphere may produce negative affect and possibly affective aggression. High positive ionic concentration leads to fatigue, stress symptoms, and irritability. If a person has been provoked in such an environment, the negative affect may lead to aggression. Negative ion concentration may create positive affect under non-provoking conditions. However, when a person has been provoked, a high concentration of ions, both positive and negative, leads to aggression. The major effect of ionic density thus appears to be the intensification of ongoing behavior.

9 Physical pain is a strong source of negative affect and aggression.

## Suggestions for further reading

Anderson, C. A. (1989). Temperature and aggression: The ubiquitous effects of heat on the occurrence of human violence. *Psychological Bulletin*, 106, 74–96. In this major review of theories and research on the temperature–aggression relationship, Anderson suggests several directions for future experimental studies.

Mueller, C. W. (1983). Environmental stressors and aggressive behavior. In R. G. Geen and E. I. Donnerstein (eds), *Aggression: Theoretical and Empirical Reviews, Vol. 2: Issues in Research*. New York: Academic Press, pp. 51–76. This review describes current studies of the role of environmental stressors in aggression and provides an integrative theoretical model of environment effects.

# 4 / THE INFLUENCE OF THE MASS MEDIA

On 22 April 1974, three people were murdered in a store in Ogden, Utah, by killers who forced them to drink a caustic drain cleaner. Police expressed horror at the grisly and novel way in which the victims were put to death. Even though he could imagine no motive for the killers' actions, one police officer noted that the murderers had earlier seen the motion picture *Magnum Force*, in which a man is shown killing a prostitute by compelling her to drink the caustic liquid. The murderers saw the motion picture three times in a single day. Police expressed the opinion that the killers intended from the start to force people to swallow the drain cleaner and knew what the deadly effects would be.

The murders in Utah were among many that have been reported in recent years in which a close temporal relationship has been shown between an act of violence and a portrayal of brutality in one of the communications media. Stories such as these naturally raise the question of possible cause and effect: does observation of violence in the media make people more aggressive than they would otherwise be? The question is critical to understanding the motives of murderers in sensational cases such as the one described above. In addition, the question may apply to more everyday and mundane aggression. To what extent is ordinary and non-lethal aggressive behavior influenced by observation of violence in the media?

Portrayals of violence are common in television and motion pictures. Williams *et al.* (1982) carried out a detailed content analysis of North American television, selecting for analysis a large number of programs watched by adults, adolescents and children. The total sample of television programs contained an average of nine acts of physical aggression and eight acts of verbal aggression per program hour. Sixty-nine per cent of the violence shown was central to the plots of the stories. Less than 6 per cent of the characters shown being involved in aggressive interchanges sought alternative, non-aggressive solutions. Moreover, this high level of violence in television is something that has remained fairly constant for many years (Signiorelli *et al.* 1982).

Before any conclusions can be drawn about the effects of violence in the media more will be needed than newspaper anecdotes and statistics on television programming. To conclude with any certainty that observation of violence affects aggressive behavior, we must turn to evidence from scientific investigations in which other possible sources of influence on aggression are controlled. The purpose of this chapter is to review some of this evidence. The review of research findings will be organized into two broad bodies of literature according to the type of studies being covered. In the first section the coverage will emphasize experimental research conducted under controlled laboratory conditions. In the second the emphasis will be on studies carried out in natural settings.

## Experimental studies of media violence

### Observational learning of aggression

One way in which violence in the media may influence aggression is by teaching new aggressive responses through a process of observational learning. In Chapter 1, the important role of social learning in the development of aggression was discussed. As was noted in that discussion, an important feature of the experiments on observational learning of aggression among children was that the modeling procedure did not involve an occasion for emission and reinforcement of aggression. Instead, it appeared to teach the children certain novel aggressive behaviors that became part of their cognitive structure. The example cited at the beginning of this chapter, in which people were killed by forced ingestion of chemicals, strongly suggests that the killers got the idea for this particular behavior from a motion picture.

### Media violence as information
Despite the ability of the modeling hypothesis to account for the

acquisition of novel or unusual aggressive behaviors, it does not explain the more general phenomenon of media-induced aggression. Most experiments on the effects of observing violence show that such observation increases the level of many aggressive responses that bear little similarity to the ones observed. Obviously, processes other than observational learning are involved in this sort of aggression.

*Reduction of inhibitions*
Observing violence in media presentations may influence aggression by providing information about aggressive behavior. It may, for example, inform the observer that aggression is a permissible or even desirable means of solving interpersonal conflicts and, by so doing, help to reduce the strengths of any inhibitions about aggressing that the person may have. Thus, violence that is presented as morally justified, because the victim deserves the attack, elicits aggressive behavior whereas morally unjustified violence either has no effect (see, for example, Berkowitz and Geen 1966) or may produce an inhibition of aggression (Goranson 1970).

*Social comparisons*
Judgments concerning the motives of the observed aggressor may also influence the ways in which media violence elicits aggression. Of the many motives that may animate aggressive behavior, vengeance is one that most people would probably agree is at least somewhat morally justified (see, for example, Carpenter and Darley 1978). Several studies have shown that when violence is described as motivated by a desire for revenge, it elicits more aggression from an observer than does the same violence attributed to other motives. For example, Geen and Stonner (1973) conducted an experiment in which some male subjects were provoked by an experimenter's confederate and then shown a short scene from a movie in which one prize-fighter beats another fighter severely. Others were shown the scene without first having been provoked. Some subjects were told that the winning fighter was motivated by desire for revenge because of an earlier beating by the other man. Other subjects were told that the fight was merely a professional match involving no hostility between the participants. All subjects then retaliated against the confederate by administering electric shocks.

Provoked subjects were more aggressive than non-provoked ones only after seeing what was regarded as vengeful violence (Table 4.1). Provoked subjects who observed a scene of revenge also reported

*Table 4.1*   Average intensities of shocks given by subjects

| Meaning of film | Treatment | |
| --- | --- | --- |
| | *Provocation* | *No provocation* |
| Revenge | $6.88^{a*}$ | $4.14^{b}$ |
| Professional | $5.57^{ab}$ | $5.74^{a}$ |

\* Cells having common superscripts are not significantly different from
each other
*Source:* Geen and Stonner (1973)
*Note:* Intensity of a shock is defined as the number of a button (from
1–10) on a Buss aggression apparatus (see Buss 1961 for details)

themselves as feeling less restrained in aggressing than did provoked
subjects who regarded the fight as merely professional. Thus,
observation of a person taking vengeance successfully on an old
enemy reduced inhibitions against aggression and also facilitated
expression of aggressive behavior. On the other hand, Geen and
Stonner (1972) also showed that when subjects observe a media
portrayal of an *unsuccessful* attempt at revenge, they are later *less*
aggressive than those who see successful vengeance.

It is important to note that in these studies, as in others showing
the aggression-facilitating effects of observing revenge (e.g., Geen
and Stonner 1974), only subjects who had first been angered behaved
aggressively after observing violence. These findings suggest that one
function of observing portrayals of revenge in the media is the
facilitation of a social comparison process. The prospects of attacking another person may ordinarily raise inhibitions and aggression
anxiety in angry subjects, thereby prohibiting retaliation. If, however, the subject is able to observe in the media an angry character
who successfully exacts revenge, the subject may consider his or her
own desire to retaliate to be more appropriate. In the same way,
observation of an unsuccessful attempt at revenge may remind the
subject that retaliation can have punishing consequences and may
thereby reinforce inhibitions.

### Identification with the aggressor
The social comparison hypothesis is further supported by studies
which have shown that when subjects are instructed to identify with
the winner of an act of observed violence, their aggression against the
victim is enhanced (Leyens and Picus 1973; Perry and Perry 1976;
Turner and Berkowitz 1972). These studies suggest that "identifica-

tion with the aggressor", or covert role-taking, facilitates the expression of media-engendered aggression. As has been proposed above, such covert role-taking may facilitate a social comparison process wherein the subject interprets the correctness of his or her motives to aggress on the basis of what is seen on television or in a motion picture.

### Realism of observed violence

Several studies have shown that when violence in the media is thought to be real it elicits more aggression than when it is regarded as fiction (see, for example, Feshbach 1972). For example, Berkowitz and Alioto (1973) found that subjects who had been angered by another person gave that person electric shocks of longer duration after witnessing a war film described as actual combat than after seeing the same footage described as a Hollywood re-enactment. Thomas and Tell (1974) showed similar results with a movie of two men fighting in a parking lot. In a similar experiment, Geen (1975) found that subjects who had been told that the parking-lot altercation was real were not only more aggressive than those who had been told that it was fiction, but showed higher levels of blood pressure as well. Thus, violence that is perceived as real is both more arousing and more likely to elicit aggressive reactions than is violence that is judged to be only fiction.

The findings that real violence is more exciting and that it elicits more arousal than fictitious violence suggest that the former has greater impact on the person than the latter. Possibly real violence is regarded as being more "concrete" than the fictitious variety. Aggressive stimuli having a high degree of concreteness have been shown to elicit more aggression than less concrete ones (Turner and Goldsmith 1976). Realistic violence is probably processed as a more intensive informational input than is fiction. As a consequence of this it may be more likely than fictitious violence to occupy the observer's attention.

### Normative judgments of violence

A series of studies by Thomas and Drabman suggests that observation of violence by children may promote a change in the children's tolerance of aggressive behavior. These investigators have found that children who are shown televised violence manifest an increased tolerance for acts of aggression that they witness first-hand. In each study, older children were given responsibility for overseeing younger ones at play. Some of the older children were first shown a violent television program while others were not. The younger children then became aggressive and destructive, and eventually began fighting with each other. Older children who had seen the violent program were slower to report the aggression of the younger ones to the experimenter than were those who had seen no program (Drabman and Thomas 1974) or an exciting but non-violent one (Thomas and Drabman 1975). In another related study, children who had just observed a violent program were more likely to predict that others would aggress in a conflict situation than were children who had seen a non-violent control program (Thomas and Drabman 1978).

The observation of violence therefore seems to change children's judgments regarding the normative nature of aggressive behavior. However, the formation of such tolerant judgments can also be prevented by moral instructions from adults. Horton and Santo-grossi (1978) conducted an experiment similar to those of Thomas and Drabman, in which older children served as caretakers of younger ones after seeing a violent film. During the showing of the film the experimenter made statements that either disapproved of the violence or suggested alternative means of conflict resolution. Children who had received these treatments were later more likely to report aggression in their young charges than were those who had seen the film without commentary.

### Symbolic catharsis

A widely-cited experiment by Feshbach (1961) stands in contrast to most of the experimental studies cited in this review. Feshbach found that males who had been instigated to aggress against another person by the latter's insulting remarks, and who had then watched a film of a prize fight, were *less* hostile in their verbal appraisal of the insulting person than were similarly provoked subjects who had seen a non-violent film. This difference between film conditions was not found among men who had not first been insulted. Feshbach concluded that the aggressive film had produced a symbolic draining-off, or *catharsis*, of hostility in the previously provoked subjects.

Several explanations have been offered for the discrepancy between Feshbach's results and those of other investigators. Goranson (1970) has argued that because the Feshbach experiment did not include an introduction to the violent film that justified the aggression, it may have increased subjects' restraints against aggressing.

Another possible explanation is suggested by an experiment by Zillmann *et al.* (1973). In this study male subjects saw the same boxing film that had been used by Feshbach, but edited so as to have two possible endings. Subjects in one condition saw the film end with the defeat of the story's hero, whereas others saw it end with a happier conclusion. The latter was the conclusion of the original film that Feshbach had used. Zillmann *et al.* found that the subjects who saw the happy ending experienced less arousal and were also less aggressive than those who saw the tragic conclusion. Thus, the happy ending of the film may have elicited a state of positive affect that offset any desire to aggress that the subject may have had. It has also been suggested by Manning and Taylor (1975) that the symbolic catharsis hypothesis applies to verbal expressions of hostility (which, as we have noted, Feshbach used as the dependent measures), whereas the opposite holds true in the case of physical aggression.

### Arousal and aggression

Observation of violence may facilitate the expression of aggression by causing an increase in autonomic arousal. Three processes may be suggested as causes for the facilitation of aggression by increased arousal. First, arousal produced by watching violence may simply raise the person's overall activity level and strengthen any responses, including aggressive ones (Doob and Kirshenbaum 1973; Geen and O'Neal 1969). A second, and as yet untested, possibility is that arousal elicited by the media, especially if it is particularly strong, may be aversive to the observer (cf. Marshall and Zimbardo 1979). It may therefore stimulate aggression in the same way as other aversive or painful stimuli have been shown to do (cf. Chapter 3). Third, arousal elicited by media portrayals of aggression may be mistaken for anger in situations involving provocation, thus producing anger-motivated aggressive behavior.

### Arousal and misattribution

This latter point of view has been proposed by Zillmann (1971). In his study, male subjects were shown a film prior to aggressing against someone who had previously provoked them. The film was either violent, erotic, or neutral in content. The erotic film, moreover, had been carefully chosen to have no violent scenes. Pretesting had shown that the erotic film elicited greater physiological arousal in subjects than did either of the other two. In addition, Zillmann found that previously provoked subjects were more aggressive after seeing the erotic film than after seeing the violent or neutral films. He concluded that arousal produced by the movie was incorrectly attributed by the subject to the provocation, so that some of the arousal due to the movie was perceived as anger (for an extended discussion of the role of attribution in aggression, see Chapter 5). Subjects who had seen the erotic film, by being more aroused than the others, therefore felt more angry as well and aggressed more as a consequence.

### Habituation to observed violence

Other evidence indicates that arousal elicited by media violence habituates with repeated exposure, leading some investigators to suggest that a "desensitization" to observed aggression may be the long-range result of such viewing (e.g., Cline *et al.* 1973). A study by Thomas *et al.* (1977) has shown that for both children and young adults, prior exposure to an arousing and violent program reduces the magnitude of subsequent skin-conductance responses to a portrayal of real-life aggression whereas exposure to an arousing but non-violent film does not. Thomas *et al.* (1977) also found a negative correlation between the amount of time subjects normally spent watching violent television and the magnitude of conductance in response to violence.

Whether reduced sensitivity to violence with increased exposure has any effect on subsequent aggression has not been studied extensively. Moreover, the processes that may be involved in such behavioral effects are not entirely clear. If arousal has a direct influence on aggression, then any condition that reduces arousal, such as habituation, should cause a decrease in aggressive behavior. A study by Geen (1981) suggests that the effects of habituation to violence on subsequent aggression may depend on the meaning of the violence to the observer. Some of the subjects in this experiment were first shown a lengthy videotaped scene from the movie *The French Connection*, in which a police officer goes through a high-speed chase after a murderer, whom he finally kills in a gunfight. Following this, some of the subjects who had seen the *French Connection* scene were shown a violent videotaped passage from the film *Rollerball*, in which one man is beaten senseless by a group of antagonists. A comparison group of subjects saw the *Rollerball* sequence after first watching a non-violent extract from *The French Connection*.

The sequence from *Rollerball* was described to some of the subjects as an example of justified aggression. The victim was described in such a way that the beating appeared to be just and deserved. Other subjects were told that the beating was gratuitous and uncalled for. Finally, after the *Rollerball* scene, all subjects retaliated verbally against another person who had previously provoked them. Table 4.2 summarizes the main findings of the study. After seeing a non-violent control tape, subjects who saw a "justified" version of the aggression from *Rollerball* were verbally more aggressive than those who had seen the "unjustified" version. However, when the violent tape had preceded the *Rollerball* scene, all differences due to justification versus non-justification disappeared. What does this mean? Possibly that prior exposure to a long scene of violence reduced overall sensitivity to subsequently presented violent stimuli. Subjects who had seen the violent *French Connection* scene were therefore less aggressive in response to justified aggression, but more aggressive in response to unjustified aggression, than they would normally be.

## Pornography and aggression

Some of the material that we call pornography represents a special case of violent stimuli. Although the content of such pornographic displays is sexual, sex is not an end in itself but rather a means whereby the real purpose of the drama is served: aggression against a human victim, who is almost always a woman. For that reason it is properly included in a discussion of violence in the mass media. The

*Table 4.2*  Average intensities of verbal aggression

|  | First videotape | |
| --- | --- | --- |
| Second videotape | Violent scene | Non-violent scene |
| Justified violence | 45.95[ab*] | 47.30[a] |
| Unjustified violence | 40.95[abc] | 33.85[c] |

* Cells having common superscripts are not significantly different from each other
Source: Geen (1981)
Note: Verbal aggression is defined as a rating of the subject's impression of the target person on a 100—point scale where 0 = a maximally positive impression and 100 = a maximally negative rating

question we will address in this section is whether observation of pornography engenders or facilitates the expression of aggression against women.

*Effects of viewing pornography*
The role of pornography in violence against women has been studied extensively (Donnerstein 1984). Much of the evidence suggests that observation of pornography is associated with violence against female victims. For example, Donnerstein (1980) arranged to have male subjects give electric shocks to another person, either another man or a woman, supposedly as punishments for errors committed in performance of a task. Before delivering the punishments, each subject watched a short videotape. Some saw a bland control tape containing neither violence nor sex. Others saw a scene depicting intimate heterosexual relations between two people, while still others watched a movie of a violent rape. The latter film, in other words, showed violence in a sexual context. Donnerstein found that whereas observation of the erotic (but non-violent) tape was followed by no more aggression than observation of the control stimulus, the violent rape scene was associated with significantly stronger shocks to a female victim. This was true, furthermore, even when the subject had no reason to be angry with his victim. The aggressive-pornographic scene also elicited more aggression against a woman than against a man. Altogether, Donnerstein's study indicates that watching violent pornography can lead to aggression against women.

A subsequent experiment by Donnerstein and Berkowitz (1981) extended the findings cited here by showing that when rape is depicted as something the female victim seems to enjoy, aggression by men against women is further enhanced. This view – that women secretly like to be sexually abused and assaulted by men – is called the "rape myth" (Burt 1980). Belief in this myth is fostered by exposure to violent pornography. Malamuth and Check (1981) carried out a large-scale field experiment in which more than 200 men and women watched either two violent pornographic movies or two neutral ones. All persons were later asked to respond to two attitude scales. One measured acceptance of violence against women, and the other measured belief in the rape myth. Among male viewers, those who had seen the pornographic movies expressed higher scores for both acceptance of violence against women and belief in the rape myth than those who had seen the control films. Women showed the opposite reactions. Among female viewers, exposure to pornography tended to depress even further what were already low scores on both variables.

*Likelihood of raping*
Drawing generalizations about male aggressiveness and attitudes toward rape from research on pornography may be somewhat misleading. Despite the obvious effects cited above, it is likley that many men are exposed to pornography without committing rape. Men show considerable individual differences in their attitudes toward women and in the likelihood of aggressing against them. Likelihood of raping (LR) is a motivational variable that has been shown to moderate some of the situational effects associated with the presentation of pornographic stimuli (Malamuth 1984). It is measured by means of a simple five-point rating scale by which men

*Figure 4.1* Self-reported arousal among men high or low in likelihood of raping in response to observation of rape, as a function of rape victim's behavior

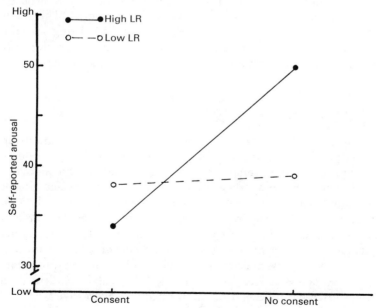

*Source:* Malamuth and Check (1983)
*Note:* Scores represent self-ratings of arousal on a raising scale, with high values indicating high arousal levels

indicate how likely they would be to commit rape if they knew that they would not be punished for it.

The LR variable is associated with both aggression toward women and attitudes toward women. Men who score high on this variable are more likely than low scorers to report that they have used force against females for sexual purposes and that they will probably do so again. Under controlled laboratory conditions, men high in LR have also been shown to be more aggressive toward women than men low in LR, but not toward other men (Malamuth 1984). A study by Malamuth and Check (1983) has also shown that LR moderates the amount of arousal that men experience while watching certain types of pornography. Men in this study listened to audiotapes of a sexual interaction between a man and a woman. The content of the tapes was varied in such a way that the woman either consented to the sexual relations or was forced to submit. In addition, the woman in each of these conditions was shown either to be aroused by the relationship, or to be disgusted by it. The results of the study (see Figure 4.1) showed that when the woman heard on the tape seemed to be enjoying the sexual act, men high in LR were more aroused when she was being forced than when she consented. This combination of conditions, indicating that a woman is being sexually aroused by rape, constitutes the rape myth. Thus, men high in LR are more aroused by the rape myth than are men low in LR.

## Aggressiveness and media preference

Little attention has been paid to the possibility that the relationship between aggressive behavior and the viewing of media violence may be reciprocal. Not only may viewing violence lead to aggression, but people who behave aggressively may seek out and prefer violent programs in their television viewing. If the latter is true, the link between television violence and aggression may be circular and self-sustaining. Fenigstein (1979) has reported evidence suggesting that aggression may influence television viewing practices. In the first of two experiments, male subjects who had been induced to create aggressive fantasies later elected to view films more violent than those chosen by subjects who had formed non-aggressive fantasies. No such effect was found among women. In a second experiment, males who had been allowed to aggress physically selected material for viewing that was more violent than that chosen by nonaggressing males. Thus, both fantasy and actual aggression led to a preference for violent over non-violent media fare among men. This finding is consistent with the report by Diener and DuFour (1978) of a positive correlation among men between scores on the aggressiveness subscale of the California Psychological Inventory and preference for violent television programs.

## Non-experimental research on media violence

Experimental research such as that reviewed in the preceding section allows investigators to test some fairly subtle hypotheses and effects. By controlling sources of extraneous variation in their studies, experimental researchers are able to isolate certain other variables (such as arousal, disinhibition, and social comparison processes) and to test whether such variables are in fact antecedents of aggression. For this reason, experimental studies constitute an important part of the literature on the effects of media violence (Geen and Thomas 1986). However, experiments have limitations as well as advantages. They examine behavior over short periods of time only. They involve behaviors that usually bear little relationship to the sort of aggressive behavior in which people engage on a daily basis. The samples of television programs that they use represent only a small portion of the wide array of programs seen on television. At best, therefore, experiments may involve analogs of aggression rather than a cross-section of it (Freedman 1984).

A more complete analysis of media effects on aggression must therefore include results from studies carried out under natural conditions. In this section we will review three types of study: the field experiment; the longitudinal study; and the study of archival material.

### Field experiments

In a field experiment, independent variables are manipulated and controlled, and dependent variables measured, much as they are in a laboratory experiment. The entire procedure takes place in a natural setting, however. The degree of control is not as high as it is in the laboratory, but, because the event takes place in a more realistic setting, external validity is perhaps greater. Some field experiments have yielded data that are largely in agreement with laboratory findings. Goldstein *et al.* (1975) carried out an experiment in which male subjects in a theater were shown a violent motion picture, an erotic non-violent one, or a non-arousing control film. After seeing the film, all subjects were given a questionnaire by means of which they expressed their opinions on how harshly lawbreakers should be punished. Aggressiveness was defined in terms of the level of punitiveness expressed. The moviegoers expressed an increase in punitive attitudes over baseline levels after having seen a violent film, but not after seeing an erotic or a neutral one. Other studies have involved more direct measures of aggression. A series of experiments conducted by Parke *et al.* (1977) showed that the behavior of delinquent boys in a penal institution became more aggressive as a result of exposure to five consecutive nights of violent television programs, and also that this high exposure to violence made the boys more punitive in a subsequent laboratory experiment.

## Longitudinal studies of observed violence

### Studies of American subjects
Longitudinal studies involve the repeated measurement of television viewing and aggressive behavior under real-life conditions over a lengthy period of time. One such project has been reported by Eron and his associates. This work began with a study of third-grade children in a rural county in the state of New York in 1960, in which each child's aggressiveness was assessed through ratings made by the child's peers and parents and by the children themselves (Eron *et al.* 1971). Each child's preference for violent television programs was also measured. Ten years later, measures of the same variables were obtained for a large number of the children used in the original sample (Lefkowitz *et al.* 1977).

The data from the two periods were analyzed by means of cross-lagged panel correlations. In cross-lagged panel correlation, measures of two variables made at one time ($A_1$ and $B_1$) are correlated with measures of the same two variables made at a later time ($A_2$ and $B_2$). If the magnitude of the correlation between $A_1$ and $B_2$ is substantially greater than the magnitude of the correlation between $B_1$ and $A_2$, this is taken as an indication that cause and effect goes from $A$ to $B$ and not vice versa. In the study by Lefkowitz *et al.*, the correlation between viewing of televised violence in grade 3 and

aggression ten years later was compared with the correlation between aggression at the early age and viewing of violence ten years
hence. This analysis revealed that preference for television violence
among third-grade boys was positively and significantly correlated
with aggressiveness ten years later, whereas aggressiveness in grade 3
was not correlated with preference for televised violence a decade
later (see Figure 4.2).

   This pattern of correlations supports the hypothesis that, for boys,
observation of television violence in childhood contributes to aggressiveness in young adulthood. Additional analyses showed that the
pattern of results was not due to differences in the level of aggressiveness among children who did or did not like violent television in third
grade. Across all levels of aggressiveness – high, moderate, and low –
in third-graders, an early preference for violent television was correlated significantly with aggressiveness ten years later. This relationship was not weakened by the controlling of several possible
contaminating variables, such as the socio-economic status of the
boys' parents, the boys' intelligence, parental aggressiveness, and the
total number of hours of television watched. Among girls, however,
preference for violent television in grade 3 was not significantly
related to aggressiveness in young adulthood.

   More recently, Huesmann *et al.* (1984) have reported the results of

*Figure 4.2*   Pattern of cross-lagged correlations between amount of violent
television watched and aggression over ten-year period

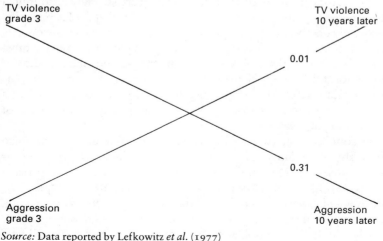

Source: Data reported by Lefkowitz *et al.* (1977)

a second follow-up study, involving 295 people from their original pool, 22 years after the original one. Data were gathered from interviews with the subjects, both face-to-face and mailed, interviews with spouses and children of the subjects, and archival records including criminal justice files. Childhood aggression was shown to be a predictor of both aggression and criminal behavior even 22 years later. Furthermore, the seriousness of the crimes for which *males* were convicted by age 30 was shown to be significantly related to the amount of television watched as eight-year-old boys. The findings of this investigation are therefore consistent with those of the ten-year follow-up reported by Lefkowitz *et al.* (1977).

The results of a study carried out by Eron and Huesmann (1980) in the Chicago area support the conclusions of the earlier research. Cross-lagged correlations over a period of one year (1977–8) showed that among boys the correlation between frequency of observing aggression in 1977 and aggressiveness in 1978 was positive and larger than the correlation between aggression in 1977 and frequency of watching violence in 1978. Among boys, therefore, the findings were much the same as they had been in the earlier study. Among girls, however, the results were different. All correlations between observation of violence on television and aggressiveness were positive, but their pattern was the *opposite* of that found for boys. The correlation between aggressiveness in 1977 and viewing of violence in 1978 was greater than the obverse.

How may this finding for girls be explained? One possibility is that girls learn a certain set of sex roles that they are strongly encouraged to play as they mature (see Chapter 6). In part, these roles prescribe generally passive and non-aggressive behavior in the face of conflicts rather than overt aggression. A girl who is typically aggressive must therefore find outlets for her emotions that do not include violent behavior. One such outlet could be vicarious aggression. From year to year during childhood the aggressive girl may come more and more to turn toward violence on television as a major means of expressing her feelings.

A connection between violence viewing and aggression has also been shown by Singer and Singer (1981) on the basis of a one-year study involving 141 children of nursery school age. On four occasions during the year, two-week periods were used as "probes", during which parents kept logs of their children's television viewing. Meanwhile, observers also recorded instances of aggressive behavior by the children in school. When data were combined across all four probes, aggressive behavior was found to be significantly correlated with the total amount of time spent viewing "action-adventure" television programs (which had a high level of violence), for both boys and girls.

The pattern of cross-lagged correlations over the four probe periods again supported the conclusion that viewing violence on television produces subsequent aggression. In general, the magnitude of the correlations between violence viewing on early probes and aggression on later ones was larger than that of correlations between aggression on early probes and violence viewing on later ones (see Figure 4.3). However, this usual effect was not found

*Figure 4.3*   Selected cross-lagged correlations between level of viewing action shows (AS) and aggressiveness across three probe periods

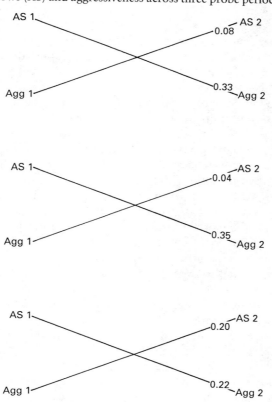

*Source:* Data reported by Singer and Singer (1981)

during the latter stages of the study, i.e. from probe 2 to probe 3. Viewing of action-adventure programs in the second probe period was correlated with aggression in the third ($r = 0.22$), but aggression in the second period was also correlated with viewing of action –adventure shows in the third ($r = 0.20$). This latter finding suggests that a liking for potentially aggressive television programs may be engendered by aggressiveness in behavior. Overall, therefore, the Singer and Singer data may indicate a circular process, by which observing violence early in the year led to subsequent aggressiveness in the children, which in turn fostered an appetite for still more of the same sort of program. The finding that aggressiveness may lead to a preference for violent television is similar to the finding reported by Fenigstein (1979), already noted, in the context of a laboratory study.

*Cross-cultural studies*
Additional evidence of a connection between the viewing of televised violence and aggression comes from a series of longitudinal studies carried out in five countries: the United States, Australia, Finland, Poland, and Israel. Two samples were studied in Israel: one from an urban setting and the other from a rural kibbutz. The findings are reported in several contributions to Huesmann and Eron (1986). The time period of the study was three years, and more than 1,000 boys and girls were tested. Aggressiveness was studied as a concomitant of such variables as the violence of preferred programs, overall viewing of violence, identification with televised aggressors, and judgments of realism of televised violence. In general, the evidence from the cross-cultural studies were consistent with those obtained from American samples in earlier research. Early television viewing was associated with aggressiveness among boys in the United States, Finland, Poland, and urban Israel. Among girls, early television viewing was related to aggression in the United States and urban Israel. Moreover, early aggression was associated with increased viewing of televised violence for boys and girls in the United States and Finland, and for girls in urban Israel.

A final interesting finding of the studies was that children whose parents were relatively aggressive and rejecting were themselves more aggressive and more likely to watch televised violence than children with less aggressive parents. This finding led Huesmann (1986a) to suggest that children who behave aggressively may thereby incur parental punishment and rejection, which in turn causes them to retreat into a fantasy world of violent television. The link between children's aggression and the viewing of violent television may therefore be less one of direct cause and effect than one mediated by parental and family variables.

## The mass media and aggression in natural settings

Experimental and longitudinal studies are different in many respects but in one way they are similar: at least some of the persons involved (e.g., the experimental subjects, the parents who monitor a child's television viewing, the teacher who rates a child's aggression) realize that they are taking part in an investigation. To some extent, therefore, the measurements are intrusive in that they break into the ongoing flow of behavior and possibly remind the participants of the purpose of the study. Another type of naturalistic study avoids this by involving the measurement of media effects and aggression after the fact and unknown to the participants. Usually this type of study consists of the analysis of public records and archival data. Inferences of cause and effect may then be drawn from evidence of a spatial or temporal relationship between media violence and aggressive reactions. For example, several writers have proposed that certain aggressive acts may occur in clusters following some spectacular violent incident, such as an airplane hijacking or mass murder, that is widely reported to the mass media (see, for example, Berkowitz 1971). The proximity of the aggressive acts to the preceding violent events may suggest the possibility that the latter somehow elicit, or facilitate the occurrence of, the former.

### Impact of introduction of television
One way to approach the question of whether television violence affects aggression in viewers is to observe whether the introduction of television to a viewing public is followed by an increase in the incidence of aggression. An assumption in such studies is that a large proportion of televised programming is devoted to violence. This assumption has been borne out by research evidence, as noted earlier in this chapter. Communities now being exposed to television for the first time are virtually non-existent in the United States but may still be found in the remote regions of northern Canada. Results of one Canadian study of behaviors following the introduction of television (Joy et al. 1986) showed that in one town differences in verbal and

physical aggression from before the introduction of television to after the introduction were greater than in two control communities that had had television prior to the time of the study. The introduction of television was thus associated with increased violence. On the other hand, a study by Hennigan *et al.* (1982) showed that the introduction of television to certain American cities in the early 1950s was not followed by any significant increase in violent crime, although at least one non-violent crime, larceny, did increase. Thus, although the introduction of television did not promote the commission of crimes like homicide and assault, it was nevertheless associated to a degree with an increase in anti-social behavior.

*Effects of media in suicides and homicides*
An ambitious and systematic attempt to account for real-world aggression with a hypothesis derived from experimental research has been made in a series of investigations by Phillips (1974; 1977; 1978; 1979; 1982; 1983). Dealing entirely with archival data, Phillips has sought to show a causal connection between violence-related events shown on television or reported in other news media and increments in aggressive acts among the public in the immediate aftermath of the reports. The connection is attributed to processes of suggestion and imitation similar to those described by Bandura in his laboratory investigations. In his first investigation, Phillips (1974) showed that the incidence of suicides increases immediately after a suicide has been reported in the newspapers, reaching a peak during the month immediately following the report. In addition, the increase in suicides was shown to be directly related to the amount of publicity given the publicly-reported suicides. Phillips (1974) described this phenomenon as the "Werther effect", after the character in Goethe's novel whose self-inflicted death was said to have elicited many real suicides among readers.

In a related study, Phillips (1979) showed a correlation between publicized suicides and the incidence of automobile fatalities. Interpretation of this finding rested on the assumption that some motor-vehicle accidents may in fact be due to suicidal intentions on the part of drivers involved. The number of motor vehicle deaths occurring over an 11-day period following each of 23 front-page suicide stories was compared with the average number of such deaths during four control periods in which no suicides were reported. In the case of all but five suicides, the number of automobile fatalities was greater following the story than during the control periods. Overall, the average number of fatalities increased significantly following suicide stories. The peak in incidence of traffic deaths occurred, on average, three days after the suicide stories were reported.

Phillips (1982) expanded upon these findings by finding a positive relationship between suicides shown in televised fiction and acts assumed to indicate suicidal motives. Thirteen suicides shown in televised soap operas during 1977 constituted the eliciting stimuli. The number of motor-vehicle deaths, non-fatal traffic accidents, and suicides all increased, compared to rates during a control period consisting of the latter part of the weeks in which the fictitious suicides were shown.

In a study that pertains more directly to evidence from experimental research, Phillips (1983) has reported a relationship between televised heavyweight prize fights and the incidence of homicides in the United States over a ten-day period following each fight. The effects of 18 fights between 1973 and 1978 were analyzed in this way. The largest increase in homicides came on the third day after a fight, a finding that parallels the peak in allegedly suicidal accidents noted above. In addition, Phillips reports that the murders of white males increased on the day that a white heavyweight was beaten, and increased again on the second day after the fight, whereas the murders of black males increased on the fourth and fifth days after the defeat of a black fighter. A race-specific modeling effect is suggested by these findings, but once again the fact that the lag time between the fight and the peak in homicides is different for the two races cannot be accounted for by a simple modeling hypothesis. Apparently, some of Phillips's findings involve the operation of variables not yet accounted for theoretically. It should also be pointed out that Phillips's findings and conclusions have been criticized on methodological grounds (see, for example, Kessler and Stipp 1984).

*Spectator aggression in sports*
The problem of aggressive behavior among spectators at sporting events is one that provokes considerable discussion. Aggression among spectators has been a part of sporting events since ancient times (Guttmann 1983), but it has attracted particular attention in the past few years following some unpleasant incidents at World Cup soccer matches and rioting among fans following the baseball World Series in the United States. In many respects the behavior of observers at sporting events, particularly those involving rough contact, is

similar to that of persons watching violence on television or in motion pictures. Several studies carried out in natural settings indicate that spectators at aggressive sporting events often tend to become more hostile and to experience less positive affect as a result. In aggressive spectator sports, as in the case of violent television, there is little evidence of symbolic catharsis.

A good example of increased hostility following an aggressive sporting event is found in a study by Goldstein and Arms (1971). Male spectators were interviewed before and after a game of American football involving two traditional rivals, with males in a control group being interviewed before and after a competitive but non-aggressive intercollegiate swimming match. Both sets of interviews contained a self-report hostility scale. Hostility after the football game was found to be greater than it had been before the game, regardless of which team the respondent had supported. The increased hostility was not, therefore, entirely due to anger over having seen a favored team defeated. No changes in hostility were found among spectators at the swimming meet. In a subsequent study, Arms et al. (1979) found evidence of increased hostility following both a hockey game and a series of wrestling matches, but not after a swimming competition.

Whereas hostility during aggressive sporting matches may be to some extent independent of what happens to the spectators' favored team, as Goldstein and Arms (1971) showed, it is not entirely unrelated to what transpires in the game. Some of the normative principles involved in aggression which were discussed in Chapter 1 may also play an important role in spectator hostility and aggressiveness. It will be recalled that aggression is defined in normative terms as an act of harm that exceeds the amount required to score, to defend one's goal, or to carry out other necessary parts of the game. It will also be recalled that persons tend to regard their own harmdoing as less aggressive than the actions of those who harm them. Given these considerations, it may follow that fans who identify closely with one team of athletes tend to regard that team as "cleaner" and less vicious than teams against whom they compete. Thus, any violence that occurs on the field will tend to be defined as an affront to the favored team, and any penalty assessed by referees against the favored team will be viewed as an injustice. In a study that suggests these possibilities, Smith (1976) conducted an analysis of 68 accounts of hostile crowd behavior at sporting events in a Toronto newspaper between 1963 and 1973, and found that the two most common causes were, in order of occurrence, "prior assaultive behavior" and "unpopular officials' decisions".

## Cognitive processes in media-induced aggression

Phillip's invocation of the idea of modeling and imitation to account for his finding once again raises the question of the limitations of this theoretical explanation. As was noted earlier in this chapter, processes of observational learning and imitation may account for the acquisition of some novel aggressive responses but hardly explain the wide range of complex effects found in studies of the effects of observing violence. Likewise, the several other explanations that have been offered – those involving disinhibition, arousal, and the acquisition of aggressive attitudes – are not sufficient to explain the general processes that underlie the results of the research studies. However, in recent years two additional theoretical explanations for the effects of media violence have been offered. Both provide more comprehensive explanations than do earlier viewpoints. Both, moreover, are derived from the premises of contemporary cognitive psychology.

### Retrieval of violent scripts

Huesmann (1986b) has proposed that when children observe violence in the mass media, they thereby learn complicated *scripts* for social behavior. The theory of scripts was originally developed by Abelson (1976). The fundamental element in a script is in the *vignette*, defined as "an encoding of an event of short duration", consisting of both a perceptual image and a "conceptual representation" of the event. A simple vignette might consist, for example, of an image of one person hitting another (image) in anger over something the other person has done (a conceptual representation). A script consists of a sequence of vignettes. Such scripts define situations and guide behavior: "Cognitively mediated social behavior depends on the occurrence of two processes: (a) the selection of a particular script to represent the given situation and (b) the taking of a participant role within that script" (Abelson, 1976, p. 42). Once a script has been learned, it may be retrieved at some later time as a guide for behavior.

How does one know which of the many scripts in a person's memory will be retrieved on a given occasion? Granted that some aggressive scripts may be learned from observation of violence, why should one of them, and not some other, be recalled when the person has been provoked and is in a state of interpersonal conflict? One answer that has been suggested to these questions involves the principle of encoding specificity (Tulving and Thomson 1973). According to this theory, the recall of information depends in large part on the similarity of the recall situation to the situation in which encoding occurred. As a child develops, she or he may observe cases in which violence has been used as means of resolving interpersonal conflicts. Such events are common in television programming. The information is then stored, possibly to be retrieved later when the child is involved in a conflict situation. Retrievability will depend partly on the similarity between cues present at the time of encoding and those present at the time of retrieval. Certain stimulus conditions may determine what happens during the encoding process. Any characteristic of observed violence that makes a scene stand out and attract attention should enhance the degree to which that scene is encoded and stored in memory (Huesmann 1982). One such characteristic may be the perceived reality of violence: acts of aggression seen as real may be regarded as more instrumental to the solving of future conflicts than less realistic ones. As noted earlier in this chapter, several studies have shown that when portrayals of violence are said to be of real events they elicit more aggression than when they are described in less realistic terms.

*Priming of aggressive associations*
A line of reasoning similar to that of Huesmann has been followed by Berkowitz (1984, p. 411), according to whom "the aggressive ideas suggested by a violent movie can prime other semantically related thoughts, heightening the chances that viewers will have other aggressive ideas in this period". Berkowitz bases this "priming" hypothesis on the notion of spreading activation (Collins and Loftus 1975): thoughts send out radiating activation along associative pathways, thereby activating other related thoughts. In this way, ideas about aggression that are not identical to those observed in the media may be elicited by the latter. In addition, thoughts are linked, along the same sort of associative lines, not only to other thoughts but also to emotional reactions and behavioral tendencies (Bower 1981; Lang 1979). Thus, observation of movie violence can engender a complex of associations consisting of aggressive ideas, emotions related to violence, and the impetus for aggressive actions.

The hypothesis of cognitive priming may also help explain the finding that the presence of weapons is sometimes associated with elevated levels of aggression. This finding, first reported by Berkowitz and LePage (1967) and since replicated and extended by others (e.g., Leyens and Parke 1975; Turner and Goldsmith 1976; Turner *et al.* 1975) may indicate that weapons, because of their associations with violence, prime aggressive thoughts, emotions, and behavioral dispositions which facilitate the expression of aggressive behavior in frustrating or provocative settings. Advocates for stricter gun control in the United States usually tend to base their case on the argument that easy availability of guns provides the means for violent crime. The work of Berkowitz and his associates suggests that widespread exposure to such weapons may have an additional effect on aggression by actually stimulating aggressive actions.

*Scripting and priming: an experimental test*
Josephson (1987) tested the scripting and priming hypotheses in a study involving school-age boys. The boys were first shown a television program on either a non-violent or a violent topic. In the latter, a group of police officers battled with a number of snipers, all of whom were eventually killed or captured. In the course of their activities, the police were shown using walkie-talkies. After the completion of the television presentation, the boys engaged in a game of floor hockey, during which observers recorded the incidence of aggressive behaviors. Just prior to beginning the game, each child was exposed to either an adult authority who carried and used a walkie-talkie or to an authority who did not carry such an instrument. All boys were, in addition, classified by their teachers according to whether they were typically aggressive or not aggressive in school.

By means of this experimental design Josephson tested three hypotheses. The first was that observation of a violent police film would activate the retrieval of aggressive scripts as Huesmann has indicated, so that boys who saw this videotape would be more aggressive while playing hockey than those who saw the non-violent presentation. This prediction was supported only for boys who had been described as highly aggressive by their teachers. Thus, retrieval of aggressive scripts is suggested, but only for boys presumed to have a large repertoire of such scripts available. The second hypothesis was that boys who had seen the violent video and who then later saw a walkie-talkie would be more aggressive than those who saw the violent video but not the walkie-talkie. Josephson's reasoning was that the walkie-talkie, which had been associated with violence in the video, would serve as a cue to prime other aggressive thoughts and emotions, in the way described by Berkowitz. This prediction was also supported, but again only among highly aggressive boys. This finding is not surprising if we consider that highly aggressive boys possess a relatively large network of aggressive associations that can be activated by a cue. The third hypothesis was that both of the aforementioned effects would occur early in the hockey game, i.e. shortly after the scripting and priming processes occurred. This, too, was found: virtually all the aggression induced by the stimuli took place in the first three minutes of the game.

*Televised violence and fear*

Viewing violence in the media may have long-range effects on behavior that do not have any obvious connection with immediate effects. In an extensive series of studies, Gerbner and his associates (e.g., Gerbner *et al.* 1980) have described one such long-range consequence of viewing violence. Briefly stated, the hypothesis of Gerbner *et al.* is that extended watching of television brings a person into contact with a high level of violence and that this violence fosters attitudes of fear, suspicion, and distrust. Over time, such attitudes may contribute to the formation of a distorted view of the world in which violence is given an importance disproportionate to its prevalence. It is not the purpose of this review to discuss research on this matter. However, evidence that televised violence elicits fear in viewers would be consistent with one of the assumptions behind Gerbner's work. Some studies have shown that fear may be an immediate consequence of watching presentations of violence (Cantor 1982; Groebel and Krebs 1983; Lagerspetz *et al.* 1978). Other evidence points to the conclusion that televised aggression is more likely to be assessed as disturbing by persons who score high in neuroticism (a variable conceptually related to anxiety) than by persons who score low in this variable (Gunter and Furnham 1983).

Additional evidence of an immediate increase in fear following exposure to media violence has been presented in a study by Bryant *et al.* (1981). Subjects received either heavy (more than four hours per day) or light (less than two hours per day) exposure to television drama over a period of days. Subjects who received the heavy exposure saw either crime dramas with socially just endings or similar dramas in which injustice prevailed. Subjects who received heavy exposure to crime drama of both types later expressed more concern about personal safety than those given lighter exposure. In addition, subjects who saw crime drama lacking justice experienced an increase in reported anxiety whereas subjects in the other conditions did not. In fact, observation of crime stories with just endings produced a reduction in anxiety among subjects who had been highly anxious at the outset.

Thus, it is possible that fear elicited by televised violence can contribute to the "scary" world view that Gerbner attributes to people who watch large amounts of television. Such an attitude could lead people to feel a need to protect themselves against a clear and present danger. Among the results could be public demands for punitive justice, authoritarian control, and vigilantism. For example, heavy users of television are more likely than lighter users to believe that too little money is being spent on fighting crime (Gerbner et al. 1982).

## Summary

1 Violence is common in the mass media of communication, especially motion pictures and television. Studies conducted in North America indicate a high level of violence in programming that has changed little over the years. Questions regarding the possible impact of such observed violence on viewers have led to extensive research in both laboratory and natural settings.

2 Observation of violence may promote the acquisition of new aggressive responses through observational learning and imitation.

3 Media violence influences aggression in ways other than observational learning, however. It may also provide information to the viewer concerning whether or not aggression is a permissible or desirable response. Observed violence that is portrayed as justified elicits aggression more than unjustified violence, and revenge elicits more aggression in the viewer than violence motivated by other concerns. Viewers who identify with the aggressor are more aggressive than those who do not. These findings may all indicate that angry viewers make social comparisons between themselves and aggressive characters in the

media and react to the violent acts of those persons with reduced inhibitions against aggressing.

4 Violence that is perceived as real elicits more aggression than that which is considered fictitious. Real violence may be more concrete to the viewer and hence more likely to attract and hold attention. It may therefore have more of an impact than fictitious violence. Observation of violence may also lead to increased tolerance of aggression, and thereby have possible long-range effects on attitudes and values where aggression is concerned.

5 Violence in the media may increase the arousal of the viewer. Increased arousal energizes dominant responses that the viewer is prepared to make, which may be aggressive ones in situations of interpersonal conflict. In addition, arousal elicited by media presentations may be misattributed to provocations and experienced as heightened anger. Prolonged exposure to media violence produces a habituation to such material. As a result, aggression in response to viewed violence will be increased or decreased by extended exposure depending on whether the violence would ordinarily facilitate or inhibit aggression.

6 The viewing of pornography by men is associated with aggression against female victims. Although non-violent sexual material does not elicit aggression against women, a depiction of violent rape does. Belief in the "rape myth" (that women secretly enjoy being sexually abused) is fostered by observation of pornography. Seeing a rape scene is especially likely to elicit greater feelings of violence toward women in male viewers when it shows the woman victim ostensibly enjoying the assault. Furthermore, men who admit to being relatively likely to commit rape are both more likely to aggress against women and to be aroused by manifestations of the rape myth than are men who are not likely rapists.

7 Research on media effects have almost all been addressed to showing that observation of violence facilitates aggression. The reverse has also been shown: both aggressive fantasizing and actual aggression are followed by increased preference for viewing violence.

8 Additional evidence that the viewing of violence promotes the development of aggressiveness in boys is found in longitudinal studies involving cross-lagged correlational analysis. In addition, aggressiveness also enhances tendencies to view violence, a finding also shown in laboratory research. Among girls, it has

been shown that aggressiveness promotes viewing of televised violence, a finding opposite to that found in boys. This finding may indicate that girls are socialized to suppress aggression and that aggressive girls may seek through watching violence a vicarious outlet for their hostile and aggressive feelings.

9  Some evidence indicates that the introduction of television into a region is accompanied by increased aggressive behavior.

10  The incidence of both suicides and homicides may be linked to presentations of violence in the media, such as in newspaper stories of suicides and television portrayals of either suicides or prize fights. These findings from archival sources parallel findings from experimental laboratories, but theoretical explanations of the naturalistic findings are not clear. More than imitative learning is obviously involved, but no overall theory has been advanced.

11  Two theoretical explanations based on cognitive psychology have been offered as to why observation of violence elicits aggression. According to one, children learn aggressive scripts as guides to behavior in situations of interpersonal conflict. The likelihood of retrieving an aggressive script as a subsequent guide to behavior depends in part on similarities between the encoding situation and the one in which retrieval is made. It has also been proposed that viewing violence primes aggressive thoughts, emotions, and action tendencies, making aggression in response to provocations more likely.

12  Observation of violence on television may have long-range effects on viewers by instilling attitudes of fear and mistrust. In extreme forms, this process may lead viewers to form unrealistically fearful views of their environments. Such fears may have social consequences, by leading viewers to demand greater use of force in the suppression of anti-social behavior.

## Suggestions for further reading

Berkowitz, L. (1984). Some effects of thoughts on anti- and prosocial influences of media events: A cognitive-neoassociationist analysis. *Psychological Bulletin,* **95**, 410–27. This paper describes an application of current theories of association and memory to the study of media-induced aggression.

Geen, R. G. and Thomas, S. L. (1986). The immediate effects of media violence on behavior. *Journal of Social Issues*, **42**, 7–27. This review discusses the literature on media-induced aggression with a heavy emphasis on laboratory studies. The entire issue of the *Journal of Social Issues* in which it appears is devoted to reviews on the effects of media violence.

Huesmann, L. R. (1986b). Psychological processes promoting the relation between exposure to media violence and aggressive behavior by the viewer. *Journal of Social Issues*, **42**, 125–39. Huesmann gives a description of the applications of script theory to the analysis of media effects on aggression.

Malamuth, N. M. and Donnerstein, E. (1984). *Pornography and Sexual Aggression*. New York: Academic Press. This book provides extensive reviews of theory and research on connections among pornography, arousal, male attitudes toward women, and rape.

# 5 / INTERVENING PROCESSES

The three preceding chapters have focused on some important conditions for aggression, such as interpersonal provocations, social and cultural factors, environmental stressors, and symbolic presentations of violence. All of these conditions are directly observable. We have argued that these antecedents lead ultimately to aggressive behavior, which is also observable. How this connection between antecedents and aggressive outcomes occurs is the subject of the present chapter. We will consider some of the processes that are alleged to occur after the conditions for aggression have been met. They are only alleged because such processes cannot be observed directly. Among these intervening states we include anger, arousal, cognitive mediations, attributions, and other such conditions. One might argue that such "invisible" states are superfluous and not necessary for explaining aggression. To a certain extent this is true. It is possible to know a great deal about aggression merely by observing situations and outcomes and noting the regularity with which the former leads to the latter. However, we have no idea why this is so. In psychology, it is common to postulate the existence of *intervening variables* which help to explain how certain conditions are related to certain behaviors. By doing so, we hope to learn more about the nature of cause and effect in behavior. As we shall see, considerable attention has been given to several intervening variables in the study of aggression.

## Arousal and aggression

### Arousal as a response activator

In Chapter 2, we observed that the frustration–aggression hypothesis was criticized and largely reformulated by theorists who rejected the notion of aggressive drive (e.g., Berkowitz 1965; 1969). Rather than accept the argument that frustration motivates consummatory aggressive responses which lead to drive reduction, these critics argued that frustrations, as well as other stimulus conditions that provoke a person, generate a state of arousal. This state in turn activates or energizes aggressive responses that the person is disposed to make. The contrast between the aggressive drive theory and the alternative described here is shown clearly in an experiment by Christy *et al.* (1971). Children first observed either an aggressive or a non-aggressive adult model, after which they engaged in one-on-one competitive behavior in which one child consistently won and the other consistently lost. Other children in a control condition interacted non-competitively. Afterwards, aggression in imitation of the model was measured. Children who had competed showed more imitative aggression than did those who had not competed. In addition, the competition winners showed as much imitative aggression as did the losers, who, presumably, should have been frustrated and driven to aggress. The results showed, therefore, that arousal elicited by competition energized aggressive behaviors that had been elicited by observation of the aggressive model.

By treating frustration or other provocations as sources of arousal, we may draw certain additional conclusions. One is that provocation need not always produce aggression. If people have been rigorously trained in non-violence, for example, provocations should activate appropriate non-aggressive behaviors. Furthermore, the provocation–arousal notion predicts the form that aggression will take when it does occur, because the nature of the aggressive behavior is determined by factors largely unrelated to the provocation. Finally, it should be noted that the concept of response energization provides for a simple mechanism by which arousal can affect aggressive behavior in ways stipulated by the model presented in Chapter 2.

# Arousal, cognition, and anger

## Arousal and cognitive labeling

Arousal may contribute to aggression in ways other than by energizing responses, however. It may combine with ideas and thoughts generated within the situation to create a state of heightened anger which leads directly to increased aggression. The original version of this idea was presented by Schachter and Singer (1962) as part of a general two-factor theory of emotion. In general, the theory postulated that an emotion is a joint function of a state of arousal and a cognition by means of which that state is understood and labeled. By arousal, Schachter and Singer mean the activation of physiological systems innervated by the autonomic nervous system; examples might be: increased heart rate and respiration, sweating of the palms, and gastric motility. More specifically, Schachter (1964) stated the theory in three premises:

1 If a person experiences a state of physiological arousal for which there is no immediate explanation, that state will be understood in terms of cognitions that are available.
2 If a person experiences a state of arousal for which an appropriate explanation exists, it is less likely that the arousal will be labeled in terms of available cognitions.
3 Given a particular set of cognitive circumstances, a person will experience emotion only to the extent that he or she feels physiologically aroused.

Manstead and Wagner (1981) have labeled these premises the *qualitative*, *null*, and *quantitative* predictions, respectively, and these terms will be used in what follows.

The particular relevance of the theory for aggression lies in its explanations of the origins of anger. This emotion should arise when a person becomes aroused and then attributes the aroused condition to some anger-related cognition. This can happen in one of two ways. The most common occurs when a person is provoked. In this case a single stimulus (the provocation) causes the increased arousal and also supplies the most likely cognition for interpretation and labeling of that state. Less common are situations in which the person is aroused for some unknown reason (such as by the unexpected side-effects of a drug). In these cases, the person presumably feels a need to understand why he or she is aroused and seeks clues in the environment. If the person happens, for example, to be a part of an angry mob that is cursing and jeering at referees in a football game, the person may decide that the arousal (which is really drug-induced) is part of an experience of anger.

In a widely-cited experiment which was designed to test their theory, Schachter and Singer (1962) created a situation similar to the second one described above. Subjects were first given an injection of either epinephrine (a drug whose effects mimic those of the autonomic nervous system and thus arouse the person) or a placebo. All subjects were then exposed to an experimental confederate who behaved in an angry and hostile way. Some subjects had been informed that the epinephrine would arouse them whereas others had not been so informed. Anger was measured both directly – through self-reports of mood by the subjects – and by inference from the subjects' behavior and verbalizations. Anger inferred in this way was found to be greater among subjects who had received epinephrine without being informed of its effects than among those who had been informed and those who had received the placebo. Self-reported anger was, however, no greater among subjects receiving epinephrine than among those given the placebo. Schachter and Singer (1962) concluded that these findings supported their theory.

Both the Schachter and Singer experiment and the theory on which it was based have been criticized on numerous grounds (see Reisenzein 1983; and Manstead and Wagner 1981, for reviews). These critiques are beyond the scope of this chapter and they will not be discussed. However, the two-factor theory of emotion has been extended by one research program to conditions different from those described by Schachter and Singer, and the work resulting from this extension has yielded some important findings. This is the program of Zillmann and his associates on *excitation transfer*.

### Excitation transfer and anger

As noted above, Schachter and Singer dealt with arousal that occurs at the same time as some emotionally relevant stimulus which provides the cognition whereby the arousal is labeled. Zillmann (1978) has described a general situation in which two arousing conditions occur in sequence. Autonomic arousal does not dissipate immediately upon termination of eliciting conditions; the processes involved in autonomic regulation follow a relatively slow and gradual time course in recovery. Given this fact, Zillmann has reasoned that if two arousing events are separated by a short amount of time, some of the arousal caused by the first event may become transferred to the second event and added to the arousal caused by the latter. If the second event is related to an emotional state, that emotion should become strengthened by the infusion of the added arousal (as would be predicted from Schachter's quantitative prediction described above).

The principle of excitation transfer can be applied to aggression in situations where "irrelevant" arousal transfers to provoking situations to intensify feelings of anger. In a typical situation of this kind the subject is first provoked by another person and then given an arousing treatment. Some time later the subject is again placed in contact with the provocateur. "As he is reconfronted with his annoyer, anger is cognitively reinstated, and residual excitation from [the arousing treatment] can potentiate anger and aggression because it is not linked to its appropriate source" (Zillmann 1978, p. 362). Residual arousal may come from a variety of sources. As will be recalled from the previous chapter, Zillmann (1971) found that male subjects who had been provoked and then shown a film of a man and a woman making love were subsequently more aggressive than similarly provoked subjects who had watched a film of a violent fight. In addition, the erotic film was more arousing than the violent one. Zillmann concluded that arousal generated by the films was in part transferred to the provocation and thus labeled as anger. Subjects who had seen the film of love-making were more angry than those who had seen violence simply because they were more aroused.

Arousal need not arise from an emotion-laden source like romantic love to be miscast as anger. Any activity that increases arousal should, when combined with sufficient provocation, serve as an antecedent of aggression. An experiment by Zillmann et al. (1972) shows this. Some of the subjects in this study were first provoked by an experimental confederate, after which half of the subjects engaged in strenuous physical exercise by riding an exercise bicycle. The other half performed a sedentary task. When subjects were later allowed to aggress against the confederate, those who had been provoked and then put through strenuous exercise were more aggressive than those who had also been provoked but who had performed the less physically demanding task. The effect of exercise on aggression was minimal among subjects who had not been provoked.

It should be noted that the temporal arrangement of the events involved in excitation transfer is critical to the process. Some time, but not too much, must intervene between the first (irrelevant) source of arousal and the second (emotional) event. If too much time elapses, of course, all excitation from the first source will dissipate. If not enough time expires, the aroused person will still experience salient and obvious symptoms of autonomic arousal (such as shortness of breath and sweating after exercise) which will easily be attributed to their true cause. In accordance with the null prediction of Schachter and Singer (see above), this clear explanation for arousal will forestall any transfer of that arousal to the emotional event. However, once the most obvious signs of activation have abated, the person will be less likely to make a correct attribution and transfer of excitation will become more likely (Cantor *et al.* 1975).

The temporal course of events described here is important because it makes possible a comparison of the excitation transfer principle with the response-energization approach described in the preceding section. Arguing from the latter position, one could dismiss excitation transfer as unnecessary and argue that the increased aggression following, say, physical exercise, is due only to increased drive which activates any response being made in the situation. We would expect that the drive arising from exercise would be at maximum strength immediately after the exercise and that it would decay over time. For that reason, the energization of aggression would be greatest when no time elapses between the two arousing events. According to Zillmann (1978), however, for reasons noted above, this should be the condition under which excitation transfer is *least* likely. There is some evidence bearing on this matter from a study that does not involve aggression and it supports Zillmann. Cantor *et al.* (1975) found that among subjects who had taken vigorous exercise, sexual arousal in response to erotic materials was greatest after a period of time had elapsed following the exercise. It was established that in this condition subjects were still autonomically aroused but no longer reporting the salient symptoms of arousal. This, of course, is exactly what Zillmann predicted.

The principle of excitation transfer is important for another reason. Once arousal has been labeled as anger, it can influence aggression far beyond the time at which arousal has dissipated. Thus, the misattribution process has implications for long-range behavior. An experiment by Bryant and Zillmann (1979) illustrates this point. Students in a class were first shown a videotape that was either highly arousing, moderately arousing, or relatively non-arousing; none of the videotapes portrayed violence or aggression. Subjects were then provoked by a hostile and insulting person described as a guest lecturer. Eight days later, the students were given an opportunity to express negative feelings about the guest lecturer, knowing that negative ratings would hurt that person's chances of obtaining a teaching position. Those students who had seen either the highly arousing or moderately arousing video eight days before were more critical and hostile in their ratings of the target than were those who had seen the non-arousing video. The arousing effects of the videotapes had undoubtedly worn off in eight days. However, when subjects made their hostile ratings of the target they could presumably recall the anger that they had felt, and the amount of anger they experienced seemed to depend on which videotape they had seen. It should be noted that anger was not directly measured, however.

*Limitations of excitation transfer*

Some problems associated with the excitation-transfer principle must be noted. One such problem has to do with the status of anger as a mediator of aggression. The literature on excitation transfer gives little evidence that anger is in fact influenced by transfer of arousal. Although a concordance between anger and aggression has been reported (cf. Donnerstein *et al.* 1976), such reports are rare. In Zillmann's research, anger is assumed to be an intervening variable, but it is not independently demonstrated. The role given by Zillmann to anger as the link between arousal and aggression is therefore in some doubt. In fairness to Zillmann, however, it must be admitted that in most experiments in which anger was measured and found not to be correlated with aggression, assessment came after the aggressive behavior. Anger may therefore have dissipated before the measurement was made.

Another problem concerns the source of irrelevant arousal. When arousal is elicited by some source that is *unlike* an aggressive provocation, it is less susceptible to transfer. For example, Bandura (1973) has argued that joyful or euphoric experiences, which customarily energize behaviors consistent with happiness, do not evoke aggression, even in angry people. Instead, they have a generally inhibiting effect on aggression. The reason for this may be that pleasant experiences elicit more than just arousal. They may also produce happy and euphoric thoughts that are antithetical to angry ones and are thus not likely to be confused with anger. The likelihood that a person will misattribute euphoric arousal to provocation is therefore small.

In support of this argument, Baron and Ball (1974) found that among subjects who had been provoked to anger by another person, exposure to non-hostile humorous cartoons led to significantly less retaliatory aggression than was found in similarly provoked subjects who had not been given cartoons. Baron (1978) also found that humor related to sex also served to render provoked subjects less aggressive than they would otherwise have been. After first arranging to have male subjects angered by an experimental accomplice, Baron showed the subjects either some neutral and non-arousing pictures or cartoons having sexual themes. Half of the latter were exploitative in that they showed one individual taking sexual advantage of another; the others were non-exploitative. Subsequent aggression against the provoking accomplice was of lower intensity among subjects who had seen the sexual cartoons than among those who had seen neutral pictures. In addition, exploitative humor reduced aggression more than non-exploitative humor. The reason for this was that subjects thought about the exploitative humor for a longer period of time after its removal than they did about the non-exploitative kind. By focusing on the humorous subject long after it was no longer present, these subjects were less likely to misattribute arousal arising from that humor to the provocation which had preceded it.

There is some reason to believe, therefore, that excitation transfer may be less likely when arousal is elicited by stimuli that evoke responses that are so different from aggression that they interfere with aggression. However, this generalization fails to account for the findings reported by Zillmann (1971), noted above. Certainly affectionate and romantic responses are quite different from aggression. Why, then, did Zillmann find that observation of an erotic non-violent film caused a high level of aggression in angry subjects? One possible answer is that excitation transfer varies with not only the type of arousing stimulus, but also the intensity of arousal evoked. It is possible that intensely arousing erotic material may facilitate a misattribution to another source, such as provocation, whereas milder erotic material does not. The results of a study by Baron and Bell (1977) support this hypothesis. In this study it was found that male subjects who were shown photographs of attractive nude women (taken from *Playboy* magazine) after having been provoked by an experimental confederate were less aggressive toward that person than were those who were shown non-sexual pictures. Possibly the still photographs used by Baron and Bell were less arousing than the motion pictures used by Zillmann.

Why should erotic material that is highly arousing be more likely to engender an excitation transfer than less arousing material? One possible answer is that people who become extremely aroused by such material have difficulty in accepting the fact that they are so influenced. In part this could be due to sexual fears and anxiety or to socialized inhibitions. The misattribution of sexual arousal to some other source could therefore be a defensive attribution. This could reconcile Zillmann's (1971) finding with the results of the Baron and Bell (1977) study.

Baron (1983) has also proposed another way in which erotic stimuli may or may not produce excitation transfer. He has suggested that erotic stimuli have two effects on viewers. The first is affective. Sexual stimuli may elicit either positive affect (pleasure and excitement) or negative affect (disgust and revulsion). Such stimuli also evoke high or low levels of arousal. The ways in which these two variables combine is the key to predicting the outcome. If, for example, arousal elicited by the erotic display is mild and the affect positive the person should easily be able to understand the state of arousal and to attribute it correctly to its cause. The result could be less aggression than would be the case if the erotic stimuli were not shown. If, however, arousal is high and affect negative, the overall strong negative feelings could be misattributed to anger arising from the provocation. The result could then be more aggression than would be the case if more neutral material had been shown. Whatever the explanation, however, it is clear that arousal does not always become misattributed to provocation, and that the excitation-transfer principle does have certain limits in explaining the relationship of arousal to aggression.

## Other viewpoints on anger

The attributional approach to aggression outlined in the previous section of this chapter assumes that anger is an intervening variable that mediates the relationship of provocation to aggression. This assumption reflects a common viewpoint concerning the role of anger in aggression, and is consistent with the approach taken by many psychologists. The revised form of the frustration–aggression hypothesis (Miller 1941), which was described in Chapter 2, held that frustration produced an *instigation* to aggression, which has commonly been considered to be a state of anger. Furthermore, attribution theorists assign to cognitive processes a central and *necessary* role in the generation of anger. Not all observers accept this definition of anger and its cognitive antecedents, however. In this section we will consider two theories of anger that depart from the attributional approach.

## Anger as an expressive-motor response

Berkowitz (1983) has taken issue with the attributional approach followed by Zillmann and his associates. While not denying the importance of cognition as one contributor to anger, Berkowitz denies that the labeling of arousal and the consequent experience of anger are necessary for either the generation of the anger state or any aggression that may follow. Instead, he argues that the experience or feeling of anger is a parallel process that accompanies but does not cause anger-relevant behavior.

In proposing his alternative to the attributional approach, Berkowitz follows the theory of emotion proposed by Leventhal (1980). This theory holds that a person's initial reaction to an emotional stimulus is a perceptual-motor reaction: the person perceives and interprets the stimulus and reacts to it immediately with certain bodily responses. These may include facial expressions, physiological activation, and muscular responses. These expressive responses are involuntary and largely outside the person's immediate awareness, even though they are later experienced as the distinctive emotion. The important point is that the person does not create an emotional experience in the deliberate and thoughtful way that attribution theorists describe in their process of cognitive labeling. Emotion, in Leventhal's theory, is a rapid, involuntary, and quickly developing process. Following the initial reaction, the person may then recall other emotional experiences similar to the one immediately felt. The input from memory causes the perception of the emotion to be richer than it would otherwise be, and also allows for the elaboration of other related emotional states, most of them more subtle than the emotion felt initially.

Applying this theory to anger, Berkowitz maintains that an aversive situation, such as an insult, a frustration, or some obnoxious environmental condition, sets off an immediate emotional reaction with all of the latter's motor and expressive features. This emotion is felt as anger. In addition, the angered person is reminded of a number of associated thoughts and feelings from past experiences in which anger was felt, and these associated thoughts and mood states amplify the feeling of anger. This entire process is associative: the associations among anger-related thoughts and feelings are a product of the person's past history of experience and learning and they are organized in a network. Anger may also be experienced as a conscious sensation, but this experience is parallel to, and not a cause of, the associative process. Thus, the person does not label an arousal state with conscious ideas in order to experience anger. The anger is present independent of the person's awareness of it.

## Anger as a social construction

The definition of anger as an intervening variable in the relationship of provocation to aggression has been challenged by Averill (1982; 1983) in ways consistent with a general theory of emotions that he has formulated. Averill considers emotions to be socially defined and constructed syndromes of affective, cognitive, and physiological processes. Emotions are complex reactions to situations and include biological, social, and cultural components. The experience of an emotion is actually the playing out of a transitory role that is defined in social and cultural terms. The common notion that anger follows provocation and in turn produces aggression is considered by Averill to be overly simplistic, even though he concedes that at the biological level this definition is acceptable to some degree.

Averill's views are supported by the results of several studies that he has conducted on the everyday experience of emotion as reported by laypersons. In these studies, people were given questionnaires by means of which they described in detail their recent experiences of anger. Several questions could be answered from analysis of the responses, such as: (1) Who or what was the target of the anger? (2) What type of person was likely to be the target of interpersonal anger? (3) How justified was the act that elicited the anger? (4) Was the act willful and deliberate? (5) Could the act have been prevented, and was it avoidable? The responses yielded more information than this sample of questions would suggest, but we will concentrate on these issues to illustrate Averill's findings.

Some of the findings from the studies were consistent with the more common findings of experimental research on aggression. For example, the incidents that led to anger were more likely to be described as willfully caused and unjustified than to be classified as unintentional or justified. In addition, a fair number of anger-causing incidents were described as having been due to mere carelessness and negligence. Averill (1982, p. 174) also found that 82 per cent of all respondents in one study reported feeling anger in response to "frustration or the interruption of some ongoing or planned activity", a finding that directly supports the frustration–aggression hypothesis. Sixty-three per cent reported feeling anger following "violation of socially accepted ways of behaving or widely shared rules of conduct", thereby supporting the argument of DaGloria and DeRidder (1977) that norm-violation is a major antecedent of anger (Chapter 2). In addition, 68 per cent reported anger as a reaction to "violation of . . . wishes which are important to you but which may not be widely shared by others", which relates to the findings of Mummendey *et al.* (1984) that the appraisals of the situation by the harmdoer and the victim of harm are quite divergent (see Chapter 2).

Some of Averill's findings are not similar to those of other research, however. Aggression, when reported, is usually on the level of verbal hostility and not physical assault. Furthermore, the most commonly reported target of anger is a friend, acquaintance, or loved one of the provoked person. Although this finding probably comes as no surprise, given that one has more interaction with close friends and family than with strangers, experimental research on aggression usually investigates anger and aggression in settings involving total strangers. Averill (1982, p. 174) also found that a commonly reported cause of anger is a "loss of personal pride, self-esteem, or sense of personal worth" that follows the harmful actions of another person. Experimental studies of anger and aggression usually do not take self-esteem into account. Analysis of the motives that underlie anger likewise provides some unusual findings. The most strongly endorsed motive for getting angry was "to reassert . . . authority or independence, or to improve (one's) image" (Averill 1982, p. 177). Seeking retaliation against the instigator of the anger was a less powerful motive for anger than was restoration of the self-image. Expression of dislike for the instigator was an even weaker motive, as was getting even for past wrongs by that person. On the other hand, a relatively potent motive was "bringing about a change in the behavior of the instigator". Such change was sought for two reasons: to effect some desirable outcome for the angry person, or to bring about a better outcome for the instigator. This latter point suggests that we sometimes become angry with other people for their own good, i.e., so that they will change in a way that is best for them.

What all of this suggests is that anger is seen by the respondents in Averill's study to be related to many outcomes other than retaliation.

From all this, Averill (1982) concludes that anger is not merely a motive for aggression. On a biological level, anger is linked to aggression to some extent, but at other levels – the psychological and social-cultural – anger has less to do with aggression than with other outcomes. On the psychological level, the major aim of anger is not aggression but the correcting of a wrong. This is reflected in the importance of lost self-esteem for anger, and the desire to restore authority and self-image by expression of anger. The need to right a wrong is also reflected in the role seen for anger in the changing of the instigator's behavior and to bring that person's actions into line with what the angry person considers to be propriety. On the social-cultural level, anger is a reaction to violation of accepted standards of conduct, and is animated by a desire to restore the instigator's behavior to those standards.

## Attributional mediators of aggression

In the preceding chapter we noted that provocations such as attacks or frustrations need not always lead to aggression. Certain interpretations of these events must be made for aggression to follow. The provocation must be regarded as intentional and malicious in intent. It must be viewed as a violation of normative behavior in social situations. It must lead to outcomes that are regarded as alternatives to more desired outcomes, i.e., it must be seen as being avoidable. A number of attributes are therefore assigned to the provocative act. In this section we will review in greater detail the nature of the attribution process that intervenes between provocation and aggression. This process has been summarized by Ferguson and Rule (1983); their conclusions will form the outline of the section.

Ferguson and Rule base their attributional analysis on the answers to three questions that a person asks after having been harmed by someone. The questions are:

1 *What was the act of harm that was done?* The answer to this question goes into the intent of the actor and whether or not the actor could foresee the harmful consequences of the act.

2 *What ought to have been done under the circumstances?* The answer to this question is based on consideration of what is

normative in the situation and what values are held by the observer.

3 *Does any discrepancy exist between what has been done and what ought to have been done?*

Depending on the answers to these questions the victim of harm will either hold the actor culpable or will absolve him or her of blame. Anger will be experienced to the extent that he or she is held responsible for the harm that has been done. Aggression is assumed to be a direct outgrowth of anger.

*Understanding the harmful act*

The first judgment that the harmed person makes is whether the other person acted intentionally or whether the harm was not intentional. If a judgment is made that the harm was intended, it is further classified as either malevolent or nonmalevolent in intent. If the act is judged to be unintentional, a further determination is made of whether or not the harmdoer could foresee the consequences of his or her actions. Hence the act of harm may be defined as one of four types: (1) intentional and malevolent; (2) intentional but not malevolent; (3) not intended but foreseeable; and (4) unintentional and unforeseeable, this last type of harm being truly accidental. Three separate attributions must be made before an act can be located within this scheme: intent, foreseeability, and motive.

*Attributions of intent*

Judgments of intentionality are made along two general lines. One has to do with the nature of the situation and the other with character of the harmdoer. In the first case, a judgment is made as to whether the harmdoing was the only act possible, whether any reasons for it (other than infliction of harm) could be imagined, and whether the consequences of the act for the actor were mainly harmful or beneficial. For example, a victim, harmed by someone but knowing that the harmful behavior was the only option that the perpetrator had, is likely to conclude that the act was not intentional but was compelled by circumstances. If, for example, a motorist swerves to avoid hitting a child and in so doing strikes and kills the child's dog, this latter act would usually be considered unintentional. Furthermore, the motorist in this case might show sorrow over killing the child's pet, indicating thereby that his or her outcomes were aversive. This, too, would elicit a judgment of unintentional harm.

Some other judgments of the immediate situation will also serve as keys to the intent of the harmdoer. Intent will often be inferred from judgments about whether the actor enjoys the harmful behavior or not. Nelson (1980) found that kindergarten children accurately used emotional expressions as clues to the intentions behind acts of transgression. When trangressors had happy facial expressions during the commission of harmful acts, the children classified the act as intentional more than when the perpetrator had a sad countenance. We also infer intent from the amount of effort that the transgressor expends in carrying out the harmful act (see, for example, Joseph *et al.* 1976). A person who overcomes many obstacles en route to doing harm to someone is more likely to be called an intentional aggressor than another person who encounters less difficulty. Planning carefully the act of harm represents such an expenditure of effort, a fact that is reflected in consideration by the legal system of "premeditation" as a condition for first-degree murder.

The second type of appraisal that leads to a judgment of intentionality has to do with characteristics of the harmdoer. If a person is known to have done a lot of harm in the past, any harmful act by that person should have a strong likelihood of being judged intentional. In addition, stereotypes based on membership in categories such as race, sex, and physical attractiveness also enter into judgments of intent behind harmdoing. For example, Duncan (1976) found that Caucasian subjects shown extracts from motion pictures regarded being shoved by a black person as being more violent (and hence probably more intentional) than a similar push by a white person.

### Attributions of motive

Once a judgment of intentionality has been made, the victim must then decide whether the intent was malicious or not. Harmful behavior that is seen as instrumental to the attainment of other ends is generally regarded as being less malevolent than harmdoing for its own sake (Rule 1978). If the harmdoing serves some prosocial purpose it also tends to be regarded as not malevolent. Hitting a mugger to restrain him from attacking an elderly woman would be considered a generally benign act by most people. Athletes who are subjected to verbal abuse by a coach who wants them to play with greater intensity also tend not to view the coach's behavior as malicious in intent. Finally, harm that is seen as retaliation for some prior provocation tends to be regarded as less malevolent than harm inflicted without an apparent desire for retaliation (Harvey and Rule 1978).

## Attributions of foreseeability

An act of harmdoing need not be intentional to be regarded as blameworthy. Ferguson and Rule (1983) point out that sometimes the failure to avoid doing unintended harm that can be foreseen is also cause for assigning moral culpability to the actor. Foreseeability can be of two types. One is negligence on the part of the person. If the person knows that something he or she is about to do to another person will cause unintended harm, but is either too lazy or too indifferent to seek an alternative course of action, we attribute negligent foreseeability to that person. The other type of foreseeability is the product of ruthlessness on the part of the actor, who makes no attempt to prevent unintentionally harming another person because some other selfish purpose would be served by the action.

One basis on which judgments of foreseeability are made is the locus of causality of the act. In general, acts of harmdoing that are regarded as due to internal causes (i.e., specific behaviors of the actor) are judged to be more foreseeable by the actor than are those attributed to external causes. For example, a study by Brickman et al. (1975) showed that subjects make judgments of greater foreseeability in the case of automobile accidents when the accident is due to an internal cause (e.g., the driver was not looking at the road) than when it is due to an external cause (e.g., failure of the steering mechanism). Another basis for judgment is the degree of control that the actor is thought to have over events. In a study that has an indirect bearing on this point, Arkkelin et al. (1979) found that drivers involved in accidents were held more responsible by subjects when the accident was due to a known mechanical fault than when it was due to daydreaming. Daydreaming may be an unforeseeable cause of an accident because the driver has no way of knowing ahead of time whether he or she will daydream while at the wheel of a car. However, driving a car with a known fault is a clear case of negligence, in which the possibility of an accident can be foreseen.

## Judging what ought to have happened

Each of the four types of harmful act can be compared to some norm that prescribes activity in the situation in question. These norms reflect the basic values of the parties involved and are determined by the culture in which the action is carried out. Most cultures have a norm that condemns the infliction of intentional malevolent harm on another person. Most also have a norm that excuses or justifies the occasional infliction of intentional but non-malevolent harm. The pain caused by a physician in treating a patient, or that inflicted by a police officer in the normal course of duties fall into this category. Thus the person who commits harm that is willfully malevolent is judged to be more culpable for the act than is someone who commits harm that is not malicious (Rule *et al.* 1975).

Another social norm that is probably fairly common is that a socially responsible person should do everything possible to avoid doing unintended harm to others. When a harmful act is seen as unintended but foreseeable, therefore, it should be judged more harshly than when it is not foreseeable, i.e. truly accidental. The latter type of act is usually not judged as one indicating blame or moral culpability. A few studies have attempted to ascertain which of the types of harmdoing elicits the strongest condemnation. The evidence indicates clearly that intentional and malevolent harm is judged to be the most blameworthy and deserving of punishment (Rule and Nesdale 1976). In addition, non-malevolent intended harm is usually rated as no more wrong than is accidentally inflicted harm (e.g., Ferguson and Rule 1980).

## Conclusion

As we noted earlier, Ferguson and Rule (1983) assumed that acts of harmdoing that are judged to be morally wrong elicit greater aggression than similar acts which are not so judged. We must ask why this is so. One possible answer involves processes similar to those described by Zillmann, which have already been described. Attributional analyses of emotion can be understood as explanations of the situational conditions under which people experience the emotion in question. When the situation is one in which one person harms another, the victim of the harm probably feels aroused by the aversive treatment. To the extent that the victim perceives the actor's behavior as either intentional and malicious in intent or unintentional but foreseen, that behavior will be considered morally wrong and worthy of blame. It is these judgements of blame that lead the person to perceive the increased arousal as a state of anger. Thus, Ferguson and Rule's (1983) analysis of cognitive judgments of harm-doing may be regarded as complementary to Zillmann's approach to anger and arousal.

## Deindividuation and aggression

A problem in human aggression that has been of interest for some time is that of collective violence. Specifically, the question is whether people may be more likely to be violent in groups than each person would be as an individual. The problem goes back to the work of certain French social philosophers of the nineteenth century who formulated various doctrines of mob behavior and the "group mind" (e.g., Le Bon 1896). In recent years this idea has been reintroduced in the psychology of "deindividuation", a process whereby individuals lose their sense of self-awareness in group settings. Deindividuation has been associated with aggressive behavior by several theorists.

### Deindividuation, anonymity, and disinhibition

Zimbardo (1970) was one of the first to indicate that aggression may be a result of the loss of individual identity. According to him, such an identity loss releases inhibitions against expressing behavior that would otherwise be suppressed because of fear of social disapproval. Zimbardo's theory describes the conditions that produce deindividuation, the nature of the deindividuated state, and the consequences of deindividuation for behavior.

### Conditions producing deindividuation
Zimbardo lists a number of situational conditions that can elicit the deindividuated state. Among these conditions are: (1) anonymity; (2) being part of a group; (3) sharing responsibility for outcomes with other people, or giving up responsibility entirely; (4) ambiguity and lack of structure in the situation; and (5) altered states of consciousness induced through drugs, alcohol, or other means. There is evidence that some of these conditions are associated with

relatively high levels of aggression, especially anonymity (see, for example, Rogers and Prentice-Dunn 1981), abdication of responsibility for aggression (Diener *et al.* 1975), and alcohol consumption (Shuntich and Taylor 1972).

## The deindividuated state

The immediate effects of deindividuation are twofold: the person experiences a reduction in self-evaluation (i.e., he or she becomes less introspective and critical of the self), and also a reduced sense of concern over being evaluated by others. From these two immediate effects follows a weakening of behavioral inhibition through such normal controls as fear, guilt, shame, or anxiety. Once these normal inhibitory controls over behavior have been weakened, the individual is more prone to express any behavior that has hitherto been suppressed because of those controls.

## Effects of deindividuation

The reduction or elimination of normal inhibitory control is followed by behavior that tends to be intense, emotional, impulsive, and atypical of the person. More important, deindividuated behavior is not under discriminative stimulus control. Normal distinctions that persons make in their surroundings become less potent in guiding behavior. Behavior instead comes under the control of previously suppressed impulses to act. In the case of aggression, this means that the deindividuated person is less influenced than the normally individuated person by such cues as the nature of the person being aggressed against and such matters as the justifiability of the aggression. In a study testing this idea, Zimbardo (1970) permitted women subjects to aggress against another woman who had previously behaved in a pleasant and polite manner or in a rude and obnoxious way. Subjects in one condition were given a high degree of anonymity by donning baggy coats over their clothing and paper bags over their heads. Those in another condition were attired normally and also wore large tags bearing their names. The results showed that whereas the subjects who wore name tags discriminated between the pleasant and obnoxious victims by increasing shocks against the latter but decreasing them against the former, deindividuated subjects made no such distinction.

## Deindividuation and self-awareness

An alternative to Zimbardo's theory of deindividuation stresses the importance of social settings in influencing a person's sense of self-awareness. Diener (1980) placed less emphasis on anonymity as an antecedent of aggression than did Zimbardo. Instead, Diener proposed that group settings serve mainly to draw the person's attention away from the self and in the direction of external stimuli. This shift of attention from the self to the environment is accompanied by a lowering of importance for internalized personal and social standards as behavioral guides. The person instead becomes more controlled by cues in the immediate situation. Thus, for example, in situations in which strong cues for aggression are present, the deindividuated person may react to these stimuli more than to internal standards of the rightness or wrongness of aggressing.

## Accountability and attention

A similar approach is taken by Prentice-Dunn and Rogers (1983), who stipulate that any conditions which promote lowering of self-awareness are, by definition, causes of deindividuation. They also recognize that self-awareness has both a private and a public aspect, and that each aspect is elicited by a specific type of situation (Buss 1980).

Public self-awareness is consciousness of one's self as an object of attention by others. The person who is in this state is especially sensitive to social evaluation and personal accountability. Hence any situation in which a lowering of personal accountability is perceived should make the person less publicly self-aware. In a study referred to earlier (Diener *et al.* 1975) it was shown that subjects who were told that the experimenter would take responsibility for the subjects' actions were more aggressive toward a passive victim than were subjects who had to take responsibility for their behavior. Passing responsibility to another person lowered individual accountability for aggression and thereby facilitated such behavior.

Private self-awareness is associated with a consciousness of one's own inner values, standards, thoughts, and feelings. Any turning of attention away from the self is followed by reduced private self-awareness. Conditions for deindividuation cause such a change in attentional focus and hence lead to behavior that is governed not by personal standards but by salient stimuli in the environment. The person who becomes deindividuated is therefore less likely to restrain aggressive behavior on the basis of personal or social values.

## Individuation and aggression

The approaches to deindividuation and aggression taken by Zimbardo, on the one hand, and by Prentice-Dunn and Rogers, on the other, differ basically in their descriptions of the locus of origin of the aggressive act. Zimbardo assumes that aggression is motivated by causes outside the immediate situation, and that deindividuation merely releases these behaviors. Prentice-Dunn and Rogers propose that aggression originates in the situation itself, being elicited by situational stimuli. These stimuli acquire their influence over behavior once public and private self-awareness have been weakened. None of the research that has been done to date permits a comparison of the two theories. However, it should be noted that the theory linking deindividuation to a lack of self-awareness is consistent with another body of literature showing that conditions which *enhance* self-awareness bring about an increased conformity of behavior to personal and social standards. This can be thought of as the opposite of deindividuation.

Two studies from this literature illustrate the effect of increased individuation on aggressive behavior. In both, aggression was defined as the level of punishment given to another person for frustrating the subject's attempts at teaching a concept; this method has been widely used in the experimental study of aggression (see, for example, Buss 1961). In one study, Carver (1975) chose two groups of subjects on the basis of their belief in whether or not physical punishment should be used in learning: one group expressed a belief in physical punishment whereas the other did not. Later, all subjects engaged in the learning task. Punishment consisted of the delivery of shocks to the learner which could vary in intensity at the subject's discretion. Half the subjects performed the task in the presence of a mirror in which they could see their reflections and the other half did not. The sight of oneself in a mirror has been shown to increase the sense of self-awareness (Wicklund 1975). Carver found that the presence of a mirror tended to reduce the intensity of shocks given by people who were opposed to the use of punishment, but to increase the intensity of shocks given by those who believed in punishment. Thus, the enhancement of self-awareness increased conformity to a personal standard for behavior, in this case aggression against another person.

In another study, Scheier *et al.* (1974) arranged to have male subjects shock a female for making errors in the task. It was assumed that aggression by men against women, in the absence of any provocation, would normally be inconsistent with social standards. The results of the study showed that men did give weaker shocks to the female victim when a mirror was present than when there was no mirror. Both this study and the one by Carver (1975) involved increased self-awareness through the use of a mirror. One showed a high level of aggression and the other a low level under conditions of self-awareness. However, in each case the subject's level of aggressiveness was determined by the personal standard governing behavior in the situation.

## Inhibition of aggression

Most theories of angry aggression stipulate that even though a person becomes angered and instigated to aggress, actual aggressive behavior may not occur if the person feels restrained by other features of the situation. The angry person may be afraid to aggress because of the threat of retaliation, or may feel anxious or guilty at the thought of doing violence. Feelings of empathy with the victim may also inhibit aggression. In each of the cases mentioned here, the situation elicits both aggressive reactions and other responses which are, for a time at least, more powerful than aggression. They therefore interfere with and block the expression of aggression.

### Aggression guilt and empathy

Acts of aggression sometimes evoke signs of pain and suffering from the victim. The person may wince, cry out, groan, or show some other evidence that the attack is causing discomfort. Early studies by Geen (1970) and Baron (1971b) showed that subjects who had been provoked by another person were less aggressive in their retaliation against that person when the latter emitted signs of distress than when he did not. This finding appeared, however, to contradict other studies which showed that victims who showed signs of suffering were treated with greater punitiveness than those who suffered in silence (e.g., Feshbach *et al.* 1967). Further analysis of the several studies suggested that the crucial cause of this apparent conflict in the data was the intensity with which subjects had been provoked by the other person (Bandura 1971). Subjects in the studies by Geen and by Baron were exposed to provocation which was relatively mild. Bandura (1971) proposed that when subjects are more intensely provoked they may well react to signs of suffering in the provocateur with a high level of aggression.

A subsequent study by Baron (1979) showed that intensity of provocation did affect the influence of pain cues from the victim on aggression against that person. Some of the subjects in this experiment were first provoked intensely by an experimental accomplice who not only gave the subject ten shocks but also made insulting comments about the subject's performance of a task. Other subjects were praised by the accomplice for their performance and given no shocks. Later all subjects were given an opportunity to shock the accomplice. The results (see Figure 5.1) strongly supported the idea that pain cues from the victim lead to inhibition of aggression among

*Figure 5.1* Effects of victim's pain cues and anger on aggression

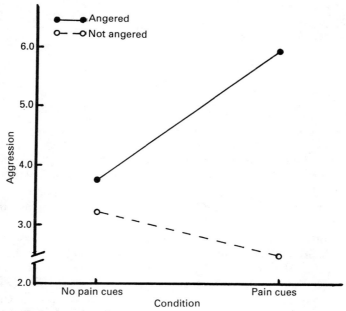

*Source:* Baron (1979)
*Note:* Intensity of a shock is defined as the number of a button (from 1–10) on a Buss aggression apparatus (see Buss 1961 for details)

subjects who have not been strongly provoked, but enhance aggression among subjects who have been provoked intensely. One explanation for this finding is that attacking another person who has done nothing to deserve the attack and who, in addition, obviously suffers from it, makes the attacker feel guilty. Aggression guilt, therefore, is an inhibitor of aggression.

Another explanation is that a state of *empathy* with the victim is induced in the aggressor by evidence of the victim's suffering (Baron 1977). Empathy is facilitated by perceptions of similarity between oneself and others (see, for example, Feshbach and Roe 1968); we might therefore expect that when similarity between the aggressor and the victim is high, empathy will be strong and aggression will be restrained (see Feshbach and Feshbach 1969). Such has been shown to be the case (Baron 1971a). In addition, the emission of pain cues by a victim who is similar to the subject, and with whom the subject should be more empathic, is more effective in inhibiting aggression than are pain cues from a more dissimilar victim. For example, Baron (1979) has shown that evidence of suffering from a victim who is racially different from the attacker does not lead to restrained aggression, whereas the same signs of suffering from a victim of the same race do have this inhibiting effect.

## Cross-sex constraints against aggression

Several studies have shown that men are less likely to aggress against women in experimental settings than they are to aggress against other men, even when provoked by the women (Buss 1966; Hoppe 1979; Taylor & Epstein 1967). At least two reasons can be suggested for such findings. One is that social customs and conventions dictate that men should not aggress against women as they might against other men. The other reason why men attack women less than they do other men may be that men may find women attractive and wish to do nothing that could possibly close the door to future interactions with them. If this is the case, then aggression against a female provocateur should be inhibited more when that person is physically attractive than when she is not. A study by Ohbuchi and Izutsu (1984) indicates that this is the case. Male subjects interacted with a female (who was actually a confederate of the experimenter) in a situation that called for the two to deliver electric shocks to each other. The woman was made to look either extremely attractive or moderately unattractive and to deliver either mild or strong shocks to the subject. When mild shocks were given the men retaliated with relatively weak shocks against both the attractive and unattractive woman. When strong shocks were given, retaliation was greater against the unattractive woman than against the attractive one.

## Fear of retaliation

Folk wisdom teaches that fear of being aggressed against is an effective inhibitor of aggression. Parents sometimes teach their children, for example, to resist those who try to intimidate them and to fight back, in hopes that counteraggression will deter attacks. Even national leaders resort to this strategy, and the assumptions behind it, in their often-stated belief that the threat of retaliation is the best deterrent of war. The formulators of the frustration–aggression hypothesis (Dollard et al. 1939) also assumed that fear of punishment, such as retaliation, could inhibit aggression instigated by a frustrator.

Some experimental evidence supports this idea. Baron (1971b) found that the level of aggression directed toward a victim by subjects decreased as the likelihood of retaliation increased. Inhibition of aggression by threat of counterattack may be especially effective if the victim's capacity for such a measure is considered to be especially great (Shortell et al. 1970). On the other hand, Baron (1973) found that if subjects are strongly provoked to aggress, threat of being aggressed against by the victim may not deter such aggression even though it successfully inhibits less provoked people. Fear of retaliation is, therefore, a negative force that blocks aggression instigated by aversive conditions unless the instigation is powerful enough to overcome the inhibition.

## Summary

1 The study of aggression involves investigation of several states that account for connections between antecedent conditions and aggressive outcomes. There are several such intervening variables, among them states of arousal, judgments of the intent of provoking persons, anger, and inhibitory and restraining states that block aggressive expression.

2  Arousal may serve as a response activator by activating or energizing aggressive responses that the person is disposed to make. If the person is ready to aggress, arousal can power aggressive behavior. Treating arousal as a response energizer helps to explain why some frustrated or provoked people do not aggress. If people have been rigorously trained in non-violence, for example, provocations should activate appropriate non-aggressive behaviors.

3  Arousal from a source that is not related to a provocation may summate with arousal elicited by a provocation. For this misattribution, called "excitation transfer", to occur, a short period of time must elapse between the provocation and the stimulus that produces the added arousal so that the most salient symptoms of the non-emotional arousal will have time to dissipate. In addition, misattribution is more likely when the source of the extraneous arousal is ambiguous. Any activity that increases arousal can, when combined with sufficient provocation, serve as an antecedent of aggression. Because of the anger-labeling that follows excitation transfer, an arousing condition may lead to aggression far beyond the time at which the arousal itself has dissipated. Thus, the misattribution process has implications for long-term behavior.

4  When arousal is elicited by some source that is unlike an aggressive provocation, it is less susceptible to misinterpretation and mistaken attribution. Exposure to non-hostile and sexually-oriented humorous cartoons, for example, renders provoked subjects less aggressive than they would otherwise have been. Thus, excitation transfer may be less likely when arousal is elicited by stimuli that evoke responses that are so different from aggression that they interfere with aggression.

5  The labeling of arousal and the consequent experience of anger may not be necessary for either the generation of the anger state or any aggression that may follow. Instead, the experience or feeling of anger can be thought of as a parallel process that accompanies but does not cause anger-relevant behavior.

6  Anger may also be defined as a social construction. Like other emotions, it may be a socially defined and constructed syndrome of affective, cognitive, and physiological processes. In studying anger in everyday settings, for example, Averill made some findings that are not similar to those coming from experimental research. He found that in people's self-reports of anger and

aggression, anger is usually caused by loss of personal pride or self-esteem. He also found that aggression is usually on the level of verbal hostility and not physical assault.

7 Provocations, such as attacks or frustrations, need not always lead to aggression. Provocations must be interpreted in certain ways in order for aggression to follow. The provocation must be regarded as intentional and malicious in intent; it must be viewed as a violation of normative behavior in social situations; and it must lead to outcomes that are regarded as alternatives to more desired outcomes, i.e., it must be seen as being avoidable.

8 Harmdoing may be classified as one of four types: (1) intentional and malevolent; (2) intentional but not malevolent; (3) not intended but foreseeable; and (4) unintentional and unforeseeable, this last type of harm being truly accidental. Three separate attributions must be made before an act can be located within this scheme: intent, foreseeability, and motive. Judgments of intentionality are made along two general lines. One has to do with the nature of the situation and the other with character of the harmdoer.

9 Aggression may follow a loss of individual identity. The immediate effects of this deindividuation are twofold: the person becomes less self-critical and less concerned about being evaluated by others. As a result, behavioral inhibitions through such normal controls as fear, guilt, shame, or anxiety are weakened. Once these normal inhibitory controls over behavior have been weakened, the individual is more prone to express any behavior that has hitherto been suppressed because of them.

10 Group settings may draw the person's attention away from the self and in the direction of external stimuli. This may produce a change in attentional focus and hence lead to behavior that is governed not by personal standards but by salient stimuli in the environment. On the other hand, increased self-awareness brings about an increased conformity of behavior to personal and social standards. Under such conditions the person will aggress or not aggress according to these standards and be less controlled by situational conditions.

11 Aggressive behavior may not occur if the person feels restrained by other features of the situation. Aggression can be inhibited by pain cues from the victim if the aggressor has not been provoked or made angry by the victim. However, when the aggressor has been provoked, pain cues from the victim serve to reinforce and

strengthen aggression. Cross-sex aggression also creates certain inhibitions. Men are less likely to aggress against women in experimental settings than they are to aggress against other men. In addition, fear of being aggressed against is an effective inhibitor of aggression.

## Suggestions for further reading

Averill, J. R. (1983). Studies on anger and aggression: Implications for theories of emotion. *American Psychologist*, 38, 1145–60. A brief overview of Averill's theory of anger and a review of data that suggest some limitations of laboratory research on anger and aggression.

Ferguson, T. J. and Rule, B. G. (1983). An attributional perspective on anger and aggression. In R. G. Geen and E. Donnerstein (eds), *Aggression: Theoretical and Empirical Review, Vol. 1: Theoretical and methodological Issues*. New York: Academic Press, pp. 41–74. This chapter provides an extensive description of attribution processes in aggressive behavior.

Zillmann, D. (1979). *Hostility and Aggression*. Hillsdale, NJ: Lawrence Erlbaum Associates. In addition to reviewing major theories of aggression, Zillmann presents a detailed description of the principles underlying the process of excitation transfer.

# 6 / THE ROLE OF INDIVIDUAL DIFFERENCES

The model of affective aggression that we have been using in this book treats aggression as the result of background variables that make aggression a likely response, and of stress-inducing conditions that elicit the aggressive act. Among the background variables already discussed have been biological inheritance, learning history, and social norms. Another class of background variables is large and varied enough to require separate treatment, and it will form the substance of this chapter. These variables are related to individual differences. In this chapter we will consider five such individual differences: (1) sex; (2) level of cognitive development; (3) tendencies to consume alcohol; (4) race; and (5) personality.

## Sex differences

In everyday life, it is commonly assumed that men are more physically aggressive than women. Statistics indicate that men are more likely than women to commit such crimes as murder, armed robbery, and aggravated assault. In addition, men describe themselves as being aggressive to a greater extent than do women and show greater potential for acting aggressively in situations of interpersonal conflict (Reinisch and Sanders 1986). Furthermore, such sex differences do not appear to be limited to any one society, but are found in several cultures besides our own (Whiting and Edwards 1973). Although most psychologists would agree that in general terms men appear to be more physically aggressive than women, differences of opinion exist concerning the basis for this phenomenon, the various conditions under which it is demonstrated, and the extent to which it is influenced by the particular measure of aggression that is being used. In this section each of these matters will be considered.

## Sex differences in disposition to aggress

Why should men be typically more aggressive than women? One possibility is that sex differences in aggressiveness are at least partially inherited. This idea has been proposed and discussed at length by Maccoby and Jacklin (1974; 1980), whose major premise is that sex differences arise from basic biological causes. Maccoby and Jacklin base their argument on four conclusions that they reach after a review of the literature:

1 Men are generally more aggressive than women in virtually all human societies.
2 Males are more aggressive than females early in life, i.e., during early childhood and the pre-school years, "a time when there is no evidence that differential socialization pressures have been brought to bear by adults to 'shape' aggression differentially in the two sexes" (Maccoby and Jacklin 1974, p. 243).
3 Greater aggressiveness in males relative to females is found not only in humans but also in subhuman primates.
4 Aggression is related to sex hormones and can be influenced by administration of these substances.

This point of view has been challenged, however. Both Tieger (1980) and White (1983) have cited studies that fail to support the assertions listed above. More traditional approaches to the etiology of sex differences tend to consider such differences to be a product of learning, not heredity. It should be emphasized, however, that Maccoby and Jacklin do not propose that inherited biologically-based sex differences account for *all* male–female differences in aggression, or even that they constitute the most important overall cause. They propose only that biological differences establish different backgrounds in the two sexes, against which environmental and situational forces operate: "We . . . believe it is highly likely that there is a biological component underlying the sex differences, although aggression, like all behavior, is subject to social shaping and undergoes successive modifications through learning" (Maccoby and Jacklin 1980, p. 964).

Two reviews of the literature on sex differences in aggression conducted since 1980 suggest that such differences are smaller than Maccoby and Jacklin had supposed. Hyde (1984) analyzed the results of 143 studies involving subjects ranging in age from 2.5 to 35 years. Included were all the studies reviewed by Maccoby and Jacklin in 1980 and a number of additional ones conducted later. The analysis revealed a smaller difference between males and females in the more recent studies than in the ones reviewed by Maccoby and Jacklin. In addition, a modest negative correlation was found between the magnitude of sex differences and age: sex differences in aggression decreased as subjects got older. Eagly and Steffen (1986), in a review of studies involving adult subjects only, also found a smaller sex difference in aggression than the one found by Maccoby and Jacklin. This corroborates Hyde's finding that sex differences in aggression diminish with age.

## Sex differences in reactivity

Both Maccoby and Jacklin (1974; 1980) and their critics are concerned with explaining sex differences in aggression in terms of different dispositions in men and women. The two viewpoints differ mainly in explaining the origins of those dispositions. Other investigators have sought the basis of sex differences not in some persistent "tendency" to aggress, but in different ways of reacting to situations (e.g., Frodi et al. 1977). For example, women and men may differ in (1) the preferred mode of aggressing; (2) the extent to which aggressive behavior elicits feelings of guilt, anxiety, or fear, all of which may inhibit aggression; (3) cognitive reactions to potentially provoking situations; and (4) responses to the observation of aggression by others.

### Response mode
Several observers (e.g., Buss 1963; Bandura 1973) have suggested that men and women may not differ in overall levels of aggression as much as they do in preferred means of aggressing, with men showing a clearer aggressive tendency than women only in the case of physical violence. Women, however, may be no less aggressive than men in non-physical ways, such as verbal expression. There is some evidence suggesting that men and women may express this sort of differential preference for physical and verbal aggression, respectively (see, for

example, Shope *et al.* 1978). In addition, as will be shown below, differences in aggression between men and women tend to be greatest when the aggression involves infliction of physical pain (Eagly and Steffen 1986). Other studies (e.g., Barrett 1979) indicate that male and female preferences in aggression depend upon a number of other situational variables. As of now, we should be cautious in drawing any conclusions about sex differences in preferred modes of aggressing (White 1983).

### Aggression inhibition

There is considerable evidence, however, that women are more likely than men to experience guilt, anxiety, and fear after aggressing (e.g., Brock and Buss 1964; Wyer *et al.* 1965). These emotional reactions may inhibit further aggression. In addition, the correlation between aggression and anxiety, which is negative for both sexes, has been shown to be of greater magnitude among women than among men (Schill and Schneider 1970), indicating that women feel more anxious when aggressing than do men. Furthermore, Schill (1972) reported that the reduction in physiological arousal that often accompanies aggressive behavior in angered men varied with aggression guilt in women, so that only those who were low in such guilt experienced the reduced arousal after aggressing. Finally, it should be noted that when situational conditions are altered in ways that should make subjects feel less guilty about aggressing, women become virtually as aggressive as men (see, for example, Larsen *et al.* 1972).

Both of the bases for sex differences noted here – men's tendencies toward physical violence and women's tendencies toward inhibition – are shown in an analysis of 63 studies of adults by Eagly and Steffen (1986). These investigators found that men tended to be more aggressive than women primarily in those studies in which aggression resulted in pain or physical injury to the victim. When aggression produced mainly psychological harm (e.g., verbal abuse), the greater aggressiveness of the men was attenuated. In addition, sex differences, with men being more aggressive than women, tended to be larger when women believed that acting aggressively would hurt the victim, produce guilt or anxiety in the aggressor, or lead to harm to the aggressor. Sex differences therefore appeared to be a function of anticipated consequences of aggression which are closely linked to traditional sex roles.

## Cognitive responses to situations

Another possible basis for sex differences in aggression may be different ways that men and women interpret situations that have the potential for eliciting aggressive behavior. Sex differences in cognitive judgments of situations may affect both emotional responses to those situations and subsequent aggression. For example, Frodi (1976) found that males typically reported being made angry to displays of physical or verbal aggression by other men, whereas they indicated that what angered them most in women was a condescending attitude. Women, on the other hand, reported being angered most by condescension from men or women. A study by Duncan and Hobson (1977) also found that men reported being angered more by interpersonal conflict than did women, whereas women reported being provoked more by such intrapersonal problems as conflicts over values. Sex differences in appraisals of what constitute proper responses to interpersonal conflicts are, moreover, found at an early age (Connor *et al.* 1978; Harden and Jacob 1978).

## Reactions to observation of aggression

In Chapter 4 a connection was shown between the observation of violence in the mass media and subsequent aggressive behavior. Relevant to the present context are some studies which show that reactions to violence in the media are moderated by the sex of the viewer. For example, Cantor *et al.* (1978) measured aggression among women subjects toward another woman who had provoked them, after viewing either a violent film, an erotic but non-violent one, or a neutral one having little arousal potential. They found that women were more aggressive after having seen the erotic film than after having seen either the aggressive or neutral one. Women who had seen the erotic film were also more physiologically aroused than those who saw either of the others. Cantor *et al.* (1978) explained these findings in terms of the "excitation-transfer" principle discussed in Chapter 4: arousal elicited by the sexual film was transferred to the provocation, hence the higher the arousal level the greater was the aggression.

Other research indicates that sex differences in reactions to observed violence may be traceable to differential experiences of boys and girls as they develop. For example, in a study by Connor *et al.* (1978) boys and girls in an elementary school read stories in which another child behaved either aggressively or passively. Boys expressed greater approval of aggressive acts than did girls; the latter stated greater approval of passive behavior than did boys. In addition, older girls expressed a stronger belief in passive behavior as means of obtaining desired ends than did younger girls; however, as boys grew older they expressed progressively less belief in the efficacy of passive behavior. It would appear that girls learn, as they grow and become socialized, that passivity and non-aggression can be more instrumental than other behaviors in obtaining desired outcomes. One implication of the data reported by Connor *et al.* (1978) is that the relation of aggression to viewing violence should diminish with age among girls but possibly become stronger among boys.

*Other variables*
Several other conditions may play some role in determining when sex differences will be found in aggression and when they will not (White 1983). These include sex-role attitudes (i.e., whether or not the person believes that women and men should act in socially stereotyped ways), induced anger, and the presence of male or female role models. Sex differences in aggression are most likely to occur only under carefully defined conditions involving these variables and others discussed above. The point of all this, and the best conclusion we may draw, is that sex differences in aggression are not uniform across persons or conditions, and are subject to the operation of numerous variables.

## Cognitive development

Individual differences in development have been shown to have important links to aggressive behavior. As a child grows from infancy to adolescence, important changes occur in the child's capacity to use information from the environment. These changes, in turn, have important consequences for behavior, including aggression. As was noted in Chapter 2, for example, the ways in which a person construes and interprets provocative acts by another person do much to determine the response that those acts will elicit. If cognitive appraisals of provocations or other stimuli to aggression are important mediators of aggression, then any variable that affects such appraisals assumes importance. Developmental changes have such effects (Parke and Slaby 1983).

## Reactions to observed violence

A series of studies by Collins and his associates has shown that youngsters vary with age in the interpretations they place on violence seen on television. Collins *et al.* (1974) showed material containing violent scenes to children at four different grade levels, from kindergarten (age 5–6) through grade 8 (age 13–14), then questioned each child about the behavior and motives of the aggressor and about the consequences of that person's acts. Children in kindergarten and grade 2 were most likely to comprehend the violence they had seen only in terms of its level of aggressiveness and its ultimate consequences, and not to be affected by the aggressor's motives. Attention to motives increased with the age of the viewer. Eighth-graders were more likely to judge the violence in terms of its motivation than in terms of its aggressiveness or consequences. Collins (1975) expanded on these findings by showing that eighth-graders were more likely than second-graders to construct the general meaning of a televised aggressive drama from a set of discrete episodes, even though the younger children were as good as the older ones in recalling the individual segments. Collins (1975) suggested that age differences in interpretations of observed violence may lead to similar differences in aggressive behavior following such observation. Older children, by being more sensitive to subtle meanings and motives, may be influenced by such factors.

## Reactions to provocation

What Collins has shown in the case of reactions to observed violence may have relevance for the child's daily life. Provocations by other children may, for example, be interpreted and understood by a child in different ways at varying levels of cognitive development, and this may translate into comparable levels of retaliatory aggression. Age plays an important part in the relationship between retaliatory aggression and a child's perception of the intent of the instigator. Shantz and Voydanoff (1973) carried out a study in which boys aged 7, 9, or 12 years indicated how aggressively they would react to a set of hypothetical provocations. In each case the provocation was made to appear either intentional or accidental. Whereas boys aged 9 and 12 differentiated between accidental and deliberate provocations, expressing greater aggressiveness toward the latter than toward the former, seven-year-olds did not. These younger children expressed as intense an aggressive reaction to unintended attacks as they did toward intended ones. Perceived intent as a mediator of retaliatory aggression is therefore a variable that assumes importance only after a certain level of cognitive development has occurred. In addition, age and development influence the reactions to provocations that are actually experienced. Rotenberg (1985) has found, for example, that as children grow older they are able to give more reasons for being angry in provocative situations than are younger children, and that the older children are less likely to regard physical aggression as the primary reaction to being angered. This finding suggests that with increasing cognitive development comes greater elaboration of understanding of the causes of anger and some degree of cognitive control over the expression of aggression.

## Cognitive deficit and aggression

It is likely, then, that poor cognitive development may influence the subtlety of judgments that children make in potentially provocative situations. The less developed the child, the more likely he or she may be to react to the simple fact of being provoked, attacked, or frustrated, and the less likely to make distinctions on the basis of other circumstances. This may also help to explain a commonly reported finding that deficits in cognitive competencies are often associated with aggressive or delinquent behavior in children (see, for example, Pitkanen-Pulkinen 1979). It has also been suggested that this relationship is mediated by the development on the child's part of a negative self-image (Feshbach and Price 1984). The slow or otherwise cognitively less capable child may, because of initial failures and disappointments in school, develop a feeling of low self-esteem, a high level of anger, and a defeatist attitude. These feelings and emotions could then produce both aggression and a low level of motivation to achieve, which could in turn exacerbate feelings of failure. A dangerous cycle could thus be established.

## Alcohol consumption

The effects of alcohol consumption on human aggression have long been recognized in popular beliefs. The man who gets drunk and advertises that he will "take on every man in the bar" is an easily recognized figure in low comedy. Unfortunately, alcohol-related aggression is not a laughing matter. Several studies have indicated a positive correlation between alcohol use and violent crime. For example, in examining police records of homicides in Philadelphia between 1948 and 1953, Wolfgang and Strohm (1956) discovered that alcohol was a contributing factor in 64 per cent of the cases. The results of several controlled experimental studies bear out the suggestion that alcohol ingestion plays a causative role in aggressive behavior.

Shuntich and Taylor (1972) found that subjects who had been intoxicated in the laboratory later behaved more aggressively than did those who had either consumed a placebo or did not receive a beverage at all. In a subsequent study Taylor and Gammon (1975) found that the effects of alcohol varied with the dosage consumed. In this experiment subjects drank mixes containing either 1.5 ounces (45 ml) or 0.5 ounces (15 ml) of vodka or bourbon per 40 pounds (18 kg) of body weight prior to aggressing against an antagonist. The large and small doses appeared to have opposite effects. Subjects who had been given a small dose tended to become slightly less aggressive across the course of the study (a total of 21 trials in which electric shock was ostensibly given) whereas subjects given a relatively large dose became significantly more aggressive across the trial series. The aggression-inducing effect of large doses was also more characteristic of subjects who received vodka than of those who drank bourbon, suggesting that the type of alcohol consumed may have effects additional to those due to the amount consumed.

Demonstrations of the effects of alcohol consumption on aggression such as those described above are interesting and worthwhile, but they do not indicate why alcohol should have such an effect on behavior. To find answers to that question we must examine other circumstances that influence the alcohol–aggression relationship. When we do, we find that the facilitation of aggression by alcohol is not invariant, but is affected by (1) situational variables; (2) the cognitive state of the drinker; and (3) certain features of the drinker's personality.

*Situational moderators*

One important situational moderator is interpersonal threat: intoxicated subjects aggress more than non-intoxicated ones when they perceive that they are threatened by someone else. Taylor *et al.* (1976), for example, found that among subjects who were not threatened by a fellow subject (a person who had previously voiced strong objections to hurting anyone), those who were intoxicated were no more aggressive than those who were sober. However, among subjects who perceived the other person as threatening, those who were intoxicated were more aggressive than those who were not.

Social pressure from peers is another situational variable that influences aggression following alcohol ingestion. Taylor and Gammon (1976) found that mild social pressure from two peers was sufficient to induce restraint in the aggressiveness of a third person as the latter responded to an aggressive opponent in a game situation. Among intoxicated subjects, however, extreme pressure was required to bring about the same restraint. Thus, intoxicated subjects were relatively resistant to social attempts at reducing their aggressiveness. On the other hand, a study by Sears (cited by Taylor and Leonard 1983), showed that intoxicated subjects were more easily persuaded to aggress in response to peers who urged them on than were sober subjects. Peer pressure thus appears to be more effective in facilitating aggression in intoxicated subjects than in inhibiting it.

One study suggests, however, that a relatively strong inhibitor of aggression among inebriated subjects may be the perception of a social norm against aggressing. Jeavons and Taylor (1985) informed some subjects that the great majority of people given the opportunity to aggress against a provocative partner actually behaved in a relatively non-aggressive way. Given this imposition of a social norm of non-violence, inebriated subjects were less aggressive toward an aggressive partner than were sober subjects. In fact, intoxicated subjects provided with the normative information were no more aggressive than sober subjects who had not been given such information. Provision of the social norm therefore served as an effective inhibitor of aggression among intoxicated subjects.

Taylor and Leonard (1983) have offered an interesting hypothesis of the interaction between alcohol and situational variables. The main effect of alcohol, they propose, is a pharmacological one. Alcohol works on the central nervous system in such a way that complex cognitive processes are impaired. As a result, the inebriated person is relatively unable to attend to and utilize subtle cues in the environment, but reacts instead to the dominant and most salient stimuli. The typical situation, Taylor and Leonard propose, is one in which the person is instigated to aggress and is also cognizant of socialized restraints and inhibitions against aggressing. Alcoholic intoxication lowers the person's ability to make subtle or complex judgments involving instigation and inhibition. Thus, ingestion of alcohol will facilitate aggression when instigational cues are strong (provocation, peer support for aggression) and inhibitory cues are weak (e.g., mild peer pressure). However, when a strong inhibitory cue is introduced (clear statement of an anti-aggression norm), alcohol drinking reduces aggression. As one can see, Taylor and Leonard's hypothesis fits the data from several of the studies in Taylor's extensive research program.

## Cognitions of the situation

Some investigators would disagree with Taylor and Leonard's contention that alcohol affects behavior primarily by disrupting cognitive processes. They would contend instead that certain cognitions *produced by* the intoxicated state may also play an important role. One such effect involves the expectancy factor: aggression may follow a person's belief that he or she is intoxicated whether or not such is actually the case. Such a finding has been reported by Lang *et al.* (1975), who found that subjects who believed that they had drunk alcohol in orange juice were more aggressive toward an insulting and provocative person than those who believed that they had consumed orange juice only. This was true regardless of whether or not they had actually drunk alcohol.

Why should the mere belief that one has drunk alcohol lead to greater aggressiveness against an antagonist? One possibility is that persons who think they have ingested alcohol may feel less responsible for their actions than those who think they are sober. They may consider the consequences of any aggression they carry out as being due to the alcohol and not to themselves. If we assume that normally socialized people experience some restraints against acting aggressively and desire not to cause great harm to their victims, any disavowal of responsibility for such possible harm could facilitate the expression of aggression.

## Recognition of social cues

A study by Borrill *et al.* (1987) indicates that ingestion of alcohol may affect cognitive judgments in still another way – by reducing the person's ability to decode accurately affective cues from other people. In this study subjects were required to identify the emotion being expressed in each of a series of pictures of faces after having drunk a large or a small dose of alcohol or a placebo. Both men and women made more mistakes in identifying expressions of anger after having drunk a large amount of alcohol than after drinking a small dose or a placebo. Among male subjects, consumption of a large dose of alcohol also led to a relatively large number of errors in identifying expressions of disgust or contempt. The authors suggest that such misreading of social cues by drinkers could contribute to both aggressing and being aggressed against. Inability to recognize anger in another person could contribute to behavior that invites attack. Incorrectly attributing contempt and disgust to another person could lead one to take needless offense and perhaps retaliate.

## Personality of the drinker

Everyday experience tells us that not all people become aggressive when they are intoxicated by alcohol. Some become maudlin and sad, others become euphoric, still others thoughtful and philosophical. Only a few people become combative, and we tend to think of these people as potentially hostile and aggressive even before they become drunk. Thus the personality of the drinking person may be a contributor to any aggression shown by that person after drinking.

This supposition has been borne out in studies of the personality of aggressive drinkers. Renson *et al.* (1978) found clear evidence that persons with aggressive dispositions are more likely also to be aggressive while intoxicated than are less normally aggressive people. In their study, a number of persons undergoing treatment at an outpatient clinic for alcohol abuse were given the Buss—Durkee Inventory, a set of scales often used to assess certain dimensions of aggressiveness. Persons who had histories of being violent while intoxicated were found to be more hostile, assaultive, irritable, verbally aggressive, and resentful in their responses to the inventory than other alcohol abusers who did not show such a history of aggressiveness.

Similar results have been reported by Pihl *et al.* (1982), in an investigation of normal "social" drinkers. Consumption of alcohol was more clearly correlated with aggression among subjects who described themselves as anxious, unfriendly, unhappy, and quick to anger than among those who did not ascribe such characteristics to themselves. Thus, with both problem drinkers and less serious ones, a certain disposition toward negativity and hostility appears to mediate the effects of alcohol on aggression.

Personality variables may be implicated in the alcohol–aggression relationship in another way. Recall Taylor and Leonard's (1983) argument that alcohol interferes with cognitive processing and thus renders the person susceptible to control by powerful situational stimuli. Such stimuli may be either instigators of aggression or inhibitors. Because of the inhibitions against aggressing normally found in well-socialized people, any deficits in such socialization could predispose a person to become aggressive after drinking. In a study supporting this hypothesis, Boyatzis (1975) found that males who scored low on measures of self-control, responsibility, and socialization showed greater aggression after heavy drinking than persons who scored higher on those variables. Thus, deficient development of personality traits that inhibit aggression may predispose a person to become aggressive after drinking in much the same way as a high level of traits associated with hostility and aggressiveness.

## Race

People living in the late twentieth century need no introduction to the subject of racially-motivated aggression. Examples are everywhere: in the threats of hostile crowds menacing black school children as they arrive at previously all-white schools, in the killing or beating of black youths who wander into suburban white neighborhoods, in the fear that whites feel about going into all-black areas in the inner cities, in generalized feelings of mutual hostility and distrust that so often characterize black–white relationships. In spite of the inter-racial hostility and aggression that characterizes so much of society, relatively few attempts have been made to analyze and understand the causes of this phenomenon. In this section we will review some of the work that has been done.

### Race prejudice and aggression

A widely held belief in our culture is that racial aggression is usually motivated by racial prejudice. It is true that much of the interracial violence that occurs in natural settings is perpetrated in a climate of prejudice and bigotry. Such natural occurrences, however, are usually determined by many factors, so that separating out prejudice as a cause of aggression independent of other causes is usually impossible. However, some experimental studies have involved the use of "minimal" social situations in which persons have been given an opportunity to aggress against another person of either the same or a different race, with nothing in the situation serving as a possible cause for aggression (i.e., subjects are not attacked, angered, or provoked in any way). In such a minimal situation, any aggression that occurs can be considered a result only of attitudes, habits, and feelings that the subject brings into the situation. Interestingly, such experiments have usually shown that race prejudice, in and of itself, does not animate aggressive behavior. Instead, highly prejudiced people tend to be more aggressive than less prejudiced ones regardless of the race of the victim (see, for example, Donnerstein *et al.* 1972; Genthner and Taylor 1973). It would therefore appear, as Genthner and Taylor (1973) have concluded, that both prejudice and aggression are products of a more basic factor: a hostile and aggressive disposition.

*Interracial aggression*

If prejudice is not an underlying factor in interracial aggression, what are the causes of such behavior? To answer this question, we must first consider a finding reported several times in the experimental literature: *in the absence of provocation*, white subjects are *less* aggressive toward black victims than they are toward fellow whites, whereas black subjects are *more* aggressive toward white victims than toward fellow blacks. Wilson and Rogers (1975) found evidence that black subjects directed more intense physical aggression as well as greater verbal hostility toward white victims than they did toward black victims. This is an interesting finding in that it contrasts sharply with studies from an earlier time (e.g., Winslow and Brainerd 1950) which indicated that blacks were more aggressive toward other blacks than toward whites. How can this change be explained? Rogers (1983) has argued that it reflects changing attitudes of blacks toward the dominant white American society. Whereas the historic role of the black person, coming out of a history of slavery and long-standing discrimination, was one of subservience and self-deprecation before whites, it has lately been shifting to one reflecting greater assertiveness, black pride, and sense of fellowship with others in the black community. Along with this has grown a greater willingness to express hostility toward the white majority.

The study of aggression by whites against blacks is somewhat more complex. Most investigators have found that such aggression is seldom a function of the race of the black victim alone, but instead the product of interactions of race with other variables, such as anger, frustration, or interpersonal attack (Donnerstein and Donnerstein 1976; Rogers and Prentice-Dunn 1981). In fact, some studies have shown that white subjects may even take pains to be less aggressive toward blacks than to fellow whites, thereby showing a sort of "reverse racial discrimination". What these findings seem to show is that well-socialized whites, in contrast to whites of earlier times, may now consider aggression against blacks to be a sign of socially unjustified racism, so that unless some powerful cause is present, such as a provocation, no such racial aggression is likely. It should be noted that most experimental research on interracial aggression takes place in college settings with students as subjects. These studies therefore reflect the behaviors of highly socialized people of each racial group, people who may be expected to show in their behaviors the effects of social changes within their respective communities. Thus, the finding mentioned earlier in this section – that blacks aggress against whites more than against blacks whereas whites aggress against blacks less than against whites – may reflect changing cultural norms in each group.

## "Regressive racism"

What, however, happens when blacks and whites interact in situations involving provocation to aggression? Here an interesting effect sometimes emerges, whereby each racial group appears to revert to a type of behavior characteristic of an earlier period in history. Rogers and Prentice-Dunn (1981) conducted an experiment in which each white subject interacted with either a black or a white person who behaved in either an insulting or a non-insulting way. When no insult was delivered, the subject was later more aggressive toward the white victim than toward the black; "reverse discrimination" occurred. However, when the other person was insulting, the subject attacked the black more than the white (see Figure 6.1). When provoked, the

*Figure 6.1*    Aggression as a function of insult and race of target

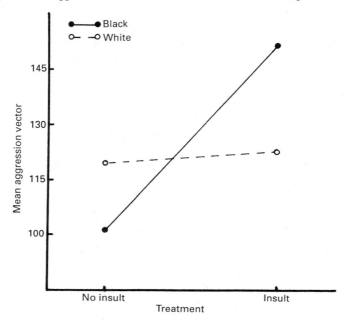

Source: Rogers and Prentice-Dunne (1981)
Note: Data are mean values of aggression vectors from a multivariate analysis of variance. The greater the value, the greater the expression expressed by the subjects (see original article for details)

white subjects "regressed" to a pattern of behavior more typical of a time when concerns about being racist were less strong than they now are. Rogers and Prentice-Dunn have therefore described this behavior as "regressive racism".

Regressive racism has also been found among black subjects. In a study already referred to, Wilson and Rogers (1975) found that when black subjects (who were all women) were insulted by another woman, they aggressed against that person more when she was black than when she was white, even though, as reported above, the reverse was found when the other person was not insulting. It should be noted, however, that this finding was restricted to a measure of shock *duration* only, and was not found when shock intensity was the dependent measure. Furthermore, the study involved women only. For reasons of these limitations, the results should be treated with some caution.

*Inhibition of interracial aggression*

The hypothesis of regressive racism is founded in part on the finding that contemporary socialized whites express less aggression toward blacks than was the case in earlier times because they do not wish to appear racist. In other words, current social norms regarding black–white relations may serve to inhibit interracial aggression. The implication seems clear that whites, as a rule, may not feel any less animosity toward blacks than they ever did, but that they now control the expression of that animosity unless they are provoked by a black. In that case, the animosity may once again lead to aggression.

Several other studies have shown that whites' aggression against blacks may be inhibited by situational constraints and that once these constraints are removed, aggression follows. One such constraint is lack of anonymity. Donnerstein *et al.* (1972) carried out an

*Figure 6.2*  Aggression as a function of anonymity of subject and race of target

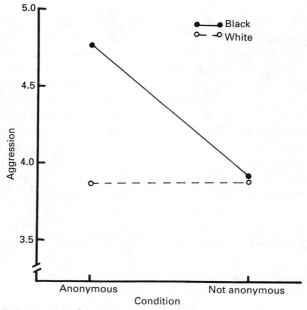

*Source:* Donnerstein *et al.* (1972)
*Note:* Intensity of a shock is defined as the number of a button (from 1–10) on a Buss aggression apparatus (see Buss 1961 for details)

experiment in which white subjects interacting with either a black or another white were either known to the latter through an earlier introduction, or unknown and anonymous. Whereas anonymity had no influence on aggression toward a white target, it greatly enhanced the expression of aggression toward a black (Figure 6.2). The reason that non-anonymous subjects were less aggressive may have been that they feared being identified later by their victims, and retaliated against or censured for their aggressiveness. Fear of retaliation has been shown to be an inhibitor of interracial aggression by Griffin and Rogers (1977). In addition, Donnerstein and Donnerstein (1973) found that white subjects were less aggressive toward blacks when they were told that their behavior was being videotaped for future analysis by the experimenter than when they were not told this. The possibility of incurring disapproval from the experimenter may have inhibited aggression against blacks that the subjects were otherwise motivated to commit.

## Conclusions

Despite the seriousness of the problem of interracial aggression, only two extensive programs of controlled investigation have been re-ported to date: those of Donnerstein and Donnerstein (1976) and Rogers (1983). The findings have been interesting but inconclusive. Conclusions can be most clearly drawn in the case of aggression of whites against blacks. The evidence indicates that in the absence of provocation, whites tend to be restrained in attacking blacks, possi-bly because of fears of social censure or retaliation. When provoked, however, whites attack blacks more than they do fellow whites. Studies of black aggression against whites are less numerous and hence less reliable. There is some evidence suggesting that blacks, while being relatively restrained in attacking other blacks, may lose some of this restraint when they are provoked. Rogers's (1983) concept of "regressive racism" may explain these findings, and it remains an interesting hypothesis for future study.

## Personality variables

Everyday experience suggests that individual differences play an important part in aggressive behavior. We are familiar with so-called "aggressive types" who supposedly make up much of the population of dangerous criminals. In fact, people who advocate harsh and punitive justice for offenders often do so on the grounds that such "types" are not likely to be reformed or rehabilitated by changing their relationships to their environments. As we will see in this section, we have solid grounds for assuming that aggressive personalities are a reality; however, it is also probably correct to think of these personalities as moderators of situational influences rather than as causes of aggression in and of themselves. As has been proposed throughout this book, aggression is best thought of as a response to situational change. Such response, however, can be affected by certain personality variables. The role of personality in reactive aggression has not always been a matter of concern to psychologists, some of whom have tended to dismiss the whole notion of personality as unnecessary in the analysis of behavior (e.g., Krasner and Ullmann 1973; Mischel 1968). Furthermore, attempts at defining and measuring individual differences in aggressiveness, as a trait, have not been generally successful (Edmunds and Kendrick 1980; Megargee 1985). In recent years, however, more and more attention has been directed to the importance of personality variables as moderators of aggression following provocation, and in this section some of the findings from this research will be reviewed.

*Stability of aggression*

Arguments against the concept of personality are usually built on the fact that behavior is sometimes unstable and variable across times and situations. An example is a study by Campbell *et al.* (1985) in which students predicted their own responses to a variety of social situations by selecting one of several possible responses from a list. These responses varied according to the degree of aggressiveness that each revealed. Campbell *et al.* found little evidence of consistency in responses across situations. The best predictor of subjects' aggressiveness was the variation within the situations. Other investigators argue that a case can be made for consistency in human aggression across times and situations. Deluty (1985) has reported that a sample of boys aged between eight and ten manifested a high level of consistency in their aggressive behaviors over a wide range of naturally occurring activities. Although the same overall level of consistency was not shown among girls, correlations among certain types of aggressive act were as high as they were among boys. The results of a major investigation by Olweus (1979) are consistent with this finding. Olweus reviewed a large number of longitudinal studies of aggressive behavior and reaction patterns in children, noting in each case the coefficient of stability in aggressive behavior from one measurement period to another (i.e., the magnitude of correlation across instances of aggression). The lengths of time intervening between measurements varied from study to study, as did the ages of the children studied at the outset of each study. Measures of aggressiveness included direct observation, teacher ratings, clinical ratings, and judgments made by other children.

Considerable evidence for stability in aggressive behavior was found. For example, clear individual differences in aggressiveness level emerged as early as the age of three, with such stability lasting for as long as 12–18 months. Among school-age children, aggressive behavior patterns at age eight to nine were found to be correlated with aggressiveness as late as 10–14 years later. In some instances the magnitude of correlation was sufficient to account for 25 per cent of the variance in aggressiveness at the later age. Aggressive behavior at ages 12–13 was also found to show a high degree of stability for periods of one to five years (with between 50 per cent and 90 per cent of the variance accounted for). Such findings strongly indicate that aggressive behavior is to some degree a function of generalized aggressiveness.

It is difficult to account for such stability in aggressiveness in terms of usual social learning explanations, according to which aggression is the product of social reinforcements or other situational inducements. In fact, as Olweus points out, children who show aggressiveness early in life are probably punished for such behavior, which, according to social learning theory, should inhibit further aggression. In addition, aggressive children are probably the object of attempts by teachers and others to make them less aggressive. Olweus (1979, p. 871) has therefore concluded that aggressive behavior "is often maintained irrespective of considerable environmental variation and in opposition to forces acting to change this same behavior".

## Personality and cognitive functioning

Do these findings indicate that people have a "trait" of aggressiveness, i.e., a stable tendency to behave aggressively most of the time and in most places? Olweus discourages such an interpretation of the findings, suggesting instead that individual differences contribute to aggression in concert with cognitive appraisals of the situation, emotional reactions, and any tendencies the person may have to inhibit aggression. Huesman and Eron (1984) have explained stable and persistent aggressive behavior in terms of the internal cognitive representations, or *schemata*, that people form of their environments. The person who, as a child, uses aggression as an approach to interpersonal conflicts exposes himself or herself, by virtue of this behavior, to a large number of aggressive events, or *scenarios*. These scenarios become encoded in memory and maintained through rehearsal. In addition, the child may elaborate upon these scenarios, and as a result develop more abstract and generalized aggressive strategies for dealing with conflict. The end result is a high probability that the child will retrieve an aggressive schema whenever conflict arises. Aggressive behavior guided by such schemata is the consequence. This in turn adds other scenarios to the cognitive structure, and the process begins again. In this way aggression can become self-perpetuating, running in ongoing cycles.

Several cognitive variables may enter into the process of encoding, rehearsal, and retrieval. Two have been examined by Huesman and Eron: (1) intellectual functioning and (2) fantasy.

*Intellectual functioning*

Intellectual functioning, manifested in such matters as reading comprehension and mathematical ability, can affect aggressiveness and in turn be affected by it. Poor intellectual functioning produces frustration and arousal in normal problem-solving settings such as children encounter in school. Several consequences follow from this. The child has a tendency to react to frustration with aggression. Because of the intellectual deficit, he or she is not as able as other children to understand the inappropriateness of aggression or to formulate alternative reactions. At the same time his or her behavior results in a low rate of reinforcement for non-aggressive responses. The child therefore encodes an aggressive strategy for such situations.

Matters do not end there, however. Once an aggressive strategy has been encoded, it tends to persist and, in turn, to exert a reciprocating effect on intellectual processes. Aggressiveness, by hindering good relationships between the child and his or her teachers and peers, interferes with intellectual opportunity and advancement. The result is continued poor achievement in school, which perpetuates the low level of intellectual functioning. Hence, the cycle is repeated. Whereas poor intellectual functioning originally led to aggression, aggression now becomes the source of continued intellectual deficits. In support of this conclusion, Huesman and Eron (1984) reported data from a 22-year longitudinal study which showed that aggressiveness in children at age eight was highly correlated with both anti-social behavior and intellectual deficit in those children when they reached adulthood. In fact, aggressiveness at age eight predicted intellectual functioning at age 30 better than intellectual functioning at age eight predicted adult aggressiveness.

*Fantasy*
In the cognitive approach to behavior, fantasizing is regarded as a type of rehearsal of a schema. Every time an idea is mulled over in fantasy it is being rehearsed and possibly elaborated. It should follow, therefore, that because rehearsal maintains the strength of a schema in memory, children who fantasize about violence should be more likely to retrieve aggressive schemata than those who do not fantasize. They should, therefore, be more likely to behave aggressively. In a three-year longitudinal study of primary-school children, Huesman and Eron (1984) did find that children who frequently fantasized about aggression were described as being more aggressive by their peers than children who fantasized less. It should also be noted that aggressive fantasizing was positively correlated with both television viewing and the extent to which children identified with television characters (cf. Chapter 4). Thus one reason why observation of televised violence is associated with aggressive behavior may be that fantasy behavior, and identification elicited by the televised violence, causes aggressive schemata to be rehearsed and strengthened in memory. As a result, these schemata become more likely to serve as guides for behavior.

*Arousability and overcontrol*

Another important basis for individual differences in aggressiveness is the degree to which people are emotionally aroused or inhibited in situations with potential for aggressive behavior. People who are considered aggressive are usually those who become affectively aroused and who act out their feelings in such situations. The non-aggressive person is identified often by the amount of self-control that she or he exerts. Where others respond to insults, attacks, or frustrations with angry outbursts, this person stays calm, does not show overt signs of anger, and maintains an acceptable level of socially acceptable behavior.

## Impulsivity

Impulse control is therefore important in the control of aggression. The opposite is also true: lack of such control is associated with relatively high levels of aggressive behavior. Hynan and Grush (1986), for example, found that among male subjects in whom a negative affective state had been induced, those subjects who had also scored high on a measure of impulsivity were more aggressive toward an experimental partner than were those who scored low in impulsivity. They concluded that the induced negative affect made all the subjects aggressive, but made impulsive ones more aggressive than non-impulsive ones.

## Irritability, emotional susceptibility, and rumination

Another aspect of arousability is seen in the concepts of *irritability* and *emotional susceptibility* described by Caprara and his associates. Irritability is defined by Caprara *et al.* (1983, p. 346) as "a stable tendency of the individual to react offensively to minimal provocation", and has been shown in the same study to be a moderator of aggressive reactions to disparaging or insulting remarks from another person.

Emotional susceptibility is defined as "the tendency . . . to experience feelings of discomfort, helplessness, inadequacy, and vulnerability" (Caprara *et al.* 1985, p. 666). Persons who score high on this variable have been found to be more aggressive than low scorers, but the variable does not interact with provocation in the same way as does irritability (Caprara *et al.* 1983). Possibly emotional susceptibility reflects a more generalized tendency to experience negative affect, which can be an antecedent of aggression in and of itself (Berkowitz 1983).

A third variable, *dissipation-rumination*, describes individual differences in tendencies to "harbor and even to enhance, with the passing of time, feelings and desires of vengeance" (Caprara 1986). Although little research has been done with the variable, Caprara

*Table 6.1* Sample items from irritability and emotional susceptibility scales

---

*Irritability*
I easily fly off the handle with those who don't listen or understand.
It makes my blood boil to have somebody make fun of me.
I never get mad enough to throw things.*
Some people irritate me if they just open their mouth.

*Emotional susceptibility*
I am too sensitive to criticism.
I don't complain about what life has given me.**
I often feel vulnerable and defenseless.
I have often felt upset.

---

* *Disagreement* signifies irritability
** Agreement signifies *low* emotional susceptibility
*Source:* Caprara *et al.* (1985)

(1986) found that persons who were low dissipators/high ruminators were more verbally hostile following an insult than were similarly insulted high dissipators/low ruminators.

*Overcontrol*
Although normal impulse control is required for inhibition of aggression, too much control can have the opposite effect. Newspapers frequently report cases in which horrible crimes of violence are committed by persons thought to be incapable of such mayhem. Such persons are often described by neighbors and friends as polite, quiet, unemotional, and soft-spoken. Usually they have no history of assaultive behavior. Why, then, do these people show murderously violent behavior in a single outburst? The reason is not that they are undercontrolled, but that their high degree of *overcontrol* makes them dangerously likely to explode.

Megargee (1966) proposed that assaultive persons may be classified into two distinct groups: the undercontrolled and the chronically overcontrolled. The first type we have already considered. The second is characterized by extremely strong defenses and inhibitions against aggressing. Because these inhibitions are also diffuse and generalized, the overcontrolled person is not only unlikely to aggress against primary targets, but also unlikely to find suitable secondary targets for displaced aggression. Tensions associated with provocations therefore summate over time and build to a point at which they exceed even the abnormally high level of defenses against aggressing. If sufficient stimuli for aggression are present in the environment, the result will be an act of violence proportional to the intense level of stored-up tensions.

To test his hypotheses about overcontrol, Megargee (1966) studied four groups of incarcerated male juvenile offenders. Some had been arrested for violent crimes (e.g., homicide, attempted homicide, assault with a deadly weapon) and were classified as extremely assaultive. Others had been charged with less severe crimes (e.g., gang fights) and were described as moderately assaultive. Two other groups of boys had been detained for non-violent offenses. On several indicators the extremely assaultive boys differed from those in the other three groups. They had better records of school attendance. They were more likely to be rated by their counselors in terms such as "self-controlled", "meek", and "conscientious". They had lower scores on a measure of verbal aggression and higher scores on the self-control, responsibility, and tolerance subscales of the California Psychological Inventory. They were also more likely to be first offenders than were the boys in the other groups. All of these characteristics point to an excessively high level of self-control in the extremely assaultive boys.

## Summary

1 Several individual difference variables moderate the effects of situational conditions on aggression. Among these are sex; race; level of cognitive development; tendencies to consume alcohol; and personality.

2 The underlying cause of sex differences in aggression is a matter of some dispute. Some evidence points to a possible genetic basis for at least some of the sex differences. This evidence indicates that men are generally more aggressive than women in most societies, that male–female differences in aggression begin too early in life to be easily attributed to learning, that similar male–female differences are found in subhuman species, and that a hormonal basis for sex differences can be shown. This evidence has been criticized by other investigators who argue that the case for a genetic basis for sex differences has not been properly established. Other studies show that sex differences in aggression diminish with age from childhood to adulthood.

3  Even proponents of a genetic link to sex differences concede that a large part of male–female differences is traceable to social learning. There is only weak evidence for the idea that men prefer physical aggression and women prefer verbal means of aggressing. Women are more likely than men to experience guilt and anxiety over aggressing. Other sex differences occur at a more cognitive level. Men and women differ somewhat in the ways in which they interpret provoking situations and may differ in aggression as a result. The two sexes also tend to react to observed violence in different ways, a difference that can be attributed to different values placed on aggression as a way of reacting to conflict.

4  Individual differences in level of cognitive development also influence aggression in response to both provocation and the observation of violence being carried out by others. Age-linked differences in attributions of the cause and meaning of events account for the developmental differences in each case. In addition, poor cognitive development may be associated with high levels of delinquency and with a generally negative self-image.

5  Consumption of alcohol may increase the chances of a person's aggressing, especially if certain situational factors are present, such as interpersonal threat or social pressure from peers. The presence of strong social norms against aggressing may have a reverse effect, by inhibiting aggression in inebriated people more than in sober ones. It has been proposed that alcohol ingestion impairs the action of the central nervous system, thereby reducing a person's ability to make complex judgments and increasing the influence of strong situational stimuli. Such influence can either inhibit or facilitate aggression, depending on the nature of the dominant cues.

6  Alcohol consumption may also directly influence the drinker's judgmental processes. Drinkers may aggress more than non-drinkers because they are able to attribute their actions to the effects of alcohol rather than having to take personal responsibility. In addition, people with aggressive dispositions are more likely to aggress when intoxicated than persons with less aggressive dispositions.

7  Race prejudice alone does not predict interracial aggression; prejudiced people tend to be more aggressive than non-prejudiced ones toward all others. In the absence of provocation, whites tend to be more aggressive toward fellow whites than

toward blacks and blacks tend to be less aggressive toward fellow blacks than toward whites. When provoked, the behaviour of both whites and blacks tends to be the opposite of their behaviour when not provoked. This may show a "regressing" back to behavior patterns that were typical before the current norms for interracial behavior took effect.

8 Aggressive behavior tends to be stable over time and situations, suggesting that aggressiveness is a fairly consistent mode of behavior. Stable individual differences interact with situations to produce varying levels of aggression. Aggressiveness as a personal characteristic operates in part through the cognitive process of retrieving scenarios and scripts to guide behavior.

9 Individual differences in aggressiveness are related to overall intellectual functioning. A low level of intellectual functioning early in life may produce aggressiveness because of frustration and failure-induced arousal. This aggressiveness, in turn, may cut a child off from opportunities for intellectual growth and may thereby maintain the child's low intellectual status.

10 Children who fantasize a great deal are more aggressive than those who do not. A reason for this may be that fantasizing causes rehearsal of existing schemata for behavior; children who fantasize about violence may thereby be increasing the likelihood of retrieving an aggressive schema on occasions of future interpersonal conflict.

11 Normal control over impulses is necessary for the control of aggression. However, too much control can have the opposite effect. Persons who commit acts of extreme violence despite appearing to be unemotional and highly restrained may exemplify the overcontrolled type. Such persons inhibit expression of aggression until they become excessive in their violence.


## Suggestions for further reading

Edmunds, G. and Kendrick, K. (1980). *The Measurement of Human Aggressiveness*. Chichester, UK: Horwood. The first half of this book describes and critically evaluates existing scales for the assessment of human aggressiveness.

Rogers, R. W. (1983). Race variables in aggression. In R. G. Geen and E. Donnerstein (eds), *Aggression: Theoretical and Empirical Reviews, Vol. 2: Issues in Research*. New York: Academic Press, pp. 27–50. An excellent review of laboratory experiments on black–white conflict and aggression.

White, J. W. (1983). Sex and gender issues in aggression research. In R. G. Geen and E. Donnerstein (eds), *Aggression: Theoretical and Empirical Reviews, Vol. 2: Issues in Research.* New York: Academic Press, pp. 1–26. This paper is superior to many analyses of sex differences in aggression for its organization and integrative discussions of research data.

# 7 / HOSTILITY, HEALTH, AND ADJUSTMENT

The emotional and affective states related to aggression have also been linked to general health and to psycho-social adjustment. In recent years extensive research has been devoted to the question of whether hostility, anger, and trait aggressiveness play important roles in the development of such health problems as high blood pressure and coronary artery disease. Interest in this problem arises from a suspicion that such psychological risk factors may be as important in the etiology of cardiovascular diseases as the more commonly recognized physical ones. Furthermore, because these diseases indicate an increased risk of death, some investigators are studying the possibility of a correlation between aggressive affective states and mortality.

A commonplace piece of folk wisdom tells us that it is unwise to hold in anger, lest we eventually explode in pent-up rage. Is there anything to this idea? Is anger accompanied by a potentially dangerous increase in arousal, and, if so, does aggression allow for some reduction in that state? Is this alleged build-up in arousal a result of active aggressiveness, or of a suspicious and hostile, but restrained, type of attitude?

Even if aggression does promote a release of potentially harmful affective arousal, does it also have a beneficial effect of psycho-social adjustment? Does aggressing when angry reduce subsequent aggressive desires and make the person less likely to be violent again? Can aggression become habitual and subject to repetition?

In this chapter we will be concerned with two aspects of aggression and its related emotional and affective states. First, we will consider the possible links among anger, hostility, trait aggressiveness and physical health. We will also consider whether aggressive behavior has a beneficial effect of regulating physiological arousal associated with those affective conditions. Second, we will consider whether aggression brings about a reduction in future tendencies to aggress, or whether it may under some circumstances have the exact opposite effect.

## Physiological effects of anger and hostility

### Physiology of anger

Cannon (1929) was among the first investigators to study the physiological concomitants of anger, noting that the pattern of autonomic activity associated with flight and withdrawal is different from that found in aggression. Similar observations were made by Ax (1953) and Schachter (1957), who carried out experiments in which fear and anger were experimentally induced and were shown to be accompanied by specific and different patterns of activation. In general, these investigators noted that states of fear produced a physiological reaction similar to that elicited by epinephrine, whereas anger appeared to be a mixed epinephrine–norepinephrine response. An important finding was also reported by Funkenstein *et al.* (1954), who proposed that the physiological reaction to anger depends in part on one's response to anger, i.e., whether it is expressed in overt aggression or whether it is repressed and held in. Male subjects were first harassed and provoked as they solved problems, after which they were classified into four groups: those who expressed their anger in aggression (anger-out), those who held anger in, those who showed a mixture of the two, and those who manifested aggression anxiety. Physiologically, the anger-in subjects responded much like the aggression-anxious ones: both groups showed increased heart rates and systolic blood pressure. The anger-out subjects, on the other hand, showed little change in heart rate and increased diastolic blood pressure. This finding prefigured later ones, reviewed below, which indicate that repressed anger is related to both hypertension and cardiovascular problems.

### Anger, hostility, and hypertension

#### Hostility and blood pressure
Attempts to link personality differences in hostility to blood pressure

have yielded mixed results. The results of two recent studies reveal no relationship between the two variables. Smith and Houston (1987) classified subjects in terms of levels of hostility and typical expression of anger (anger-in versus anger-out), then gave subjects challenging mental tasks to perform. The magnitude of correlations between the various anger and hostility measures and both systolic and diastolic blood pressure during the tasks was virtually zero. Similar results have been reported by Sallis *et al.* (1987) in a study in which subjects were exposed to both mental and physical stressors. Again, no consistent evidence was found of a relationship between hostility and either systolic or diastolic blood pressure during the stressful tasks.

In contrast to these findings, Hardy and Smith (1987) found that subjects who participated in a role-playing analog of a situation involving strong interpersonal conflict did show a relationship between hostility level and hypertension, at least in the case of diastolic blood pressure. Highly hostile subjects performing under these conditions revealed higher levels of diastolic blood pressure than did less hostile subjects. The main difference between the Hardy and Smith study and the other two cited here is that it involved a situational manipulation (the role-play situation) that could engender feelings of anger whereas the others involved stressful but impersonal circumstances. Thus, hostility may be related to hypertension only when situational cues for conflict and anger are present.

*Repressed anger and blood pressure*
Other studies suggest a connection between repressed anger and high blood pressure. In an early review, Wolf and Wolff (1951) noted that essential hypertension was often accompanied by a personality in which affability was mixed with suspiciousness and mistrust of others and an underlying desire to aggress. In a study from the same period, Harris *et al.* (1953) noted that persons classified as potential hypertensives described themselves on an adjective checklist as not only "hot-headed" and "rash", but also as "submissive" and "docile". One implication of these early investigations is that hypertension may be related to a particular personality marked by both strong anger and hostility and a need to repress and hold in such feelings out of concern for social approval and conformity. More recently, Baer *et al.* (1979) noted that the item on their 16-item screening questionnaire which best discriminated between hypertensives and people with normal blood pressure was "I tend to harbor grudges that I don't tell anybody about." Thirty-seven per

cent of hypertensives endorsed this item whereas only 27 per cent of normotensives did.

One of the more important research programs on the relationship between anger and hypertension is that of Harburg *et al.* (1979), who studied these variables within samples of black Americans. Harburg *et al.* speculated that suppressed hostility and anger could be contributors to the high levels of hypertension found in blacks, levels considerably higher on average than those found in whites. Black males who showed high levels of suppressed hostility were, as predicted, found to have higher diastolic blood pressure levels than those who did not reveal this pattern of suppression. In addition, males who tended to cope with stress in their lives by holding in anger and by experiencing aggression guilt were, in general, more likely to become hyptertensives than those who coped with stress more expressively.

Additional evidence of the relationship between suppressed anger and hypertension in black Americans has been reported by Gentry *et al.* (1982). These investigators isolated four specific risk factors for hypertension: (1) sex (with men being at greater risk than women); (2) race (with blacks at greater risk than whites); (3) area of habitation (with people from high-stress neighborhoods being at greater risk than those from less stressful ones); and (4) coping style (with anger expressors being at less risk than anger suppressors). Overall, the group at least risk of developing hypertension were white women who live in low-stress neighborhoods and express anger directly, whereas the group at greatest risk were black men living in high-stress areas and who hold anger in.

Gentry (1985) has also shown that coping style moderates the effects of interracial hostility on blood pressure. Blacks who were high in hostility toward whites and who also tended to suppress their anger had higher average diastolic blood pressure than similarly angry blacks who expressed their anger. Furthermore, Gentry (1985) has shown that subjects who have anger-in coping styles react with high blood pressure to tensions in the workplace and in their everyday lives to a greater extent than do people who let their anger out. Apparently, both job strain and everyday-life strain generate anger, and the way in which this anger is handled determines to some extent the consequences of these strains for health (Figure 7.1). In general, therefore, there does appear to be a connection among hostility, coping style, and hypertension among black Americans.

Evidence that connects anger expression with hypertension in

*Figure 7.1* Effects of anger expression on relation of job strain to blood pressure

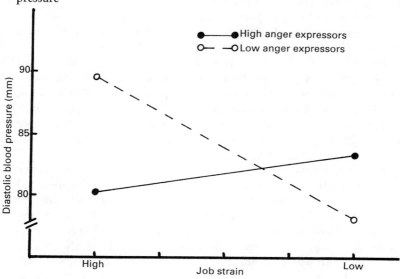

*Source:* Gentry (1985)

whites as well as blacks comes from a study by Johnson *et al.* (1987). Adolescent males of both racial groups were tested for the tendency to suppress expression of anger as well as for other traditional risk factors such as smoking, excess weight, and family history of hypertension. Both groups showed a clear relationship between suppression of anger and elevation in blood pressure. Among blacks, suppression of anger even outweighed the more traditional risk variables in predicting hypertension whereas in whites the anger-in variable was less related to hypertension than was excess weight. Thus, although anger suppression appears to be a predictor of hypertension in both blacks and whites, it is a more powerful one among blacks than among whites.

### Heart disease, hostility, and the Type A pattern

#### The Type A behavior pattern

Research on the connection between hostility, anger, and coronary disease has tended to be concentrated in investigations of the Type A coronary-prone behavior pattern (TABP). This pattern is a cluster of behaviors, dispositions, and emotional reactions including a hard-driving and competitive motivational state, a sense of time urgency, impatience, hostility, and elevated physiological arousal (Rosenman and Chesney 1982; Houston 1983). The TABP is also related to a relatively high level of aggressiveness (Strube *et al.* 1984).

Interest in the TABP originated among heart specialists who sought psychological risk factors in coronary heart disease to go along with the better-known physical ones such as serum cholesterol, smoking, lack of exercise, and hypertension. It was suspected that people who manifest the characteristics listed above may be more susceptible to coronary disease than others, called Type Bs, who do not show such tendencies.

Early conceptualizations of the TABP led to a major *prospective* study (i.e., one in which occurrence of coronary disease is predicted from risk factors measured earlier) called the Western Collaborative Group Study. A structured interview method was devised as the means of distinguishing Type A persons from their Type B counterparts. After eight-and-a-half years, the results of the study showed that the TABP was a significant predictor of coronary disease, with Type As being approximately twice as likely to have the disease as Type Bs (Brand 1978). The two-to-one ratio of risk was found even when all other risk factors were controlled. Moreover, the TABP was as reliable a predictor of heart disease as any of the more traditional and agreed-upon physical ones. Although a causal link between the TABP and coronary disease has not been unequivocally established (Matthews and Haynes 1986), considerable additional correlational evidence has been reported that suggests some connection between the two (Rosenman and Chesney 1982). As a consequence, it has been suggested that one or more of the components of the TABP may be involved in coronary disease even though the entire configuration is not.

### Hostility and the Type A pattern

Several investigators have suggested that the component of the TABP most clearly related to coronary heart disease is hostility (e.g., Dembroski and Costa 1987). Several studies support this idea. For example, Theorell and Rahe (1972) found that persons who become hostile when held up in queues are at greater risk of subsequent heart problems than are people who do not show this characteristic. Matthews *et al.* (1977) noted that a TABP factor from the structured interview labeled "potential for hostility" is the best single discriminator of coronary disease. They also found that coronary heart disease could be predicted from such matters as the extent to which a person becomes irritated when having to wait in a queue, explosiveness in speech, and the frequency of experience of anger. Mac-Dougall *et al.* (1985) corroborated the finding that potential for hostility was a valid predictor of coronary artery disease. They also found that another TABP factor − the anger-in tendency, which describes a tendency to suppress displays of anger − was significantly related to the disease. This latter finding indicates that suppression of anger may be implicated in coronary problems much as it is in hypertension. Hostility has also been linked to incidence of coronary heart disease independently of the TABP. Barefoot *et al.* (1983), for example, examined both the incidence of coronary heart disease and mortality from all causes in a number of physicians, each of whom had been assessed for hostility level while enrolled in medical school 25 years earlier. Barefoot *et al.* found a significant relationship of hostility to both coronary disease and mortality during the 25 years studied. In another investigation, Shekelle *et al.* (1983) found that hostility predicted the incidence of both heart attacks and cardiac-related deaths in a sample of men over a ten-year period. In both of these studies hostility was measured by means of scales specifically constructed for that purpose (see, for example, Cook and Medley 1954). One recent study indicates that another scale assessing hostility may also be a potential indicator of coronary disease. Siegman *et al.* (1987) ascertained the existence of a factor in the Buss−Durkee Hostility Inventory (Buss and Durkee 1957) which they labeled "expressive anger". This factor was found to be positively correlated with coronary disease. Persons scoring high on scale items linked to this factor indicate that they frequently argue with others, that they do so in a loud voice, that they easily express their anger verbally, and that they are capable of physical aggression if they are provoked.

None of the studies reviewed here necessarily shows, of course, that the TABP is irrelevant to coronary heart disease. Because hostility is a part of the TABP by definition, the studies in which it is independently assessed may simply be suggesting it is the major component in the link between the TABP and the disease. This possibility was addressed in a study by Williams *et al.* (1980), in which the TABP and hostility, as measured by an independent scale (Cook and Medley 1954), were both found to predict coronary heart disease. Thus, Type As showed evidence of more coronary disease than Type Bs and highly hostile people showed more disease than did less hostile people. The two variables did not interact with each other. This convergence of the two indicators in predicting heart disease led to the conclusion that it is probably the hostility component of the TABP that is most closely related to coronary problems.

The joint contribution of hostility and the TABP to coronary disease is further shown in a study by Weidner *et al.* (1987). These investigators used both a measure of the TABP and an independent measure of hostility to assess coronary risk in young adult men and women. In addition, they measured elevation of plasma lipids (cholesterol and triglycerides), a common physical risk factor. The main purpose of the investigation was to discover whether an elevation in blood lipids linked to hostility could be the source of the connection between hostility and coronary heart disease. The results showed that whereas neither hostility nor the TABP alone was consistently related to lipid elevation, the interaction between the two was highly related. A high level of hostility was associated with elevated lipid level among Type A men and women, but not among Type Bs. How can this finding be explained? Weidner *et al.* suggest that highly hostile people tend to be suspicious and mistrustful of others. This tendency alone may mean little, but when combined with the highly competitive nature of the Type A person, it may create a strong need to be constantly vigilant and watchful of other people. The stress of this behavior may initiate activity in the autonomic nervous system, leading to a release of catecholamines such as norepinephrine. The latter in turn stimulates lipid mobilization.

*Suppressed anger and coronary disease*
Earlier it was noted that the connection between hostility and hypertension is probably brought about by a characteristic anger-in style of coping. The same may be true in the case of heart disorders. Some evidence exists linking suppressed hostility to coronary heart disease. Dembroski *et al.* (1985) gave a structured interview to patients undergoing diagnosis for heart problems in order to isolate two components of the TABP, potential for hostility and anger-in, described earlier. Persons who manifested either high or low levels of each of these two characteristics were then compared in terms of several indicators of coronary heart disease. For every indicator, potential for hostility and anger-in were found to have an interactive effect: persons who had strong tendencies to hold in anger showed progressively greater likelihood of developing coronary problems as potential for hostility increased. Figure 7.2 illustrates one of these

*Figure 7.2*    Relationship between anger expression, potential for hostility, and incidence of coronary occlusion

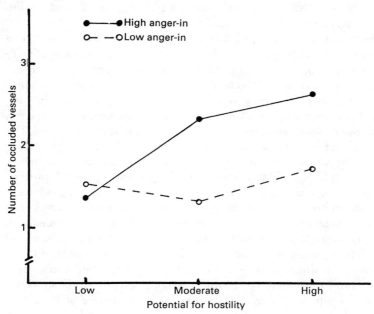

*Source:* Dembroski *et al.* (1985)

interactions. The dependent measure is the number of coronary arteries showing blockage of 75 per cent or more. Among persons high in anger-in, the number of such arteries is greater when potential for hostility is high than when it is low. No such effect for hostility potential is found in patients low in anger-in. Coronary risk is therefore relatively high for hostile people only if they exert too much control over it and suppress it.

*Cynical hostility*
In several of the studies reviewed here, the test used to assess hostility was the Cook and Medley (1954) scale. This scale has been analyzed by Smith and Frohm (1985) and found to correlate with several other variables. It is significantly positively correlated with six subscales of the Buss–Durkee Hostility Inventory, particularly with those assessing resentment, suspicion, irritability, and negativism. It also correlates positively with a measure of cynicism and negatively with a measure of trust. Finally, it correlates only slightly with the TABP.

Taken together, these findings led Smith and Frohm to conclude that the Cook–Medley scale measures a tendency of people to be angry, bitterly resentful, suspicious, and mistrusting. Smith and Frohm label this tendency *cynical hostility*.

Futher analysis showed that cynical hostility was related to a number of other variables. Persons having this tendency were marked by characteristically higher levels of anger than their less hostile counterparts and by less ability to cope with stressors encountered in daily life. They reported experiencing a relatively high number of everyday annoyances. They also expressed dissatisfaction with the amount and quality of social support that they received. The overall picture of the cynically hostile person that emerges is that of someone who carries around a great deal of anger and resentment, often over little daily problems, but who possesses poor adaptive or adjustive mechanisms. The anger therefore tends to become expressed in hostile and irritating ways that alienate other people and lead to social rejection and lack of support. Aversive social feedback simply reinforces the bleak expectations of the cynical person and helps to maintain his or her hostile behavior. Several of the factors involved in this process – the high level of anger and consequent autonomic arousal, the poor ability to cope and adjust, the low level of social support – may all keep the person in a state of stress and render him or her vulnerable to coronary disease and other health problems.

*Factor L*
A construct that is conceptually similar to cynical hostility has been described by Barefoot *et al.* (1987). Factor L of the Cattell 16PF (a widely used personality assessment test) measures a tendency to be hostile, suspicious, jealous of others, irritable, and intolerant. Barefoot *et al.* measured mortality from all causes in a sample of 500 people from whom Factor L scores had been obtained approximately eight years previously. The results showed that people scoring in the 80th percentile in hostility on Factor L were almost 1.5 times as likely to die in the eight-year interval as those scoring in the 20th percentile.

## Aggression and physiological recovery

The literature on the relationship between the anger-in style of coping and some of the health problems reviewed above leads us to ask whether the expression of aggression brings about a reduction of arousal and tension. A number of experimental investigations have been addressed to this problem. In each case, subjects were first provoked in some way so that arousal would be increased, after which the subjects were given an opportunity to aggress. The main dependent measure in most of the studies was blood pressure. The conclusion most warranted from this body of research is that aggression leads to autonomic recovery under some conditions but not others, and that in some cases it may actually bring about *increased* autonomic activation. Briefly stated, the data indicate that autonomic recovery after aggression is likely to occur *except* when the target person appears to be powerful and potentially threatening, aggression is considered to be an inappropriate response, or the aggressor characteristically feels guilty after aggressing.

## Status of the victim

When the victim of aggression is a person of high status, aggression does not produce autonomic recovery. This is true, moreover, even when that person has provoked the subject and is the cause of the subject's agitated state. Hokanson and Shetler(1961) showed this in a study in which subjects were first abused and harassed by a male experimenter, after which some were required to give electric shocks to the experimenter and others were not. The experimenter presented himself as a person of relatively low status (a student) or high status (a young member of the faculty). Subjects who were harassed showed higher levels of blood pressure following this treatment than did those in a control group who were treated in a less frustrating and provoking way. Provoked subjects who then attacked a low-status experimenter revealed a sharp decline in blood pressure after shocking, whereas those who attacked a person of high status showed no significant change in blood pressure.

The finding that aggression against a person of high status does not promote physiological recovery underlines a problem inherent in the use of blood pressure as an indicator of anger and aggressive arousal. Other studies have shown that when subjects are free to aggress or not aggress against a provocateur, they choose not to aggress against a high-status person as much as against one of low status (Hokanson 1961). However, subjects in the Hokanson and Shetler (1961) experiment were given no choice: they had to shock the high-status experimenter. Aggression in this case may have seemed inappropriate to the subjects and was therefore likely to elicit feelings of discomfort and anxiety. Blood pressure may be susceptible to influence by several emotional states in addition to anger and hostility. Thus, subjects who aggressed against a high-status person may have shown steadily high levels of blood pressure because blood pressure was in this case reflecting fear or anxiety.

### Aggression guilt

People who feel guilty about behaving aggressively may also fail to show reduced autonomic arousal after aggressing. For example, Schill (1972) carried out a study in which women subjects were first classified as high or low in aggression guilt and then frustrated by an experimenter. Later, each subject was given an opportunity to aggress verbally against the experimenter. Schill found that frustration caused increased blood pressure, regardless of level of aggression guilt. However, subjects low in guilt showed greater blood pressure reduction after verbally aggressing than did subjects high in guilt. Thus, aggression guilt hindered autonomic recovery in this experiment in much the same way as did perception of the victim's high status in the Hokanson and Shetler (1961) study.

   Taken together, the two studies reviewed above suggest one possible conclusion: when aggression is likely to create an emotional state of fear, anxiety, or guilt, it leads to an increase in autonomic arousal which offsets any reduction in arousal that accompanies aggression. These two antagonistic processes may summate and cancel each other out, so that there is no net change in arousal. In the absence of anxiety, fear, or guilt, however, arousal reduction does occur as a consequence of aggression.

### The nature of the response

### Fantasy and vicarious aggression

A question that has received little attention is whether or not autonomic recovery would be more likely following some kinds of aggression than following others. Although little evidence exists, a few conclusions are suggested by what is known. One is that whereas either physical or verbal aggression may promote recovery, fantasizing about aggression does not (Baker and Schaie 1969). Even though some observers have suggested that aggressive fantasy may serve a drive-reducing function (e.g., Feshbach 1955), it would appear at the very least that such fantasizing is not as effective as overt aggression. Nor does vicarious aggression lead to autonomic recovery. Geen *et al.* (1975) conducted an experiment in which subjects who had been provoked by a fellow subject either aggressed against the latter or merely observed as the experimenter aggressed against him. Subjects who aggressed personally showed a significant reduction in blood pressure, but those who observed as the experimenter aggressed remained as aroused as they had been immediately after being provoked.

### Non-aggressive responses

Reacting to a provocation with a friendly pro-social response has also been found to be ineffective in bringing about autonomic recovery, at least among men. In an experiment by Hokanson and Edelman (1966), male subjects were able to react to an attack by another person either by retaliating, by ignoring the attack, or making a friendly and rewarding response. Those who retaliated showed a faster return to baseline blood pressure levels than did those who made rewarding responses. The latter showed no more autonomic recovery than control subjects who were not allowed to respond to the attack at all. Refraining from retaliation and "blessing one's enemies", while possibly being of some benefit to society, does not appear to reduce the arousal level of a provoked person as well as does aggressing.

### Social learning and physiological recovery

The study by Hokanson and Edelman (1966), as noted, shows that aggression produces autonomic recovery in men. Two questions follow from this observation. The first is whether a similar reduction in arousal is found among aggressing women. The second is why aggression has this effect in men (and possibly in women also). Both questions were addressed in an experiment by Hokanson *et al.* (1968), who concluded that a person's history of socialization and social learning is involved. These histories may differ in men and women. In the first part of the experiment, women subjects interacted with another woman who behaved in an aggressive way. Subjects could respond to her either by aggressing or by giving her a reward. Subjects showed a more rapid reduction in blood pressure after rewarding her than after attacking her. The investigators reasoned that this finding can be attributed to normal socialization practices, whereby girls are trained not to behave violently and, as a consequence, experience no reduction in arousal after aggressing. It is also possible that women may experience more anxiety and guilt after aggressing than do men (Frodi *et al.* 1977); as was proposed above, if anxiety and guilt produce increased arousal, this increase may overpower physiological recovery following aggression. Subsequently, Hokanson *et al.* gave their women subjects a series of rewards for behaving aggressively toward their antagonist. Following this treatment, the subjects showed more rapid autonomic recovery after aggressing than after rewarding the other person. When these rewards were later withdrawn, subjects reverted to their original pattern of recovery, showing faster recovery after rewarding responses than after aggression (See Figure 7.3).

In the second part of the experiment men served as subjects in a

*Figure 7.3*    Blood pressure following non-aggressive and reinforced aggressive responses in women

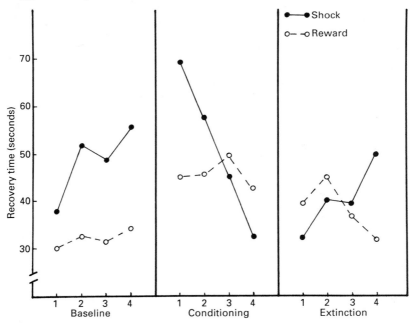

*Source:* Hokanson *et al.* (1968)

*Figure 7.4* Blood pressure following aggressive and reinforced non-aggressive responses in men

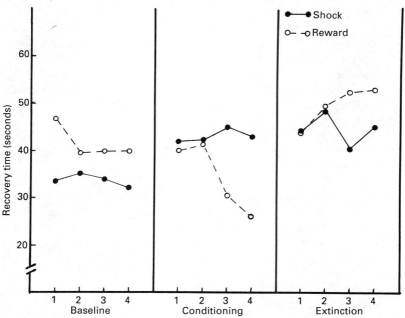

*Source:* Hokanson *et al.* (1968)

similar procedure. The results were almost a mirror image of those obtained with women. Males originally showed more rapid auto-nomic recovery after aggressing against their male antagonist than after rewarding him – the exact opposite of what the women had shown. The males were then given a series of rewards for behaving *non-aggressively*, with the result that they revealed faster recovery following rewarding behavior than after aggressing. When rewards for non-aggression were withdrawn, the men also reverted to their earlier pattern, this being in their case faster recovery following aggression than following reward (see Figure 7.4). Altogether, the study by Hokanson *et al.* indicates that people experience the optimal degree of physiological recovery after responding to provo-cation in a way that has led to reinforcement in the past. A person's history of social learning is therefore an important contributor to the physiological outcome of aggressive behavior.

Additional evidence indicting that socialization history influences physiological recovery following aggression has been reported by Scarpetti (1974). In this study, which was similar to that of Hokanson *et al.* (1968), persons classified as "sensitizers" (i.e., those who tend to be open and non-defensive under stress) experienced greater recovery following aggression than did "repressors" (i.e., those who react to stress with denial and other defensive responses). When repressors were rewarded for aggressing, however, their autonomic recovery rate following aggression increased greatly. If we assume that sensitizing and repressive coping styles are acquired through social learning experience, this study supports and extends the earlier findings of Hokanson *et al.*

## The behavioral consequences of aggression

A few years ago, an American manufacturer advertised a product consisting of a short pole with large foam balls attached to each end. The device was sold in pairs. The photograph which accompanied the advertisement showed two men, each holding one of the instruments, squaring off in a jousting position and apparently preparing to strike each other with the foam balls. The text of the advertisement suggested that by using these objects two people could work off hostility and tensions in a harmless way. Implicit in this claim was the hypothesis that aggression helps people reduce their violent and hostile urges and is beneficial provided that it leads to no real harm in the process.

The phenomenon by which aggressive feelings, motives, and impulses are supposedly "drained off" through violent action has been called *aggression catharsis*. It is related to an earlier theory that originated in ancient Greece. The notion that one can purge emotions by experiencing them intensely goes back to Aristotle, who, in the *Poetics*, taught that classical tragedy induces in the viewer feelings of pity and fear, and thereby allows the viewer to experience a catharsis of these affective states. Over the years many psychologists have argued that feelings of anger and hostility may likewise be drained away through behavior associated with these emotions. Experimental research on aggression catharsis has taken two approaches. One, already reviewed in Chapter 4, studies symbolic catharsis, whereby the angry subject is exposed to aggression carried out by others such as actors or athletes. The other involves giving the angry subject an opportunity to attack either the antagonist or some substitute. Two questions are raised by this latter procedure: (1) does aggression reduce the attacker's level of arousal, and (2) does aggression make the person less likely to aggress again?

We have already explored evidence pertaining to the first question, and have seen that under some conditions aggression does produce a reduction of the arousal state associated with anger. In this section we will consider the second question and concentrate on the behavioral outcomes of aggression.

## Catharsis in psychoanalytic theory

Much of the current thinking on catharsis originated with Freud, who first used the idea in connection with the treatment of hysteria. Breuer and Freud (1894/1961) proposed that therapy for hysteria requires the re-experiencing (called "abreaction") of an affective state previously associated with a psychological trauma. They held that the best sort of abreaction for traumas such as insults is obtained through direct aggression: "The reaction of an injured person to a trauma has really only . . . a 'cathartic' effect if it is expressed in an adequate reaction like revenge" (Breuer and Freud 1894/1961, p. 5). The form of revenge may be physical or verbal, but whatever the mode, expression of hostility is considered preferable to no expression at all: "An insult retaliated, be it only in words, is differently recalled from one that had to be taken in silence . . . Man finds a substitute for . . . (direct aggression) . . . in speech through which help the affect can be well-nigh abreacted." In relating catharsis to hysteria Freud originally stressed its importance in the treatment (and, by implication, the possible prevention) of symptoms. This idea is reflected in the modern belief that expressing anger is better for the person than holding it in, and that suppression of hostility can lead to hypertension or other psychosomatic disorders.

The idea of catharsis was also implicit in Freud's later writing, especially in his principle of the death wish. This principle is expressed in the statement that "the aim of all life is death" (Freud 1920/1959) and the corollary that the death wish, in which this purpose is manifested, is ultimately self-destructive. The expression of anger toward others through aggression is an alternative available to the person, however, so that the death wish may be turned away from the self. This idea had serious consequences for Freud's overall view of life. He believed, for example, that war is inevitable because the "destructive instinct" is really a form of self-preservation: we kill each other in order to avoid turning our destructive wishes inside and destroying ourselves (Freud 1932/1963).

The Freudian position may therefore be summarized by saying that psychic energy arising from the death wish creates a tension that must be relieved either through aggression against the self or aggression against others. Aggressive behavior reduces aggressive motivation and decreases the probability of further violence until such time as violent tensions and drives build up again to intolerable levels. This view is not limited to psychoanalytic theory. It forms a part of the "human ethology" position described in Chapter 1 of this book. In addition, certain popular psychology approaches, such as those found in advice columns in the newspapers, hold that expression of aggression is desirable because it removes or reduces aggressive urges and hence makes people less aggressive in the future.

*Catharsis and reduction of inhibitions*

There is no reason to assume, however, that reduced physiological arousal following aggression will generally lead to reduced aggressiveness. It is possible that the act of aggressing may bring about not only autonomic recovery but also a lowering of socialized inhibitions against aggressing further. Instigation to aggression may arouse both the desire to aggress and socialized restraints against aggressing (Taylor & Leonard 1983). People can, however, lose some of their restraints under certain conditions, so that expression of aggressive motives becomes more probable.

A considerable body of research supports this hypothesis. The experimental studies fall into two groups. In some a subject aggressed against an antagonist after first having engaged in aggressive behavior with an inanimate object. In others the subject aggressed against an antagonist twice. If the catharsis hypothesis is correct, less aggression would be found after prior aggression against either an inanimate object or a provoking person than would be the case if no such prior aggression took place.

*Verbal expression of hostility*
Several experiments have shown that verbal expression of hostility does not bring about catharsis, but instead leads to increased verbal aggressiveness (e.g., Wheeler and Caggiula 1966). The findings of a natural experiment by Ebbesen *et al.* (1975) concur with those of

laboratory studies. In this study, technicians who had been allowed to verbalize hostility toward former employers or supervisors following a layoff were subsequently more punitive in their descriptions of those persons than were other discharged workers who had not previously voiced their feelings. Expression of hostility against either the company or the supervisors facilitated expression of aggression only toward the same target, however, and did not lead to a general tendency toward greater aggressiveness.

*Effects of aggressive play*

The idea that taking part in vigorous physical activity such as contact sports can provide a means of discharging aggressive motives has been propounded by both psychodynamic psychologists (e.g., Menninger 1948) and advocates of human ethology (e.g., Lorenz 1966). Some evidence bearing on this idea has been found in controlled studies. In one such study, Ryan (1970) provided an opportunity for catharsis to subjects who had been angered by an experimenter's accomplice. Some subjects pounded on a box with a rubber hammer. Of these, some competed with the person who had angered them and some did not. Of those who competed, half defeated the accomplice and half lost to that person. A group of control subjects did not hammer the box. When subjects were later allowed to aggress against the accomplice, no sign of catharsis was found. Subjects who had pounded on the box, whether in competition or not, were no less aggressive than the control subjects who had not had this opportunity for catharsis.

Evidence which disputes the catharsis hypothesis has also been found in the case of the less vigorous, but perhaps more violent, act of firing a gun. Mallick and McCandless (1966) used this activity as a means of aggressive play in an experiment with children. After having been frustrated by another child, the subject engaged in either target shooting or talking with the experimenter. Half of those who conversed with the experimenter merely chatted, whereas the other half were informed that the frustration caused by the other child had not been deliberate. Later, every subject had a chance to hurt the other child by preventing that child's attainment of a valued goal. Children who had done the target-shooting were as punitive as those who had merely talked with the experimenter, and more aggressive than those to whom the other child's behavior had been rationalized. Aggression in the form of shooting a gun had not reduced the probability of future aggression.

The findings of a field study by Patterson (1974) corroborate the data from laboratory studies. High school American football players and physical education students were given hostility self-rating scales one week before the football season began and again one week after the season's end. Whereas physical education students showed a slight but non-significant decrease in hostility over the course of the season, football players showed a significant increase. Whether playing football caused this increase in hostility over the course of the season we cannot say. Of one conclusion we can, however, be certain: the experience of playing the rough and aggressive game did nothing to diminish hostility in the players.

*Effects of physical aggression*
We must now ask whether physical aggression against another person increases or, as the catharsis hypothesis would predict, decreases the strength or likelihood of subsequent physical aggression. The evidence tends to be somewhat equivocal. Berkowitz (1966) showed that subjects who were first provoked and then given two opportunities to aggress against their antagonist were more aggressive on the second occasion than were other subjects not given the initial opportunity. It has also been shown that when subjects who have been provoked are given a chance to aggress over a long series of occasions, they tend to increase in their level of aggressiveness, not to decrease as the catharsis hypothesis would imply (Geen 1968).

Other studies have, however, reported findings consistent with the catharsis hypothesis. Doob and Wood (1972), for example, found that subjects who had aggressed against an antagonist tended later to be less aggressive toward that person than others who had not aggressed the first time. In addition, subjects who merely watched as the experimenter attacked their antagonist also tended to be less aggressive later than those who had not observed. Doob (1970) reported similar findings of reduced aggressiveness among subjects who had, following provocation, learned that their provocateur had lost money. Konecni and Doob (1972) also found that subjects who were allowed to "displace" aggression by punishing a third party were later less aggressive toward an enemy than were others who had not aggressed. All of these findings are consistent with the catharsis hypothesis, yet, as some observers (e.g., Quanty 1976) have pointed out, they may also be explained in terms of increased inhibitions. In each case, certain features of the experiment could have induced restraints against aggressing in the subjects which resulted in less aggression later on.

To help answer this question, Geen *et al.* (1975) conducted a study in which the conditions for a possible catharsis were created and subjects' levels of restraint against aggressing were also measured. In addition, the study included a measurement of physiological arousal. Subjects, all of whom were males, first interacted with an experimental confederate posing as a fellow subject. This person provoked half the subjects but not the others. Some subjects were then given a chance to deliver electric shocks to the confederate. Other subjects did not shock, but watched as the experimenter shocked the confederate. Another group of subjects merely sat and waited for a given period of time. Finally, every subject was given an opportunity to shock the confederate.

The main measure of the experiment was the average intensity of shocks given during the last shocking session (in which every subject gave shocks). As Table 7.1 shows, subjects who had been provoked and who had also shocked the confederate previously were *more* aggressive during the final session than were both those who had not shocked previously and those who had merely watched the experimenter shock their antagonist. A second measure in the experiment was a questionnaire rating by each subject of how much he had "held back" (i.e., been inhibited) from shocking the other person. Provoked subjects who had previously shocked felt less restrained about shocking during the second session than did those who had not shocked before. Thus, the original act of aggressing appears to have facilitated subsequent aggression instead of diminishing it. A final measure was that of blood pressure, taken at several points during

*Table 7.1*  Average intensities of shocks given by subjects

| Treatment of confederate | Treatment | |
| --- | --- | --- |
| | *Provocation* | *No provocation* |
| Subject shocks | $6.65^{a*}$ | $3.92^{bc}$ |
| Experimenter shocks | $4.13^{bc}$ | $3.62^{c}$ |
| No shock | $5.20^{b}$ | $3.20^{c}$ |

\* Cells having common superscripts are not significantly different from each other

*Source:* Geen *et al.* (1975)

the experiment. The main finding of this measurement was that provoked subjects who shocked the confederate in the first session experienced a reduction of blood pressure after this act, whereas the blood pressure of provoked subjects who did not aggress in the first session remained high until they aggressed in the second session. In other words, "physiological catharsis" *did* occur; aggression was accompanied by a return of blood pressure to normal levels. However, "behavioral catharsis", defined as a reduction in aggression following aggression, did not occur – in fact, the opposite was found.

*Summary*

At the beginning of this chapter two questions were raised. The first was whether aggressive behavior promotes reduction of arousal levels that have been elevated by provocation. The other was whether aggression reduces motivation to aggress further and, as a consequence, makes further aggressive behavior less likely. According to the hypothesis of aggression catharsis, the answer to both questions would be affirmative because the two phenomena are related. The presumed reduction in physiological arousal should have as a consequence the reduced likelihood of subsequent aggression. The evidence from research tends to support the idea that aggression promotes physiological recovery following provocation, at least under conditions in which anxiety, fear, or guilt are not produced. When these latter conditions are produced, they may increase arousal and offset physiological recovery. The premise that aggression reduces the likelihood of future aggression is generally not supported. When conditions are such that strong inhibitions against aggression are not engendered, aggression tends to reduce inhibitions against violence and to facilitate further aggression.

*Aggression and reinforcement*

Despite evidence to the contrary, the catharsis hypothesis continues to have some appeal. It makes some intuitive sense to assume that a reduction in arousal following aggression should reduce motivation toward further aggression. Such an idea is also consistent with the "aggressive drive" theory discussed earlier in this book (see Chapter 2). The frustration–aggression hypothesis placed catharsis at the end of a series of events that were related in a cause–effect chain: frustration arouses aggressive drive which leads to aggression,

aggression reduces aggressive drive and thereby eliminates the motive force for aggression. The result should be a reduction in further aggressive behavior. This formulation raises one important question, however: why should drive reduction reduce the probability of the behavior that precedes it? According to the reinforcement principle, if reduction of drive is a desirable (i.e., rewarding) state, it should strengthen the preceding response and *increase* its probability. The result would therefore be that after aggressing the person should feel less aroused than before, but more likely to react to future provocation with aggression.

One way in which aggression may be reinforced, and hence maintained, is by being successful in causing the termination or modification of the aversive conditions that produced it. When retaliatory aggression eliminates or reduces the severity of aversive conditions, it is by definition rewarded. Although this may produce a short-term reduction in the retaliator's aggression (see, for example, Epstein and Taylor 1967), receiving this sort of reinforcement for aggressive behavior may, over the long run, make the person more and more likely to resort to aggression under similar conditions (Dengerink and Covey 1983). Dengerink and his colleagues have used an experimental procedure in which interacting partners appear to administer shocks of various intensity to each other, but in which shocks are actually under the control of the experimenter. In one such study, O'Leary and Dengerink (1973) created the impression that the intensity of shocks chosen by one subject was gradually decreased because the other subject retaliated with intense shocks of his own. In other words, the behavior of the retaliating subject punished, and hence reduced, the aggressive behavior of the other person. The immediate result of this was a decrease in the intensity with which the retaliator shocked the attacker.

However, in a subsequent study, Dengerink et al. (1978) found that subjects who experienced a decrease in their antagonist's attacks contingent on their retaliatory behavior shocked the latter more than subjects who experienced the same reduction but did not regard it as due to their own aggressiveness. Subjects who saw their aggression as the cause of the other person's ceasing and desisting in his own violence were therefore given feedback that their aggressive behavior was serving a useful purpose, and this feedback maintained their aggressiveness. Successful use of punishment may therefore have an undesirable side-effect for the person using it by making him or her even more likely to use such punishment in the future. For this reason

Dengerink and Covey (1983, p. 172) have concluded that "persons who employ aggressive means of controlling another's aversive behavior may find that successful use of such tactics [is] ultimately self-corrupting".

## *Is there an alternative to aggression?*

On the basis of the several topics covered in this chapter the reader may be forgiven for wondering exactly what advice psychologists would give about how to handle anger and hostility. A word or two by way of summing up may therefore be in order. First, suppressing and holding in anger is not advised. This response is closely tied to hypertension and is also a risk factor in coronary heart disease. Expressing hostile and angry feelings in some way is clearly better for overall physical health. Second, aggression is one response that can reduce tension and probably prevent a dangerous build-up of suppressed hostility. However, aggression may have an undesirable side effect in that it may lead to a person's becoming more aggressive in the future. The angry person may therefore be faced with a difficult choice between two unattractive alternatives. Perhaps the best solution to the dilemma for someone who has been provoked and aroused to anger by another person is to express his or her feelings clearly but without hostility, and to seek a dialogue in which both persons can find mutually satisfactory outcomes to their conflict (cf. Holt 1970). This solution requires assertiveness, honesty, and self-control on the part of both persons and may for that reason be difficult to implement. However, it may be worth the effort in that it can help to reduce undesirable tensions without risking an escalation of aggression.

## Summary

1 The emotion of anger is associated with a pattern of autonomic activity that resembles a mixture of epinephrine-like and norepinephrine-like responses. The autonomic pattern associated with suppressed anger resembles that which accompanies anxiety.

2 Individual differences in hostility are not associated with

elevated blood pressure in all situations. High hostility accompanies hypertension only in situations characterized by interpersonal conflict.

3 Repressed anger is closely related to hypertension. Although this relationship is found among both black and white people, among blacks it outweighs the relationship between hypertension and other more traditional risk factors.

4 Although the Type A behavior pattern as a whole is not closely linked to incidence of coronary heart disease, the component of the Type A pattern labeled "potential for hostility" is so related. The Type A component labeled "anger-in", which describes tendencies to suppress anger, is also related to incidence of coronary disease.

5 Independent measures of hostility in combination with the Type A pattern provide the best overall predictor of coronary disease and of lipid elevation, itself a risk factor in coronary problems. Hostility which is manifested in resentment, suspiciousness, irritability, and mistrust is especially linked to health problems and mortality.

6 Provocation produces increased levels of physiological activation. Aggression promotes reduction of activation to normal except when the target is a powerful and threatening person, aggression is considered an inappropriate response, or the person is likely to experience guilt after aggressing. In situations in which aggression elicits fear, anxiety, or guilt, it is likely to produce increased arousal associated with these emotions.

7 Physiological recovery following aggression is promoted by behaviors for which the person has been reinforced. A social learning history of reinforcement for aggressing facilitates autonomic recovery following aggression, whereas a history of reinforcement for pro-social responses promotes recovery following such behavior.

8 Although aggression may bring about reduction in arousal, it does not necessarily produce reduced aggressiveness as predicted by the catharsis hypothesis. Aggressing may also lead to reduced inhibitions against aggression, with consequent facilitation of aggression. The facilitation of aggression by aggression has been found in verbal behavior, aggressive play, and physical retaliation.

9 If aggression is reinforced, the likelihood of future aggression is enhanced. Reinforcement may come about as a consequence

of aggression itself, as is the case when aggression causes a provocateur to cease provocation.

10 The catharsis hypothesis therefore appears to be only partially supported. Aggression leads to reduction of arousal that had been elevated by provocative circumstances, but only under certain conditions. In addition, aggression may have effects other than arousal reduction, such as weakening of inhibitions, which promote further aggression.

## Suggestions for further reading

Chesney, M. A. and Rosenman, R. H. (eds) (1985). *Anger and Hostility in Cardiovascular and Behavioral Disorders*. Washington, DC: Hemisphere. A collection of review papers on various aspects of the relationship between anger and cardiovascular problems.

Geen, R. G. and Quanty, M. B. (1977). The catharsis of aggression: An evaluation of a hypothesis. In L. Berkowitz (ed.), *Advances in Experimental Social Psychology*, Vol. 10, pp. 1–37 New York: Academic Press. A discussion of the doctrine of catharsis and a review of evidence bearing on both physiological and behavioral effects predicted by a catharsis hypothesis.

# 8 / POSTSCRIPT

As the reader of this book is probably well aware, the material in it has not been organized along rigorous theoretical lines. To be sure, theories of aggression have been described in brief terms at various places. The emphasis of the book has, however, been upon organizing and explaining what is known about human aggression in a factual sense, with relatively little emphasis placed on theoretical explanation. For that reason I have presented a simple model in Chapter 2 which affirms only that aggression is a reaction to a stressful situation, mediated by certain cognitive processes, and occurring against a background of personal, social and cultural antecedents. Nowhere does this simple model explain why any of this happens, nor was it intended to do so.

In this final chapter I hope to summarize the current state of thinking on human aggression by contrasting it with the state of the science that prevailed early in the period in which most of the research reviewed in Chapters 1–7 was begun: the period from approximately 1955 to 1965. Possibly the changes that have taken place in our ideas of aggression from that period until now will cast their shadow ahead of our time. Perhaps by knowing how we got where we are today we may have some basis for imagining how developments in the field will proceed in the years to come. For this, we must pay more attention to theories of aggression than we have so far.

A few years ago, Geen and Donnerstein (1983, p. 247) summarized a book devoted mainly to theoretical issues in the study of aggression by concluding that theorizing in the 1980s differed from that in the 1960s in two major respects: "First, higher levels of theoretical integration are now being attained than was formerly the case. Second, this integration reveals more and more explanation in terms of general psychology, rather than strictly social psychology". The chapters of the present volume show these same tendencies in contemporary studies. The works of such psychologists as Huesmann (Chapter 4), Berkowitz (Chapter 4), Ferguson and Rule (Chapter 5) and Zillmann (Chapter 5) are couched in terms like *schemata, affect, emotion, association*, and *priming* – all terms from general psychology which in recent years have found new applications in social psychology and, through it, in the psychology of aggression.

Three theoretical approaches that dominated much of the thinking on aggression in the period 1955–65 were the theories of (1) aggressive instinct; (2) aggressive drive; and (3) social learning of aggression. Each still exists, but in modified forms, as will be shown below.

## Theoretical formulations of aggression

### Innate bases of aggression

The idea that aggressive behavior arises out of some innate features of the person took two forms in the earlier period being considered. One was the doctrine of human ethology, reviewed in Chapter 1. The other was psychoanalysis, which has been touched on only in passing in the seven preceding chapters. As was noted in Chapter 1, ethological approaches to aggression emphasize the adaptive nature of aggressive responses, which are regarded as pre-programmed or "wired-in" reactions to specific stimuli. Although this approach was based on systematic observation of lower animals, some ethologists (e.g., Eibl-Eibesfeldt 1977; Lorenz 1966) argued that some part of human aggression is also based on innate structures.

Many students of animal aggression maintain a strong interest in the possibility of reconciling human and animal studies on the basis of ethology. The reader is referred to a volume edited by Brain and Benton (1981), in which a number of chapters take this approach. Furthermore, even though the idea of a human ethology of aggression has been criticized, sophisticated defenses of the position based on careful use of the concepts of homology and analogy have been made. It will be recalled that Rajecki (1983) made such a defense, as summarized in Chapter 1.

Even so, it must be admitted that a sophisticated human ethology of aggression matching that for lower animals has never been produced. It would seem unlikely at this late date that such an undertaking will be attempted. The search for causes of human aggression will probably continue to be guided by hypotheses which emphasize unique human abilities, such as those derived from attribution theory and other cognitive points of view. If there is any shift in the study of human aggression in the direction of innate factors, it may well come from research on *temperament*. This research, which attempts to establish the existence of general and broadly-defined inherited tendencies in human behavior, has been greatly facilitated by the widespread use of the twin-study method in human behavior genetics (cf. Buss & Plomin 1984). To date, little evidence exists linking aggressiveness to inherited temperamental factors. However, in one study that has been reported, Rushton *et al.* (1986) found a significant heritability component in aggressiveness. This study was described in Chapter 1.

Although it has had considerable influence on psychiatry and on the sort of psychology that one reads in the popular press, the psychoanalytic approach has never been a major contributor to mainstream psychological theorizing on aggression. Some psychoanalysts (e.g., Fenichel 1945) have treated aggression as reactive behavior, but for the most part the psychoanalytic approach emphasizes the operation of deep-seated instincts which drive aggressive behavior. The doctrine of catharsis, which has been referred to in Chapters 4 and 7, is the one element in psychoanalytic theory that has endured in the study of human aggression. However, as has been shown in the case of both symbolic catharsis (Chapter 4) and direct catharsis (Chapter 7), most research on human subjects fails to support the idea.

*Aggressive drive*

As was noted in Chapter 2, the frustration–aggression hypothesis in its original form (Dollard *et al.* 1939) stated that frustration always leads to aggression and that aggression always presupposes some frustration. Stated in this way the hypothesis has much in common with the ethological and psychoanalytic theories in that each describes aggression as a specific response to specific stimulus conditions. For this reason the original frustration–aggression hypothesis is often thought of as a theory of *specific* aggressive drive. In a subsequent revised version, Miller (1941) proposed that frustration produces only an instigation to aggress (commonly associated with anger) which does not necessarily lead to aggression. This formulation led to several attempts to define the conditions under which frustration leads to aggression, with the result, as discussed in Chapter 2, that frustration became commonly thought of as a source of generalized or *non-specific* drive which energizes responses that the person is ready to make. This point of view was widely accepted during the 1960s (see also Chapter 5).

Both the specific and non-specific versions of aggressive drive theory were based on one assumption: that emotions such as anger function as intervening variables between stimuli and responses. Thus, it was assumed that once anger is aroused it somehow motivates the emission of aggressive acts, whether it does this in a direct way or in the guise of a generalized energizer. In either case, anger or some emotion like it is a necessary element in aggression. Contrast this with the most recent statement of the frustration–aggression hypothesis (Berkowitz 1989), which differs from the earlier one in at least three important ways: (1) frustration is considered to be a stimulus for increased negative affect rather than increased drive; (2) negative affect elicits through associative links a number of aggression-related expressive motor reactions, emotions, and thoughts; and (3) anger is an experience that may parallel aggression but is not a direct cause (see Chapter 2). In this formulation the concept of motivation has almost disappeared completely, being replaced by a combination of cognitive and affective reactions.

Does this mean that motivational approaches to aggression have been abandoned? Not entirely. It will be recalled from the discussion of excitation transfer in Chapter 5 that Zillmann (1978) still assigns an important role to anger as an antecedent of aggression. However, Zillmann's whole viewpoint is a cognitive one that is more or less in the tradition begun by Schachter and Singer (1962). What we may conclude from all this (and from the work of Huesmann and his associates cited below) is that current explanations of aggression fit neatly into the area of social psychology known as social cognition. Interestingly, this area is changing at the present time in that it is becoming more and more open to constructs like emotion and motivation (cf. Sorrentino and Higgins 1986). In the future, we might expect theorizing on human aggression to move in this direction and to show how cognitive, affective, behavioral, and emotional variables interact.

## Social learning

Theories of social learning of aggression originally served as alternatives to theories of specific aggressive drives. Aggression was treated by these theories as simply another behavior that is learned and maintained through such processes as observation and reinforcement. The social learning approach to aggression was discussed in Chapter 1. That approach has been refined and expanded over the years, and today it finds expression in the work of Huesmann (1986b) and his associates and of attribution theorists like Ferguson and Rule (1983). It will be recalled from Chapter 5 that Huesmann interprets aggression in the context of cognitive encoding and retrieval. To summarize this viewpoint briefly, people encode information about their environment and themselves in the form of scenarios and schemata which thereafter become guides or scripts for behavior in situations that resemble the ones involved in the encoding. If aggression is usually associated with interpersonal conflict, people encode aggressive scenarios that are built out of these experiences and which subsequently become elaborated and refined into more general scripts. Instances of interpersonal conflict in the future may then cause these scripts to be called up as guides or plans for decision-making and action.

This idea of scripting is a development that has grown out of earlier theorizing on schemata from the general psychology of memory. It represents a significant development beyond the simple early ideas of observational learning and imitation in that it accounts for the emission of a broad range of aggressive behaviors and not just the ones observed in a given situation. Like the ideas discussed above, it is firmly anchored in contemporary principles of social cognition and its future development is obviously linked to developments in that area.

## Methods of investigation

At the end of Chapter 1 a short section described some common experimental methods in the study of human aggression. This was included mainly to help the reader understand the means whereby much of the data from experimental studies, which constitute the bulk of the evidence cited in Chapters 1–7, was obtained. As was stated in that section, these do not represent the only means of studying aggression. Indeed, as times goes by it appears that they will become less and less representative of aggression research.

The laboratory experiment is, of course, by no means a thing of the past in aggression research. A search of Chapters 1–7 will show that it is still an important method of testing causal hypotheses. However, there is little doubt that the laboratory experiment no longer dominates the field as it once did. No single method has replaced it; aggression research today involves the use of a number of methods. Some studies which use longitudinal methods, observational techniques, questionnaires, and other practices common to field research will be designed to test hypotheses that have been derived from the findings of laboratory research. In this way controlled experimental studies and more naturalistic field studies will serve jointly to keep aggression research conceptually and theoretically valid even while it is being addressed to important social problems.

On a more technical level, modern techniques of multivariate statistical analysis will undoubtedly come to be used more and more in aggression research in the coming years. Chapter 4 contained a review of several longitudinal research studies in which cross-lagged correlational analysis was used as a basis for inference of cause and effect involving aggression and media violence. It is unlikely that many such analyses will be seen in the future. Newer statistical approaches which utilize multiple regression as a method for evaluating alternative cause–effect models are now widely used in social and personality psychology, and it would seem only a matter of time before they are generally applied to aggression research. Just as theorizing on human aggression will take place in the mainstream of social psychological theories of cognition and motivation, so, too, will methodology for studying aggression be found in the mainstream of methodology and analysis.

## Emphases in the study of aggression

What may we expect to see in the years ahead as the major topics of investigation in aggression research? In gathering material for this book, I tried to find representative studies relating aggression to each of a number of problem areas that are dominant in the 1980s, such as (among others) environmental stressors, effects of the mass media, race relations, gender differences, and health. In so far as these problems remain central to our society, their manifestations in aggression should remain a matter of interest to psychologists. A few such problems may be especially noteworthy.

## Drugs and aggression

As these words are being written, an American presidential election campaign is drawing to a close. It has been the first such campaign in which a widespread public fear of illegal drugs has been a major issue. Much of this fear is animated by the belief that persons under the influence of drugs may become more aggressive and dangerous, and more likely to commit crimes of violence. Despite abundant anecdotal evidence that drugs such as marijuana, amphetamines, and cocaine may have links to aggression, to date no systematic analysis of their behavioral effects has been conducted and the findings that have been reported are inconclusive (e.g., Meyerscough and Taylor 1985). Of all the drugs suspected of being related to aggression, only alcohol has received this kind of scientific scrutiny (see Chapter 6). The study of drugs such as cocaine or heroin under experimental conditions would be beset by serious ethical problems and may never be done for that reason. However, studies of aggression in real life among persons known to use these drugs are quite possible and may, given the multivariate analytic techniques now available, yield valuable results.

## Pornography and sexual aggression

Concern over the availability of erotic literature in the United States recently moved the Attorney General to establish a panel of inquiry into the matter. One fact that appeared to be clearly established by the deliberations of that group was that very little is known about the effects of pornography as a result of controlled scientific studies. As more becomes known of the dimensions of the problem of sexual violence, however, research on this matter should continue. The roots of male violence against women are complex, involving both personality factors and attitudes that develop out of manifold experiences. To implicate pornography as the main cause of such aggression would be premature. However, the research to date by Malamuth, Donnerstein, and others (see, for example, Malamuth and Donnerstein 1984) appears to implicate pornography as at least one cause of the problem. Research that has been reported to date indicates that an important link in the relationship between viewing pornography and committing aggression against women is provided by certain attitudes, such as the "rape myth" that women enjoy being violated. Future research should be addressed to the question of how attitudes of this type articulate with other anti-women attitudes and beliefs, such as those which motivate behaviors like wife-abuse.

## Individual differences

As was noted in Chapter 6, research on aggression has not to date included an emphasis on individual differences in personality. To some extent this indifference was the result of a belief that aggression is a function of situational causes and does not manifest much consistency over time and across situations. This viewpoint is still being debated, with some investigators favoring it (e.g., Campbell *et al.* 1985) and others disagreeing (e.g., Olweus 1979). Meanwhile, evidence is accumulating to indicate that personality variables appear to interact with situational stressors to influence aggressive behavior. In this regard the work of G. V. Caprara and his associates at the University of Rome is especially promising. As was noted in Chapter 6, Caprara and his associates have identified three variables (emotional susceptibility, irritability, and dissipation-rumination) which predict individual differences in aggressive behavior in various situations. Future research on these variables should consist of attempts to describe further the exact situational conditions with which the variables interact. Given the growth of interest in personality research in contemporary psychology, aggression research will probably also bring forth additional person-situation models similar to those proposed by Caprara.

A good case could probably be made for including every other major area of aggression research reviewed in Chapters 1–7 as a source of future investigation. A good example would be interracial aggression. Aside from the pioneering work of Donnerstein and Donnerstein (1976) and the more recent studies of Rogers (1983), little controlled research on interracial conflict and aggression has been reported. This apparent lack of interest comes, ironically, at a time when racial and ethnic tensions appear to be increasing in many countries. Certainly, more must be learned about the social-psychological antecedents of this problem. Another example is aggression in response to environmental stressors. As these stressors proliferate in virtually every country on earth, their role in eliciting aggression will become a problem of increasing importance for psychology.

I would summarize by concluding that the study of aggression in the years to come will probably be marked by three characteristics. One is a continuation of present trends toward theoretical models derived from general psychology, especially from contemporary theories of cognition and emotion. A second is an increase in research conducted in natural settings, analyzed by means of multiple regression techniques that test various alternative cause–effect hypotheses. The third is increased application of theories and methods of research to social problems. In this book I have tried to summarize the state of the field as we know it today. It is hoped that this level of knowledge will be a mere prolegomenon to a wider and deeper understanding of the psychology of aggression in the future.

# REFERENCES

Abelson, R. P. (1976). Script processing in attitude formation and decision making. In J. S. Carroll and J. W. Payne (eds), *Cognition and Social Behavior*. Hillsdale, NJ: Lawrence Erlbaum Associates.

Aiello, J. R., Epstein, Y. M. and Karlin, R. A. (1975). Effects of crowding on electrodermal activity. *Sociological Symposium*, **14**, 43–57.

Anderson, C. A. (1987). Temperature and aggression: Effects on quarterly, yearly, and city rates of violent and nonviolent crime. *Journal of Personality and Social Psychology*, **52**, 1161–73.

Anderson, C. A. (1989). Temperature and aggression: The ubiquitous effects of heat on the occurrence of human violence. *Psychological Bulletin*, **106**, 74–96.

Anderson, C. A. and Anderson, D. C. (1984). Ambient temperature and violent crime: Tests of the linear and curvilinear hypotheses. *Journal of Personality and Social Psychology*, **46**, 91–7.

Arkkelin, D., Oakley, T. and Mynatt, C. (1979). Effects of controllable versus uncontrollable factors on responsibility attributions: A single-subject approach. *Journal of Personality and Social Psychology*, **37**, 110–15.

Arms, R. L., Russell, G. W. and Sandilands, M. L. (1979). Effects of viewing aggressive sports on the hostility of spectators. *Social Psychology Quarterly*, **42**, 275–9.

Averill, J. R. (1982). *Anger and Aggression: An Essay on Emotion*. New York: Springer-Verlag.

Averill, J. R. (1983). Studies on anger and aggression: Implications for theories of emotion. *American Psychologist*, **38**, 1145–60.

Ax, A. F. (1953). The psychophysiological differentiation between fear and anger in humans. *Psychosomatic Medicine*, **15**, 433–42.

Azrin, N. H. (1970). Punishment of elicited aggression. *Journal of the Experimental Analysis of Behavior*, **14**, 7–10.

Azrin, N. H., Hutchinson, R. R. and Hake, D. F. (1967). Attack, avoidance, and escape reactions to aversive shock. *Journal of the Experimental Analysis of Behavior*, 10, 131–48.

Baer, P. E., Collins, F. H., Bourianoff, G. C. and Ketchel, M. F. (1979). Assessing personality factors in essential hypertension with a brief self-report instrument. *Psychosomatic Medicine*, 16, 321–30.

Baker, J. W. and Schaie, K. W. (1969). Effects of aggressing "alone" or "with another" on physiological and psychological arousal. *Journal of Personality and Social Psychology*, 12, 80–6.

Bancroft, J. and Backstrom, T. (1985). Premenstrual syndrome. *Clinical Endocrinology*, 22, 313–36.

Bandura, A. (1965). Influence of models' reinforcement contingencies on the acquisition of imitative responses. *Journal of Personality and Social Psychology*, 1, 589–95.

Bandura, A. (1971). Social learning theory of aggression. In J. F. Knutson (ed.), *Control of Aggression: Implications from Basic Research*. Chicago: Aldine-Atherton, pp. 201–50.

Bandura, A. (1973). *Aggression: A Social Learning Analysis*. Englewood Cliffs, NJ: Prentice-Hall.

Bandura, A., Ross, D. and Ross, S. A. (1963). Imitation of film-mediated aggressive models. *Journal of Abnormal and Social Psychology*, 66, 3–11.

Barefoot, J. C., Dahlstrom, W. G. and Williams, R. B. (1983). Hostility, CHD incidence and total mortality: A 25-year followup study of 255 physicians. *Psychosomatic Medicine*, 45, 59–63.

Barefoot, J. C., Siegler, I. C., Nowlin, J. B., Peterson, B. L., Haney, T. L. and Williams, R. B. (1987). Suspiciousness, health, and mortality: A followup study of 500 older adults. *Psychosomatic Medicine*, 49, 450–7.

Barker, R., Dembo, T. and Lewin, K. (1941). Frustration and regression: An experiment with young children. *University of Iowa Studies in Child Welfare*, no. 18.

Baron, R. A. (1971a). Aggression as a function of magnitude of victim's pain cues, level of prior anger arousal, and aggressor–victim similarity. *Journal of Personality and Social Psychology*, 18, 48–54.

Baron, R. A. (1971b). Magnitude of victim's pain cues and level of prior anger arousal as determinants of adult aggressive behavior. *Journal of Personality and Social Psychology*, 17, 236–43.

Baron, R. A. (1972). Aggression as a function of ambient temperature and prior anger arousal. *Journal of Personality and Social Psychology*, 21, 183–9.

Baron, R. A. (1973). Threatened retaliation from the victim as an inhibitor of physical aggression. *Journal of Research in Personality*, 7, 103–15.

Baron, R. A. (1977). *Human Aggression*. New York: Plenum.

Baron, R. A. (1978). Aggression-inhibiting influence of sexual humor. *Journal of Personality and Social Psychology*, 36, 189–97.

Baron, R. A. (1979). Aggression, empathy, and race: Effects of victim's pain cues, victim's race, and level of instigation on physical aggression. *Journal of Applied Social Psychology*, 9, 103–14.

Baron, R. A. (1983). The control of human aggression: A strategy based on incompatible responses. In R. G. Geen and E. Donnerstein (eds), *Aggression: Theoretical and Empirical Reviews, Vol. 2: Issues in Research.* New York: Academic Press, pp. 173–90.

Baron, R. A. (1987). Effects of negative ions on interpersonal attraction: Evidence for intensification. *Journal of Personality and Social Psychology*, 52, 547–53.

Baron, R. A. and Ball, R. L. (1974). The aggression-inhibiting influence of nonhostile humor. *Journal of Experimental Social Psychology*, 10, 23–33.

Baron, R. A. and Bell, P. A. (1975). Aggression and heat: Mediating effects of prior provocation and exposure to an aggressive model. *Journal of Personality and Social Psychology*, 31, 825–32.

Baron, R. A. and Bell, P. A. (1977). Sexual arousal and aggression by males: Effects of type of erotic stimuli and prior provocation. *Journal of Personality and Social Psychology*, 35, 79–87.

Baron, R. A., Russell, G. W. and Arms, R. L. (1985). Negative ions and behavior: Impact on mood, memory, and aggression among Type A and Type B persons. *Journal of Personality and Social Psychology*, 48, 746–54.

Barrett, D. E. (1979). A naturalistic study of sex differences in children's aggression. *Merrill-Palmer Quarterly*, 25, 193–207.

Berkowitz, L. (1965). The concept of aggressive drive: Some additional considerations. In L. Berkowitz (ed.), *Advances in Experimental Social Psychology, Vol. 2.* New York: Academic Press, pp. 301–29.

Berkowitz, L. (1966). On not being able to aggress. *British Journal of Social and Clinical Psychology*, 5, 130–9.

Berkowitz, L. (1969). The frustration–aggression hypothesis revisited. In L. Berkowitz (ed.), *Roots of Aggression.* New York: Atherton.

Berkowitz, L. (1971). The contagion of violence: An S–R mediational analysis of some effects of observed aggression. In W. J. Arnold and M. M. Page (eds), *Nebraska Symposium on Motivation, 1970.* Lincoln: University of Nebraska Press.

Berkowitz, L. (1983). The experience of anger as a parallel process in the display of impulsive "angry" aggression. In R. G. Geen and E. Donnerstein (eds), *Aggression: Theoretical and Empirical Reviews, Vol. 1: Theoretical and Methodological Issues.* New York: Academic Press, pp. 103–33.

Berkowitz, L. (1984). Some effects of thoughts on anti- and prosocial influences of media events: A cognitive-neoassociationist analysis. *Psychological Bulletin*, 95, 410–27.

Berkowitz, L. (1989). The frustration–aggression hypothesis: An examination and reformulation. *Psychological Bulletin*, 106, 59–73.

Berkowitz, L. and Alioto, J. (1973). The meaning of an observed event as a determinant of its aggressive consequences. *Journal of Personality and Social Psychology*, 28, 206–17.

Berkowitz, L., Cochran, S. and Embree, M. (1981). Physical pain and the goal of aversively stimulated aggression. *Journal of Personality and Social Psychology*, 40, 687–700.

Berkowitz, L. and Donnerstein, E. (1982). External validity is more than skin deep: Some answers to criticisms of laboratory experiments (with special reference to research on aggression). *American Psychologist*, 37, 245–57.

Berkowitz, L. and Geen, R. G. (1966). Film violence and the cue properties of available targets. *Journal of Personality and Social Psychology*, 3, 525–30.

Berkowitz, L. and LePage, A. (1967). Weapons as aggression–eliciting stimuli. *Journal of Personality and Social Psychology*, 7, 202–7.

Billig, M. (1976). *Social Psychology and Intergroup Relations*. New York: Academic Press.

Blanchard, R. J., Blanchard, D. C. and Takahashi, L. K. (1977). Reflexive fighting in the albino rat: Aggressive or defensive behavior? *Aggressive Behavior*, 3, 145–55.

Borrill, J. A., Rosen, B. K. and Summerfield, A. B. (1987). The influence of alcohol on judgment of facial expressions of emotion. *British Journal of Medical Psychology*, 60, 71–7.

Bower, G. (1981). Mood and memory. *American Psychologist*, 36, 129–48.

Boyatzis, R. E. (1975). The predisposition toward alconol-related interpersonal aggression in men. *Journal of Studies on Alcohol*, 36, 1196–207.

Brain, P. F. and Benton, D. (eds) (1981). *Multidisciplinary Approaches to Aggression Research*. Amsterdam: Elsevier/North Holland.

Brand, R. (1978). Coronary-prone behavior as an independent risk factor for coronary heart disease. In T. M. Dembroski, S. M. Weiss, J. L. Shields, S. G. Haynes and M. Feinleib (eds), *Coronary-prone behavior*. New York: Springer-Verlag, pp. 11–24.

Breuer, J. and Freud, S. (1894/1961). *Studies in Hysteria*. Boston: Beacon Press.

Brickman, P., Ryan, K. and Wortman, C. (1975). Causal chains: Attribution of responsibility as a function of immediate and prior causes. *Journal of Personality and Social Psychology*, 32, 1060–7.

Briere, J. (1987). Predicting self-reported likelihood of battering: Attitudes and childhood experiences. *Journal of Research in Personality*, 21, 61–9.

Brock, T. C. and Buss, A. H. (1964). Effects of justification for aggression and communication with the victim on postaggression dissonance. *Journal of Abnormal and Social Psychology*, 68, 403–12.

Brown, G. L. and Goodwin, F. K. (1984). Diagnostic, clinical and personality characteristics of aggressive men with low 5-HIAA. *Clinical Neuropharmacology*, 7(1), 756–7.

Bryant, J., Carveth, R. A. and Brown, D. (1981). Television viewing and anxiety: An experimental examination. *Journal of Communication*, 31, 106–19.

Bryant, J. and Zillmann, D. (1979). Effect of intensification of annoyance through unrelated residual excitation on substantially delayed hostile behavior. *Journal of Experimental Social Psychology*, 15, 470–80.

Burt, M. R. (1980). Cultural myths and support for rape. *Journal of Personality and Social Psychology*, 38, 217–30.

Buss, A. H. (1961). *The Psychology of Aggression*. New York: Wiley.

Buss, A. H. (1963). Physical Aggression in relation to different frustrations. *Journal of Abnormal and Social Psychology*, 67, 1–7.

Buss, A. H. (1966). Instrumentality of aggression, feedback, and frustration as determinants of physical aggression. *Journal of Personality and Social Psychology*, 3, 153–62.

Buss, A. H. (1980). *Self-Consciousness and Social Anxiety*. San Francisco: Freeman.

Buss, A. H. and Durkee, A. (1957). An inventory for assessing different kinds of hostility. *Journal of Consulting Psychology*, 221, 342–8.

Buss, A. H. and Plomin, R. (1984). *Temperament: Early Developing Personality Traits*. Hillsdale, NJ: Lawrence Erlbaum Associates.

Campbell, A., Bibel, D. and Muncer, S. (1985). Predicting our own aggression: Person, subculture, or situation? *British Journal of Social Psychology*, 24, 169–80.

Cannon, W. B. (1929). *Bodily Changes in Pain, Hunger, Fear, and Rage*. New York: Appleton-Century.

Cantor, J. R. (1982). Adolescent fright reactions from TV programming. *Journal of Communication*, 32, 87–99.

Cantor, J. R., Zillmann, D. and Bryant, J. (1975). Enhancement of experienced sexual arousal in response to erotic stimuli through misattribution of unrelated residual excitation. *Journal of Personality and Social Psychology*, 32, 69–75.

Cantor, J. R., Zillmann, D. and Einsiedel, E. F. (1978). Female responses to provocation after exposure to aggressive and erotic films. *Communication Research*, 5, 395–411.

Caprara, G. V. (1986). Indicators of aggression: The dissipation-rumination scale. *Personality and Individual Differences*, 7, 763–9.

Caprara, G. V., Cinanni, V., D'Imperio, G., Passerini, S., Renzi, P. and

Travaglia, G. (1985). Indicators of impulsive aggression: Present status of research on irritability and emotional susceptibility scales. *Personality and Individual Differences*, 6, 665–74.

Caprara, G. V., Renzi, P., Alcini, P., D'Imperio, G. and Travaglia, G. (1983). Instigation to aggress and escalation of aggression examined from a personological perspective: The role of irritability and of emotional susceptibility. *Aggressive Behavior*, 9, 345–51.

Carlsmith, J. M. and Anderson, C. A. (1979). Ambient temperature and the occurrence of collective violence: A new analysis. *Journal of Personality and Social Psychology*, 37, 337–44.

Carpenter, B. and Darley, J. M. (1978). A naive psychological analysis of counteraggression. *Personality and Social Psychology Bulletin*, 4, 68–72.

Carver, C. S. (1975). Physical aggression as a function of objective self-awareness and attitudes toward punishment. *Journal of Experimental Social Psychology*, 11, 510–19.

Charry, J. M. and Hawkinshire, F. B. W. V. (1981). Effects of atmospheric electricity on some substrates of disordered social behavior. *Journal of Personality and Social Psychology*, 41, 185–97.

Christy, P. R., Gelfand, D. M. and Hartmann, D. P. (1971). Effects of competition-induced frustration on two classes of modelled behavior. *Developmental Psychology*, 5, 104–11.

Cline, V. B., Croft, R. G. and Courrier, S. (1973). Desensitization of children to television violence. *Journal of Personality and Social Psychology*, 27, 360–5.

Cohen, J. (1941). The geography of crime. *Annals of the American Academy of Political and Social Sciences*, 217, 29–37.

Collins, A. and Loftus, E. (1975). A spreading-activation theory of semantic memory. *Psychological Review*, 82, 407–28.

Collins, W. A. (1975). The developing child as viewer. *Journal of Communication*, 25, 35–44.

Collins, W. A., Berndt, T. J. and Hess, V. L. (1974). Observational learning of motives and consequences for television aggression: A developmental study. *Child Development*, 45, 799–802.

Connor, J. M., Serbin, L. A. and Ender, R. A. (1978). Responses of boys and girls to aggressive, assertive, and passive behaviors of male and female characters. *Journal of Genetic Psychology*, 133, 59–69.

Cook, W. W. and Medley, D. M. (1954). Proposed hostility and pharisaic-virtue scales for the MMPI. *Journal of Applied Psychology*, 38, 414–18.

Court-Brown, W. M. (1968). Males with an XYY sex chromosome complement. *Journal of Medical Genetics*, 5, 341–59.

Crosby, F. (1976). A model of egoistical relative deprivation. *Psychological Review*, 83, 85–113.

Cummings, E. M., Iannotti, R. J. and Zahn-Waxler, C. (1985). Influence of conflict between adults on the emotions and aggression of young children. *Developmental Psychology*, 21, 495–507.

Cummings, E. M., Zahn-Waxler, C. and Radke-Yarrow M. (1981). Young children's responses to expressions of anger and affection by others in the family. *Child Development*, 52, 1274–82.

Dabbs, J. M., Jr, Frady, R. L., Carr, T. S. and Besch, N. F. (1987). Saliva testosterone and criminal violence in young adult prison inmates. *Psychosomatic Medicine*, 49, 174–82.

DaGloria, J. and DeRidder, R. (1977). Aggression in dyadic interaction. *European Journal of Social Psychology*, 7, 189–219.

DaGloria, J. and DeRidder, R. (1979). Sex differences in aggression: Are current notions misleading? *European Journal of Social Psychology*, 9, 49–66.

Dalton, K. (1964). *The Pre-menstrual Syndrome*. Springfield, IL: Thomas.

Dalton, K. (1977). *The Pre-menstrual Syndrome and Progesterone Therapy*. London: Heinemann.

Daly, R. F. (1969). Neurological abnormalities in XYY males. *Nature*, 221, 472–3.

DeFronzo, J. (1984). Climate and crime: Tests of an FBI assumption. *Environment and Behavior*, 16, 185–210.

Deluty, R. H. (1985). Consistency of assertive, aggressive, and submissive behavior for children. *Journal of Personality and Social Psychology*, 49, 1054–65.

Dembroski, T. M. and Costa, P. T. (1987). Coronary prone behavior: Components of the Type A pattern and hostility. *Journal of Personality*, 55, 212–35.

Dembroski, T. M., MacDougall, J. M., Williams, R. B., Haney, T. L. and Blumenthal, J. A. (1985). Components of Type A, hostility, and anger-in: Relationship to angiographic findings. *Psychosomatic Medicine*, 47, 219–33.

Dengerink, H. A. and Covey, M. K. (1983). Implications of an escape-avoidance theory of aggressive responses to attack. In R. G. Geen and E. I. Donnerstein (eds), *Aggression: Theoretical and Empirical Reviews, Vol. 1: Theoretical and Methodological Issues*, New York: Academic Press, pp. 163–88.

Dengerink, H. A., Schnedler, R. S. and Covey, M. K. (1978). The role of avoidance in aggressive responses to attack and no attack. *Journal of Personality and Social Psychology*, 36, 1044–53.

DeRidder, R. (1985). Normative considerations in the labeling of harmful behavior as aggressive. *Journal of Social Psychology*, 125, 659–66.

Diamond, E. L., Schneiderman, N., Schwartz, D., Smith, J. C., Vorp, R. and Pasin, R. D. (1984). Harassment, hostility, and Type A as determinants of cardiovascular reactivity during competition. *Journal of Behavioral Medicine*, 7, 171–89.

Diener, E. (1980). Deindividuation: The absence of self-awareness and self-regulation in group members. In P. Paulus (ed.), *The Psychology of Group Influence*. Hillsdale, NJ: Erlbaum.

Diener, E., Dineen, J., Westford, K., Beaman, A. L. and Fraser, S. C. (1975). Effects of altered responsibility, cognitive set, and modelling on physical aggression and deindividuation. *Journal of Personality and Social Psychology*, 31, 328–37.

Diener, E. and DuFour, D. (1978). Does television violence enhance program popularity? *Journal of Personality and Social Psychology*, 36, 333–41.

Dodge, K. A. (1980). Social cognition and children's aggressive behavior. *Child Development*, 51, 162–70.

Dodge, K. A. and Coie, J. D. (1987). Social-information-processing factors in reactive and proactive aggression in children's peer groups. *Journal of Personality and Social Psychology*, 53, 1146–58.

Dodge, K. A., Murphy, R. R. and Buchsbaum, K. (1984). The assessment of intention-cue detection skills in children: Implications for developmental psychopathology. *Child Development*, 55, 163–73.

Dollard, J., Doob, L. W., Miller, N. E., Mowrer, O. H. and Sears, R. R. (1939). *Frustration and Aggression*. New Haven, CT: Yale University Press.

Donnerstein, E. (1980). Aggressive erotica and violence against women. *Journal of Personality and Social Psychology*, 39, 269–77.

Donnerstein, E. (1984). Pornography: Its effects on violence against women. In N. Malamuth and E. Donnerstein (eds), *Pornography and Sexual Aggression*. New York: Academic Press, pp. 53–81.

Donnerstein, E. and Berkowitz, L. (1981). Victim reactions in aggressive erotic films as a factor in violence against women. *Journal of Personality and Social Psychology*, 41, 710–24.

Donnerstein, E. and Donnerstein, M. (1973). Variables in interracial aggression: Potential ingroup censure. *Journal of Personality and Social Psychology*, 27, 143–50.

Donnerstein, E. and Donnerstein, M. (1976). Research in the control of interracial aggression. In R. G. Geen and E. C. O'Neal (eds), *Perspectives on Aggression*. New York: Academic Press, pp. 133–68.

Donnerstein, E., Donnerstein, M. and Barrett, G. (1976). Where is the facilitation of media violence? The effects of nonexposure and placement of anger arousal. *Journal of Research in Personality*, 10, 386–98.

Donnerstein, E., Donnerstein, M., Simon, S. and Ditrichs, R. (1972). Variables in interracial aggression: Anonymity, expected retaliation, and a riot. *Journal of Personality and Social Psychology*, 22, 236–45.

Donnerstein E. and Wilson, D. W. (1976). The effects of noise and perceived control upon ongoing and subsequent aggressive behavior. *Journal of Personality and Social Psychology*, 34, 774–83.

Doob, A. N. (1970). Catharsis and aggression: The effect of hurting one's enemy. *Journal of Experimental Research in Personality*, 4, 291–6.

Doob, A. N. and Kirshenbaum, H. M. (1973). The effects on arousal of frustration and aggressive films. *Journal of Experimental Social Psychology*, 9, 57–64.

Doob, A. N. and Wood, L. E. (1972). Catharsis and aggression: Effects of annoyance and retaliation on aggressive behavior. *Journal of Personality and Social Psychology*, 22, 156–62.

Drabman, R. S. and Thomas, M. H. (1974). Does media violence increase children's toleration of real-life aggression? *Developmental Psychology*, 10, 418–21.

Duncan, B. L. (1976). Differential social perception and attribution of intergroup violence: Testing the lower limits of stereotyping of blacks. *Journal of Personality and Social Psychology*, 34, 590–8.

Duncan, P. and Hobson, G. N. (1977). Toward a definition of aggression. *Psychological Record*, 3, 545–53.

Eagly, A. H. and Steffen, F. J. (1986). Gender and aggressive behavior: A meta-analytic review of the social psychological literature. *Psychological Bulletin*, 100, 309–30.

Eastwood, L. (1985). Personality, intelligence, and personal space among violent and non-violent delinquents. *Personality and Individual Differences*, 6, 717–23.

Ebbesen, E. G., Duncan, B. and Konecni, V. J. (1975). Effects of content of verbal aggression on future verbal aggression. *Journal of Experimental Social Psychology*, 11, 192–204.

Edmunds, G. and Kendrick, D. (1980). *The Measurement of Human Aggressiveness*. Chichester, UK: Horwood.

Eibl-Eibesfeldt, I. (1977). Phylogenetic adaptation as determinants of aggressive behavior in man. In W. Hartup and J. DeWit (eds), *Origins of Aggression*. The Hague: Mouton, pp. 27–55.

Eisenberg, G. J. (1980). Children and aggression after observed film aggression with sanctioning adults. *Annals of the New York Academy of Science*, 347, 304–18.

Epstein, S. and Taylor, S. P. (1967). Instigation to aggression as a function of degree of defeat and perceived aggressive intent of the opponent. *Journal of Personality*, 35, 265–89.

Epstein, Y. M., Woolfolk, R. L. and Lehrer, P. M. (1981). Physiological, cognitive, and nonverbal responses to repeated exposure to crowding. *Journal of Applied Social Psychology*, 11, 1–13.

Eron, L. D. and Huesmann, L. R. (1980). Adolescent aggression and television. *Annals of the New York Academy of Science*, 347, 319–31.

Eron, L. D., Walder, L. O. and Lefkowitz, M. M. (1971). *Learning of Aggression in Children*. Boston: Little, Brown.

Evans, G. W. (1979). Behavioral and physiological consequences of crowding in humans. *Journal of Applied Social Psychology*, 9, 27–46.

Eysenck, S. B. G and Eysenck, H. J. (1972). The questionnaire measurement of psychoticism. *Psychology and Medicine*, 2, 50–5.

Feierabend, I. K. and Feierabend, R. L. (1972). Systemic conditions of political aggression: An application of frustration–aggression theory. In I. K. Feierabend, R. L. Feierabend and T. R. Gurr (eds), *Anger, Violence, and Politics*. Englewood Cliffs, NJ: Prentice-Hall, pp. 136–83.

Fenichel, O. (1945). *The Psychoanalytic Theory of Neurosis*. New York: Norton.

Fenigstein, A. (1979). Does aggression cause a preference for viewing media violence? *Journal of Personality and Social Psychology*, 37, 2307–17.

Ferguson, T. J. and Rule, B. G. (1980). Effects of inferential set, outcome severity, and basis for responsibility on children's evaluations of aggressive acts. *Developmental Psychology*, 16, 141–6.

Ferguson, T. J. and Rule, B. G. (1983). An attributional perspective on anger and aggression. In R. G. Geen and E. Donnerstein (eds), *Aggression: Theoretical and Empirical Reviews, Vol. 1: Theoretical and Methodological Issues*. New York: Academic Press, pp. 41–74.

Feshbach, N. D. and Feshbach, S. (1969). The relationship between empathy and aggression in two age groups. *Developmental Psychology*, 1, 102–7.

Feshbach, N. D. and Roe, K. (1968). Empathy in six and seven year olds. *Child Development*, 39, 133–45.

Feshbach, S. (1955). The drive-reducing function of fantasy behavior. *Journal of Abnormal and Social Psychology*, 50, 3–11.

Feshbach, S. (1961). The stimulating versus cathartic effects of a vicarious aggressive activity. *Journal of Abnormal and Social Psychology*, 63, 381–5.

Feshbach, S. (1964). The function of aggression and the regulation of aggressive drive. *Psychological Review*, 71, 257–72.

Feshbach, S. (1972). Reality and fantasy in filmed violence. In J. P. Murray, E. A. Rubinstein and G. A. Comstock (eds), *Television and Social Behavior, Volume 2: Television and Social Learning*. Washington, DC: United States Government Printing Office.

Feshbach, S. and Price, J. (1984). Cognitive competencies and aggressive behavior: A developmental study. *Aggressive Behavior*, 10, 185–200.

Feshbach, S., Stiles, W. B. and Bitter, E. (1967). The reinforcing effect of witnessing aggression. *Journal of Experimental Research in Personality*, 2, 133–9.

Flynn, J. P., Edwards, S. B. and Bandler, R. J. (1971). Changes in sensory and motor systems during centrally elicited attack. *Behavioral Science*, 16, 1–20.

Freedman, J. L. (1984). Effect of television violence on aggressiveness. *Psychological Bulletin*, 96, 227–46.

Freedman, J. L., Levy, A., Buchanan, R. and Price, J. (1972). Crowding and human aggressiveness. *Journal of Experimental Social Psychology*, 8, 528–48.

Freud, S. (1920/1959). *Beyond the Pleasure Principle*. New York: Bantam Books.

Freud, S. (1932/1963). Why war? In P. Rieff (ed.), *Freud: Character and Culture*. New York: Collier Books.

Frodi, A. (1976). Experiential and physiological processes mediating sex differences in behavioral aggression. *Psychological Reports*, 6, 113–14.

Frodi, A., Macaulay, J. and Thome, P. R. (1977). Are women always less aggressive than men? A review of the experimental literature. *Psychological Bulletin*, 84, 634–60.

Funkenstein, D. H., King, S. H. and Drolette, M. E. (1954). The direction of anger during a laboratory stress-inducing situation. *Psychosomatic Medicine*, 16, 404–13.

Geen, R. G. (1968). Effects of frustration, attack, and prior training in aggressiveness upon aggressive behavior. *Journal of Personality and Social Psychology*, 9, 316–21.

Geen, R. G. (1970). Perceived suffering of the victim as an inhibitor of attack-induced aggression. *Journal of Social Psychology*, 81, 209–15.

Geen, R. G. (1975). The meaning of observed violence: Real vs. fictional violence and consequent effects on aggression. *Journal of Research in Personality*, 9, 270–81.

Geen, R. G. (1978). Effects of attack and uncontrollable noise on aggression. *Journal of Research in Personality*, 12, 15–29.

Geen, R. G. (1981). Behavioral and physiological reactions to observed violence: Effects of prior exposure to aggressive stimuli. *Journal of Personality and Social Psychology*, 40, 868–75.

Geen, R. G. (1983). Aggression and television violence. In R. G. Geen and E. I. Donnerstein (eds), *Aggression: Theoretical and Empirical Reviews, Vol. 2: Issues in Research*. New York: Academic Press, pp. 103–25.

Geen, R. G. and Berkowitz, L. (1967), Some conditions facilitating the occurrence of aggression after the observation of violence. *Journal of Personality*, 35, 666–76.

Geen, R. G. and Donnerstein, E. I. (1983). A concluding comment. In R. G. Geen and E. I. Donnerstein (eds), *Aggression: Theoretical and Empirical Reviews, Vol. 1: Theoretical and Methodological Issues*, New York: Academic Press, pp. 247–9.

Geen, R. G. and McCown, E. J. (1984). Effects of noise and attack on aggression and physiological arousal. *Motivation and Emotion*, 8, 231–41.

Geen, R. G. and O'Neal, E. C. (1969). Activation of cue-elicited aggression by general arousal. *Journal of Personality and Social Psychology*, 11, 289–92.

Geen, R. G. and Pigg, R. (1970). Acquisition of an aggressive response and its generalization of verbal behavior. *Journal of Personality and Social Psychology*, **15**, 165–70.

Geen, R. G. and Stonner, D. (1971). Effects of aggressiveness habit strength on behavior in the presence of aggression-related stimuli. *Journal of Personality and Social Psychology*, **17**, 149–53.

Geen, R. G. and Stonner, D. (1972). The context of observed violence: Inhibition of aggression through displays of unsuccessful retaliation. *Psychonomic Science*, **27**, 342–4.

Geen, R. G. and Stonner, D. (1973). Context effects in observed violence. *Journal of Personality and Social Psychology*, **25**, 145–50.

Geen, R. G. and Stonner, D. (1974). The meaning of observed violence: Effects on arousal and aggressive behavior. *Journal of Research in Personality*, **8**, 55–63.

Geen, R. G., Stonner, D. and Shope, G. L. (1975). The facilitation of aggression by aggression: Evidence against the catharsis hypothesis. *Journal of Personality and Social Psychology*, **31**, 721–6.

Geen, R. G. and Thomas, S. L. (1986). The immediate effects of media violence on behavior. *Journal of Social Issues*, **42**, 7–27.

Genthner, R. W. and Taylor, S. P. (1973). Physical aggression as a function of racial prejudice and the race of the target. *Journal of Personality and Social Psychology*, **27**, 207–10.

Gentry, W. D. (1985). Relationship of anger-coping styles and blood pressure among black Americans. In M. A. Chesney and R. H. Rosenman (eds), *Anger and Hostility in Cardiovascular and Behavioral Disorders*. Washington, DC: Hemisphere, pp. 139–47.

Gentry, W. D., Chesney, A. P., Gary, H. E., Hall, R. P. and Harburg, E. (1982). Habitual anger-coping styles: I. Effect on mean blood pressure and risk for essential hypertension. *Psychosomatic Medicine*, **44**, 195–202.

Gerbner, G., Gross, L., Morgan, M. and Signiorelli, N. (1980). The "mainstreaming" of America: Violence profile no. 11. *Journal of Communication*, **30**(3), 10–29.

Gerbner, G., Gross, L., Morgan, M. and Signiorelli, N. (1982). Charting the mainstream: Television's contributions to political orientations. *Journal of Communication*, **32**, 100–27.

Gilmour, D. R. and Walkey, F. H. (1981). Identifying violent offenders using a video measure of interpersonal distance. *Journal of Consulting and Clinical Psychology*, **49**, 287–91.

Glass, D. C. (1977). *Behavior Patterns, Stress, and Coronary Disease*. Hillsdale, NJ: Erlbaum.

Glass, D. C. and Singer, J. E. (1972). *Urban Stress*. New York: Academic Press.

Goldstein, J. H. and Arms, R. L. (1971). Effects of observing athletic contests on hostility. *Sociometry*, **34**, 83–90.

Goldstein, J. H., Rosnow, R. L., Raday, T., Silverman, I. and Gaskell,

G. D. (1975). Punitiveness in response to films varying in content: A cross-national field study of aggression. *European Journal of Social Psychology*, 5, 149–65.

Goranson, R. E. (1970). Media violence and aggressive behavior: A review of experimental research. In L. Berkowitz (ed.), *Advances in Experimental Social Psychology, Vol. 5*. New York: Academic Press.

Green, M. R. (ed.) (1980). *Violence and the Family*. Washington, DC: American Association for the Advancement of Science.

Griffin, B. Q. and Rogers, R. W. (1977). Reducing interracial aggression: inhibiting effects of victim's suffering and power to retaliate. *Journal of Psychology*, 95, 151–7.

Griffitt, W. and Veitch, R. (1971). Hot and crowded: Influences of population density and temperature on interpersonal affective behavior. *Journal of Personality and Social Psychology*, 17, 92–8.

Groebel, J. and Krebs, D. (1983). A study of the effects of television on anxiety. In C. D. Spielberger and R. Diaz-Guerrero (eds), *Cross Cultural Anxiety, Vol. 2*. Washington, DC: Hemisphere, pp. 89–98.

Gunter, B. and Furnham, A. (1983). Personality and the perception of TV violence. *Personality and Individual Differences*, 4, 315–22.

Gurr, T. R. (1970). *Why Men Rebel*. Princeton, NJ: Princeton University Press.

Guttmann, A. (1983). Roman sports violence. In J. H. Goldstein (ed.), *Sports Violence*. New York: Springer-Verlag, pp. 7–19.

Harburg, E., Blakelock, E. H. and Roeper, P. J. (1979). Resentful and reflective coping with arbitrary authority and blood pressure: Detroit. *Psychosomatic Medicine*, 41, 189–202.

Harden, R. R. and Jacob, S. H. (1978). Differences in young children's expectations of women's and men's intervention in aggression. *Perceptual and Motor Skills*, 46, 1303–9.

Hardy, J. and Smith, T. W. (1987). Cynical hostility and vulnerability to disease: Social support, life stress, and physiological response to conflict. Unpublished manuscript, University of Utah.

Harries, K. D. and Stadler, S. J. (1983). Determinism revisited: Assault and heat stress in Dallas, 1980. *Environment and Behavior*, 15, 235–56.

Harris, R. E., Sokolow, M., Carpenter, L. G., Freedman, D. and Hunt, S. P. (1953). Response to psychological stress in persons who are potentially hypertensive. *Circulation*, 7, 874–9.

Harvey, M. D. and Rule, B. G. (1978). Moral evaluations and judgments of responsibility. *Personality and Social Psychology Bulletin*, 4, 583–8.

Haskins, R. (1985). Public school aggression among children with varying day-care experience. *Child Development*, 56, 689–703.

Hennigan, K. M., DelRosario, M. L., Heath, L., Cook, T. D., Wharton, J. D. and Calder, B. J. (1982). Impact of the introduction of television crime in the United States: Empirical findings and theoretical implications. *Journal of Personality and Social Psychology*, 42, 461–77.

Hildreth, A. M., Derogatis, L. R. and McCuster, K. (1971). Body buffer zone and violence: A reassessment and confirmation. *American Journal of Psychiatry*, **129**, 77–81.

Hokanson, J. E. (1961). The effect of frustration and anxiety on overt-aggression. *Journal of Abnormal and Social Psychology*, **62**, 346–51.

Hokanson, J. E. and Edelman, R. (1966). Effects of three social responses on vascular processes. *Journal of Personality and Social Psychology*, **3**, 442–7.

Hokanson, J. E. and Shetler, S. (1961). The effect of overt aggression on physiological arousal. *Journal of Abnormal and Social Psychology*, **63**, 446–8.

Hokanson, J. E., Willers, K. R. and Koropsak, E. (1968). The modification of autonomic responses during aggressive interchanges. *Journal of Personality*, **36**, 386–404.

Holmes, T. H. and Rahe, R. H. (1967). The social readjustment rating scale. *Journal of Psychosomatic Research*, **11**, 213–18.

Holt, R. R. (1970). On the interpersonal and intrapersonal consequences of expressing or not expressing anger. *Journal of Consulting and Clinical Psychology*, **35**, 8–12.

Hoppe, C. M. (1979). Interpersonal aggression as a function of subject's sex, subject's sex role identification, opponent's sex, and degree of provocation. *Journal of Personality*, **47**, 317–29.

Horton, R. W. and Santogrossi, D. A. (1978). The effect of adult commentary on reducing the influence of televised violence. *Personality and Social Psychology Bulletin*, **4**, 337–40.

Houston, B. K. (1983). Psychophysiological responsivity and the Type A behavior pattern. *Journal of Research in Personality*, **17**, 40–7.

Huesmann, L. R. (1982). Television violence and aggressive behavior. In D. Pearl, L. Bouthilet and J. Lazar (eds), *Television and Behavior: Ten Years of Scientific Progress and Implications for the Eighties, Vol. 2: Technical Reviews*. Washington, DC: United States Government Printing Office, pp. 126–37.

Huesmann, L. R. (1986a). Cross-national commonalities and differences in the effects of media violence on children. In L. R. Huesmann and L. D. Eron (eds), *Television and the Aggressive Child: A Cross-national Comparison*. Hillsdale, NJ: Erlbaum, pp. 239–57.

Huesmann, L. R. (1986b). Psychological processes promoting the relation between exposure to media violence and aggressive behavior by the viewer. *Journal of Social Issues*, **42**, 125–39.

Huesmann, L. R. and Eron, L. D. (1984). Cognitive processes and the persistence of aggressive behavior. *Aggressive Behavior*, **10**, 243–51.

Huesmann, L. R. and Eron, L. D. (eds) (1986). *Television and the Aggressive Child: A Cross-national Comparison*. Hillsdale, NJ: Erlbaum.

Huesmann, L. R., Eron, L. D., Lefkowitz, M. M. and Walder, L. O. (1984).

Stability of aggression over time and generations. *Developmental Psychology*, 20, 746–75.

Hutt, C. and Vaizey, M. J. (1966). Differential effects of group density on social behavior. *Nature*, 209, 1371–2.

Hyde, J. S. (1984). How large are gender differences in aggression? A developmental meta-analysis. *Developmental Psychology*, 20, 722–36.

Hynan, D. J. and Grush, J. E. (1986). Effects of impulsivity, depression, provocation, and time on aggressive behavior. *Journal of Research in Personality*, 20, 158–71.

Jacobs, P. A., Brunton, M., Melville, M. M., Brittain, R. P. and Mc-Clermont, W. F. (1965). Aggressive behaviour, mental sub-normality, and the XYY male. *Nature*, 208, 1351–2.

Jeavons, C. M. and Taylor, S. P. (1985). The control of alcohol-related aggression: Redirecting the inebriate's attention to socially appropriate conduct. *Aggressive Behavior*, 11, 93–101.

Johansson, G. G. (1981). Neural stimulation as a means for generating standardized threat under laboratory conditions. In P. F. Brain and D. Benton (eds), *Multidisciplinary Approaches to Aggression Research*. Amsterdam: Elsevier/North Holland, pp. 93–100.

Johnson, E. H., Spielberger, C. D., Worden, T. J. and Jacobs, G. A. (1987). Emotional and familial determinants of elevated blood pressure in black and white adolescent males. *Journal of Psychosomatic Research*, 31, 287–300.

Johnson, T. E. and Rule, B. G. (1986). Mitigating circumstance information, censure, and aggression. *Journal of Personality and Social Psychology*, 50, 537–42.

Jones, J. W. and Bogat, G. A. (1978). Air pollution and human aggression. *Psychological Reports*, 43, 721–2.

Joseph, J. M., Kane, T. R., Gaes, G. G. and Tedeschi, J. T. (1976). Effects of effort on attributed intent and perceived aggressiveness. *Perceptual and Motor Skills*, 42, 706.

Josephson, W. L. (1987). Television violence and children's aggression: Testing the priming, social script, and disinhibition predictions. *Journal of Personality and Social Psychology*, 53, 882–90.

Joy, L. A., Kimball, M. M. and Zabrack, M. L. (1986). Television and aggressive behavior. In T. M. Williams (ed.), *The Impact of Television: A Natural Experiment Involving Three Towns*. New York: Academic Press.

Kanner, A. D., Coyne, J. C., Schaefer, C. and Lazarus, R. S. (1981). Comparisons of two modes of stress measurement: Daily hassles and uplifts versus major life events. *Journal of Behavioral Medicine*, 4, 1–39.

Kaufmann, H. (1970). *Aggression and Altruism*. New York: Holt.

Kelly, J. F. and Hake, D. (1970). An extinction-induced increase in aggressive response with humans. *Journal of the Experimental Analysis of Behavior*, 14, 153–64.

Kenrick, D. T. and MacFarlane, S. W. (1986). Ambient temperature and horn honking: A field study of the heat/aggression relationship. *Environment and Behavior*, 18, 179–91.

Kessler, R. C. and Stipp, H. (1984). The impact of fictional television suicide stories on US fatalities: A replication. *American Journal of Sociology*, 90, 151–67.

Kinzel, A. F. (1970). Body buffer zone in violent prisoners. *American Journal of Psychiatry*, 127, 59–64.

Klein, M. W. (1969). Violence in American juvenile gangs. In D. J. Mulvihill and M. M. Tumin, *Crimes Violence: A Staff Report Submitted to the National Commission on the Causes and Prevention of Violence, Vol. 13*. Washington, DC: United States Government Printing Office, pp. 1427–60.

Konecni, V. J. and Doob, A. N. (1972). Catharsis through displacement of aggression. *Journal of Personality and Social Psychology*, 23, 378–87.

Krasner, L. and Ullmann, L. P. (1973). *Behavior Influence and Personality*. New York: Holt, Rinehart, and Winston.

Lagerspetz, K. (1979). Modification of aggressiveness in mice. In S. Feshbach and A. Fraczek (eds), *Aggression and Behavior Change*. New York: Praeger, pp. 66–82.

Lagerspetz, K., Wahlroos, C. and Wendelin, C. (1978). Facial expressions of pre-school children while watching televised violence. *Scandinavian Journal of Psychology*, 19, 213–22.

Lang, A. R., Goeckner, D. J., Adesso, V. J. and Marlatt, G. A. (1975). Effects of alcohol on aggression in male social drinkers. *Journal of Abnormal Psychology*, 84, 508–18.

Lang, P. J. (1979). A bio-informational theory of emotional imagery. *Psychophysiology*, 16, 495–512.

Lange, H., Mueller, C. and Donnerstein, E. (1979). The effects of social, spatial, and interference density on performance and mood. *Journal of Social Psychology*, 109, 283–7.

Larsen, K. S., Coleman, D., Forbes, J. and Johnson, R. (1972). Is the subject's personality or the experimental situation a better predictor of a subject's willingness to administer shock to a victim? *Journal of Personality and Social Psychology*, 22, 287–95.

Lazarus, R. S. and Folkman, S. (1984). *Stress, Appraisal and Coping*. New York: Springer-Verlag.

Le Bon, G. (1896). *The Crowd: A Study of the Popular Mind*. London: Ernest Benn.

Lefkowitz, M. M., Eron, L. D., Walder, L. O. and Huesmann, L. R. (1977). *Growing Up To Be Violent*. New York: Pergamon.

Leventhal, H. (1980). Toward a comprehensive theory of emotion. In L.

Berkowitz (ed.), *Advances in Experimental Social Psychology, Vol. 13*. New York: Academic Press, pp. 139–207.

Lewis, D. O., Moy, E., Jackson, L. D., Aaronson, R., Restifo, N., Serra, S. and Simos, A. (1985). Biopsychological characteristics of children who later murder: A prospective study. *American Journal of Psychiatry*, 142, 1161–7.

Leyens, J.-P., Herman, G. and Dunand, M. (1982). The influence of an audience upon the reactions to filmed violence. *European Journal of Social Psychology*, 12, 131–42.

Leyens, J.-P. and Parke, R. D. (1975). Aggressive slides can induce a weapons effect. *European Journal of Social Psychology*, 5, 229–36.

Leyens, J.-P. and Picus, S. (1973). Identification with the winner of a fight and name mediation: Their differential effects upon subsequent aggressive behavior. *British Journal of Social and Clinical Psychology*, 12, 374–7.

Loeber, R. and Dishion, T. J. (1984). Boys who fight at home and school: Family conditions influencing cross-setting consistency. *Journal of Consulting and Clinical Psychology*, 52, 759–68.

Loew, C. A. (1967). Acquisition of a hostile attitude and its relationship to aggressive behavior. *Journal of Personality and Social Psychology*, 5, 335–41.

Loo, C. M. (1972). The effects of spatial density on the social behavior of children. *Journal of Applied Social Psychology*, 2, 372–81.

Lorenz, K. (1966). *On Aggression*. New York: Harcourt Brace Jovanovich.

Maccoby, E. E. and Jacklin, C. N. (1974). *The Psychology of Sex Differences*. Stanford, CA: Stanford University Press.

Maccoby, E. E. and Jacklin, C. N. (1980). Sex differences in aggression: A rejoiner and reprise. *Child Development*, 51, 964–80.

MacDougall, J. M., Dembroski, T. M., Dimsdale, J. E. and Hackett, T. P. (1985). Components of Type A, hostility, and anger-in: Further relationships to angiographic findings. *Health Psychology*, 4, 137–52.

Malamuth, N. (1984). Aggression against women: Cultural and individual causes. In N. Malamuth and E. Donnerstein (eds), *Pornography and Sexual Aggression*. New York: Academic Press, pp. 19–52.

Malamuth, N. and Check, J. (1981). The effects of violent-sexual movies: A field experiment. *Journal of Research in Personality*, 15, 436–46.

Malamuth, N. and Check, J. (1983). Sexual arousal to rape depictions: Individual differences. *Journal of Abnormal Psychology*, 92, 55–67.

Malamuth, N. M. and Donnerstein, E. (eds) (1984). *Pornography and Sexual Aggression*. New York: Academic Press.

Mallick, S. K. and McCandless, B. R. (1966). A study of catharsis of aggression. *Journal of Personality and Social Psychology*, 4, 591–6.

Mandler, G. (1972). Helplessness: Theory and research in anxiety. In C. D. Spielberger (ed.), *Anxiety: Current Trends in Theory and Research, Vol. 2*. New York: Academic Press, pp. 363–74.

Manning, S. A. and Taylor, D. A. (1975). The effects of viewed violence and aggression: Stimulation and catharsis. *Journal of Personality and Social Psychology*, 31, 180–8.

Manstead, A. S. R. and Wagner, H. L. (1981). Arousal, cognition and emotion: An appraisal of two-factor theory. *Current Psychological Reviews*, 1, 35–54.

Marshall, G. D. and Zimbardo, P. G. (1979). Affective consequences of inadequately explained physiological arousal. *Journal of Personality and Social Psychology*, 37, 970–85.

Matthews, K. A., Glass, D. C., Rosenman, R. H. and Bortner, R. W. (1977). Competitive drive, Pattern A, and coronary heart disease: A further analysis of some data from the Western Collaborative Group Study. *Journal of Chronic Diseases*, 30, 489–98.

Matthews, K. A. and Haynes, S. G. (1986). Type A behavior pattern and coronary risk: Update and critical evaluation. *American Journal of Epidemiology*, 123, 923–60.

Matthews, R. W., Paulus, P. B. and Baron, R. A. (1979). Physical aggression after being crowded. *Journal of Nonverbal Behavior*, 4, 5–17.

McGurk, B. J., Davis, D. D. and Grehan, J. (1981). Assaultive behavior personality and personal space. *Aggressive Behavior*, 7, 317–24.

Megargee, E. I. (1966). Undercontrolled and overcontrolled personality types in extreme antisocial aggression. *Psychological Monographs*, 80(3).

Megargee, E. I. (1985). The dynamics of aggression and their application to cardiovascular disorders. In M. A. Chesney and R. H. Rosenman (eds), *Anger and Hostility in Cardiovascular and Behavioral Disorders*. Washington: Hemisphere, pp. 31–57.

Menninger, W. C. (1948). Recreation and mental health. *Recreation*, 42, 340–6.

Meyerscough, R. and Taylor, S. P. (1985). The effects of marijuana on human physical aggression. *Journal of Personality and Social Psychology*, 49, 1541–6.

Milgram, S. (1963). Behavioral study of obedience. *Journal of Abnormal and Social Psychology*, 67, 371–8.

Milgram, S. and Shotland, R. L. (1973). *Television and Antisocial Behavior: Field Experiments*. New York: Academic Press.

Miller, N. E. (1941). The frustration–aggression hypothesis. *Psychological Review*, 48, 337–42.

Mischel, W. (1968). *Personality and Assessment*. New York: Wiley.

Montagu, M. F. A. (ed.) (1973). *Man and Aggression*, 2nd edn. New York: Oxford University Press.

Moser, G. and Levy-Leboyer, C. (1985). Inadequate environment and situation control: Is a malfunctioning phone always an occasion for aggression? *Environment and Behavior*, 17, 520–33.

Moyer, K. E. (1976). *The Psychobiology of Aggression*. New York: Harper & Row.

Muecher, H. and Ungeheuer, H. (1961). Meteorological influence on reaction time, flicker-fusion frequency, job accidents, and medical treatment. *Perceptual and Motor Skills*, 12, 163–8.

Mueller, C. W. (1983). Environmental stressors and aggressive behavior. In R. G. Geen and E. I. Donnerstein (eds), *Aggression: Theoretical and Empirical Reviews, Vol. 2: Issues in Research*. New York: Academic Press, pp. 51–76.

Mulvihill, D. J. and Tumin, M. M. (1969). *Crimes Violence: A Staff Report Submitted to the National Commission on the Causes and Prevention of Violence*. Washington, DC: United States Government Printing Office.

Mummendey, A. and Mummendey, H. D. (1983). Aggressive behavior of soccer players as social interaction. In J. H. Goldstein (ed.), *Sports Violence*. New York: Springer-Verlag, pp. 111–28.

Mummendey, A., Linneweber, V. and Loschper, G. (1984). Actor or victim of aggression: Divergent perspectives – divergent evaluations. *European Journal of Social Psychology*, 14, 297–311.

Nasby, W., Hayden, B. and DePaulo, B. M. (1979). Attributional bias among aggressive boys to interpret unambiguous social stimuli as displays of hostility. *Journal of Abnormal Psychology*, 89, 459–68.

Nelson, S. A. (1980). Factors influencing young children's use of motives and outcomes as moral criteria. *Child Development*, 51, 823–9.

Ohbuchi, K. (1982). On the cognitive integration mediating reactions to attack patterns. *Social Psychology Quarterly*, 45, 213–18.

Ohbuchi, K. and Izutsu, T. (1984). Retaliation by male victims: Effects of physical attractiveness and intensity of attack of female attacker. *Personality and Social Psychology Bulletin*, 10, 216–24.

Ohbuchi, K. and Saito, M. (1986). Power imbalance, its legitimacy, and aggression. *Aggressive Behavior*, 12, 33–40.

O'Leary, M. R. and Dengerink, H. A. (1973). Aggression as a function of the intensity and pattern of attack. *Journal of Research in Personality*, 7, 61–70.

Olweus, D. (1979). Stability of aggressive reaction patterns in males: A review. *Psychological Bulletin*, 86, 852–75.

Olweus, D., Mattsson, A., Schalling, D. and Low, H. (1980). Testosterone, aggression, physical, and personality dimensions in normal adolescent males. *Psychosomatic Medicine*, 42, 253–69.

O'Neal, E. C., Brunault, M., Carifio, M., Troutwine, R. and Epstein, J. (1980). Effects of insult upon personal space preferences. *Journal of Nonverbal Behavior*, 5, 56–62.

O'Neal, E. C., Macdonald, P. J., Cloninger, C. and Levine, D. (1979). Coactor's behavior and imitative aggression. *Motivation and Emotion*, 3, 373–9.

Palamarek, D. L. and Rule, B. G. (1979). The effects of ambient temperature and insult on the motivation to retaliate or escape. *Motivation and Emotion*, 3, 83–92.

Parke, R. D., Berkowitz, L., Leyens, J.-P., West, S. G. and Sebastian, R. J. (1977). Some effects of violent and nonviolent movies on the behavior of juvenile delinquents. In L. Berkowitz (ed.), *Advances in Experimental Social Psychology, Vol. 10*. New York: Academic Press, pp. 135–71.

Parke, R. D. and Slaby, R. G. (1983). The development of aggression. In P. Mussen (ed.) *Handbook of Child Psychology*, 4th edn. New York: Wiley, pp. 547–642.

Patterson, A. H. (1974). Hostility catharsis: A naturalistic quasi-experiment. Paper presented to the annual convention of the American Psychological Association, New Orleans, LA.

Patterson, G. R. (1980). Mothers: The unacknowledged victims. *Monographs of the Society for Research in Child Development*, no. 45.

Patterson, G. R., Chamberlain, P. and Reid, J. B. (1982). A comparative evaluation of parent training procedures. *Behavior Therapy*, 13, 638–50.

Perry, D. G. and Perry, L. C. (1976). Identification with film characters, covert aggressive verbalization, and reactions to film violence. *Journal of Research in Personality*, 10, 399–409.

Phillips, D. P. (1974). The influence of suggestion on suicide: Substantive and theoretical implications of the Werther effect. *American Sociological Review*, 39, 340–54.

Phillips, D. P. (1977). Motor vehicle fatalities increase just after publicized suicide stories. *Science*, 196, 1464–5.

Phillips, D. P. (1978). Airplane accident fatalities increase just after stories about murder and suicide. *Science*, 201, 148–50.

Phillips, D. P. (1979). Suicide, motor vehicle fatalities, and the mass media: Evidence toward a theory of suggestion. *American Journal of Sociology*, 84, 1150–74.

Phillips, D. P. (1982). The impact of fictional television stories on US adult fatalities: New evidence on the effect of the mass media on violence. *American Journal of Sociology*, 87, 1340–59.

Phillips, D. P. (1983). The impact of mass media violence on US homicides. *American Sociological Review*, 48, 560–8.

Pihl, R. O., Zacchia, C. and Zeichner, A. (1982). Predicting levels of aggression after alcohol intake in men social drinkers: A preliminary investigation. *Journal of Studies on Alcohol*, 43, 599–602.

Pitkanen-Pulkinen, L. (1979). Self-control as a prerequisite for constructive behavior. In S. Feshbach and A. Fraczek (eds), *Aggression and Behavior Change: Biological and Social Processes*, New York: Praeger, pp. 250–70.

Pontius, A. A. (1984). Specific stimulus-evoked violent action in psychotic trigger reaction: A seizure-like imbalance between frontal lobe and limbic system? *Perceptual and Motor Skills*, **59**, 299–333.

Prentice-Dunn, S. and Rogers, R. W. (1983). Deindividuation in aggression. In R. G. Geen and E. I. Donnerstein (eds), *Aggression: Theoretical and Empirical Reviews, Vol. 2: Issues in Research*. New York: Academic Press, pp. 155–71.

Price, W. H. and Whatmore, P. B. (1967). Behavior disorders and pattern of crime among XYY males identified at a maximum security hospital. *British Medical Journal*, **1**, 533–6.

Quanty, M. B. (1976). Aggression catharsis: Experimental investigations and implications. In R. G. Geen and E. C. O'Neal (eds), *Perspectives on Aggression*. New York: Academic Press, pp. 99–132.

Rajecki, D. W. (1983). Animal aggression: Implications for human aggression. In R. G. Geen and E. Donnerstein (eds), *Aggression: Theoretical and Empirical Reviews, Vol. 1: Theoretical and Methodological Issues*. New York: Academic Press, pp. 189–211.

Reinisch, J. M. and Sanders, S. A. (1986). A test of sex differences in aggressive response to hypothetical conflict situations. *Journal of Personality and Social Psychology*, **50**, 1045–9.

Reisenzein, R. (1983). The Schachter theory of emotion: Two decades later. *Psychological Bulletin*, **94**, 239–64.

Renson, G. J., Adams, J. E. and Tinklenberg, J. R. (1978). Buss–Durkee assessment and validation with violent versus nonviolent chronic alcohol abusers. *Journal of Consulting and Clinical Psychology*, **46**, 360–1.

Rogers, R. W. (1983). Race variables in aggression. In R. G. Geen and E. Donnerstein (eds), *Aggression: Theoretical and Empirical Reviews, vol. 2: Issues in Research*. New York: Academic Press, pp. 27–50.

Rogers, R. W. and Prentice-Dunn, S. (1981). Deindividuation and anger-mediated interracial aggression: Unmasking regressive racism. *Journal of Personality and Social Psychology*, **41**, 63–73.

Rosenman, R. H. (1985). Health consequences of anger and implications for treatment. In M. A. Chesney and R. H. Rosenman (eds), *Anger and Hostility in Cardiovascular and Behavioral Disorders*. Washington, DC: Hemisphere, pp. 103–25.

Rosenman, R. H. and Chesney, M. A. (1982). Stress, Type A behavior and coronary disease. In L. Goldberger and S. Breznitz (eds), *The Handbook of Stress: Theoretical and Clinical Aspects*. New York: Macmillan, pp. 547–65.

Rotenberg, K. J. (1985). Causes, intensity, motives, and consequences of children's anger from self-reports. *Journal of Genetic Psychology*, **146**, 101–6.

Rotton, J. (1986). Determinism redux: Climate and cultural correlates of violence. *Environment and Behavior*, **18**, 346–68.

Rotton, J., Barry, T., Frey, J. and Soler, E. (1978). Air pollution and interpersonal attraction. *Journal of Applied Social Psychology*, 8, 57–71.

Rotton, J. and Frey, J. (1985). Air pollution, weather, and violent crimes: Concomitant time-series analysis of archival data. *Journal of Personality and Social Psychology*, 49, 1207–20.

Rotton, J., Frey, J., Barry, T., Milligan, M. and Fitzpatrick, M. (1979). The air pollution experience and physical aggression. *Journal of Applied Social Psychology*, 9, 397–412.

Rule, B. G. (1978). The hostile and instrumental functions of human aggression. In W. W. Hartup and J. DeWit (eds) *Origins of Aggression*. The Hague: Mouton, pp. 121–41.

Rule, B. G., Dyck, R., McAra, M. and Nesdale, A. R. (1975). Judgments of aggression serving personal versus prosocial purposes. *Social Behavior and Personality*, 3, 55–63.

Rule, B. G. and Nesdale, A. R. (1976). Emotional arousal and aggressive behavior. *Psychological Bulletin*, 83, 851–63.

Rule, B. G. and Percival, E. (1971). The effects of frustration and attack on physical aggression. *Journal of Experimental Research in Personality*, 5, 111–18.

Rule, B. G., Taylor, B. R. and Dobbs, A. R. (1987). Priming effects of heat on aggressive thoughts. *Social Cognition*, 5, 131–43.

Rushton, J. P., Fulker, D. W., Neale, M. C., Nias, D. K. B. and Eysenck, H. J. (1986). Altruism and aggression: The heritability of individual differences. *Journal of Personality and Social Psychology*, 50, 1192–8.

Ryan, E. D. (1970). The cathartic effect of vigorous motor activity on aggressive behavior. *Research Quarterly*, 41, 542–51.

Sallis, J. F., Johnson, C. C., Trevorrow, T. R., Kaplan, R. M. and Hovell, M. F. (1987). The relationship between cynical hostility and blood pressure reactivity. *Journal of Psychosomatic Research*, 31, 111–16.

Scarpetti, W. L. (1974). Autonomic concomitants of aggressive behavior in repressors and sensitizers: A social learning approach. *Journal of Personality and Social Psychology*, 30, 772–81.

Schachter, J. (1957). Pain, fear, and anger in hypertensives and normotensives. *Psychosomatic Medicine*, 19, 17–29.

Schachter, S. (1964). The interaction of cognitive and physiological determinants of emotional state. In L. Berkowitz (ed.), *Advances in experimental social psychology, Vol. 1*. New York: Academic Press, pp. 49–80.

Schachter, S. and Singer, J. (1962). Cognitive, social, and physiological determinants of emotional state. *Psychological Review*, 69, 379–99.

Scheier, M. F., Fenigstein, A. and Buss, A. H. (1974). Self-awareness and physical aggression. *Journal of Experimental Social Psychology*, 10, 264–73.

Schill, T. R. (1972). Aggression and blood pressure responses of high- and low-guilt subjects following frustration. *Journal of Consulting and Clinical Psychology*, 38, 461.

Schill, T. R. and Schneider, L. (1970). Relationships between hostility guilt and several measures of hostility. *Psychological Reports*, 27, 967–70.

Schmidt, D. E. and Keating, J. P. (1979). Human crowding and personal control: An integration of the research. *Psychological Bulletin*, 36, 680–700.

Schopler, J. and Stockdale, J. E. (1977). An interference analysis of crowding. *Environmental Psychology and Nonverbal Behavior*, 1, 81–8.

Selmanoff, M. and Ginsburg, B. E. (1981). Genetic variability in aggression and endocrine function in inbred strains of mice. In P. F. Brain and D. Benton (eds), *Multidisciplinary Approaches to Aggression Research*. Amsterdam: Elsevier/North Holland, pp. 247–68.

Shah, S. A. (1970). Report on the XYY chromosomal abnormality. *NIMH Conference Report*. Washington, DC: United States Government Printing Office.

Shantz, D. W. and Voydanoff, D. A. (1973). Situational effects on retaliatory aggression at three age levels. *Child Development*, 44, 149–53.

Shekelle, R. B., Gale, M., Ostfeld, A. M. and Paul, O. (1983). Hostility, risk of CHD, and mortality. *Psychosomatic Medicine*, 45, 109–14.

Sherrod, D. R. and Downs, R. (1974). Environmental determinants of altruism: The effects of stimulus overload and perceived control on helping. *Journal of Experimental Social Psychology*, 10, 468–79.

Shope, G. L., Hedrick, T. E. and Geen, R. G. (1978). Physical/verbal aggression: Sex differences in style. *Journal of Personality*, 46, 23–42.

Shortell, J., Epstein, S. and Taylor, S. P. (1970). Instigation to aggression as a function of degree of defeat and the capacity for massive retaliation. *Journal of Personality*, 38, 313–28.

Shuntich R. J. and Taylor, S. P. (1972). The effects of alcohol on human physical aggression. *Journal of Experimental Research in Personality*, 6, 34–8.

Siegman, A. W., Dembroski, T. M. and Ringel, N. (1987). Components of hostility and the severity of coronary artery disease. *Psychosomatic Medicine*, 49, 127–35.

Signiorelli, N., Gross, L. and Morgan, M. (1982). Violence in television programs: Ten years later. In D. Pearl, L. Bouthilet and J. Lazar (eds), *Television and Behavior: Ten Years of Scientific Progress and Implications for the Eighties, Vol. 2: Technical Reviews*. Washington, DC: US Department of Health and Human Services, pp. 158–73.

Singer, J. L. and Singer, D. G. (1981). *Television, Imagination, and Aggression: A Study of Preschoolers*. Hillsdale, NJ: Erlbaum.

Smith, M. D. (1976). Precipitants of crowd violence. *Sociological Inquiry*, 48, 121–31.

Smith, M. A. and Houston, B. K. (1987). Hostility, anger expression, cardiovascular responsivity, and social support. *Biological Psychology*, 24, 39–48.

Smith, T. W. and Frohm, K. D. (1985). What's so unhealthy about hostility? Construct validity and psychosocial correlates of the Cook and Medley Ho Scale. *Health Psychology*, 4, 503–20.

Sorrentino, R. M. and Higgins, E. T. (eds) (1986). *Handbook of Motivation and Cognition*. New York: Guilford.

Straus, M. A. (1980). A sociological perspective on the causes of family violence. In M. R. Green (ed.), *Violence and the Family*. Washington, DC: American Association for the Advancement of Science.

Straus, M. A., Gelles, R. J. and Steinmetz, S. K. (1980). *Behind Closed Doors: Violence in the American Family*. New York: Anchor Press.

Strube, M. J., Turner, C. W., Cervo, D., Stevens, J. and Hinchey, F. (1984). Interpersonal aggression and the Type A coronary-prone behavior pattern. A theoretical distinction and practical implications. *Journal of Personality and Social Psychology*, 47, 839–47.

Taylor, S. P. and Epstein, S. (1967). Aggression as a function of the interaction of the sex of the aggressor and the sex of the victim. *Journal of Personality*, 35, 474–86.

Taylor, S. P. and Gammon, C. B. (1975). Effects of type and dose of alcohol on human physical aggression. *Journal of Personality and Social Psychology*, 32, 169–75.

Taylor, S. P. and Gammon, C. B. (1976). Aggressive behavior of intoxicated subjects: The effect of third-party intervention. *Journal of Studies on Alcohol*, 37, 917–30.

Taylor, S. P., Gammon, C. B. and Capasso, D. R. (1976). Aggression as a function of alcohol and threat. *Journal of Personality and Social Psychology*, 34, 938–41.

Taylor, S. P. and Leonard, K. E. (1983). Alcohol and human physical aggression. In R. G. Geen and E. Donnerstein (eds), *Aggression: Theoretical and Empirical Reviews, Vol. 2: Issues in research*. New York: Academic Press, pp. 77–101.

Tedeschi, J. T. (1983). Social influence theory and aggression. In R. G. Geen and E. Donnerstein (eds), *Aggression: Theoretical and Empirical Reviews, Vol. 1: Theoretical and Methodological Issues*. New York: Academic Press, pp. 135–62.

Theorell, T. and Rahe, R. H. (1972). Behavior and life satisfaction characteristics of Swedish subjects with myocardial infarction. *Journal of Chronic Diseases*, 25, 139–47.

Thomas, M. H. and Drabman, R. S. (1975). Toleration of real life aggression as a function of exposure to televised violence and age of subject. *Merrill-Palmer Quarterly*, 21, 227–32.

Thomas, M. H. and Drabman, R. S. (1978). Effects of television violence on expectations of others' aggression. *Personality and Social Psychology Bulletin*, 4, 73–6.

Thomas, M. H., Horton, R. W., Lippincott, E. C. and Drabman, R. S. (1977). Desensitization to portrayals of real-life aggression as a function of exposure to television violence. *Journal of Personality and Social Psychology*, 35, 450–8.

Thomas, M. H. and Tell, P. M. (1974). Effects of viewing real versus fantasy violence upon interpersonal aggression. *Journal of Research in Personality*, 8, 153–60.

Tieger, T. (1980). On the biological basis of sex differences in aggression. *Child Development*, 51, 943–63.

Toch, H. (1969). *Violent Men: An Inquiry into the Psychology of Violence*. Chicago: Aldine.

Tulving, E. and Thomson, D. M. (1973). Encoding specificity and retrieval processes in episodic memory. *Psychological Review*, 80, 352–73.

Turner, C. W. and Berkowitz, L. (1972). Identification with film aggressor (covert role taking) and reactions to film violence. *Journal of Personality and Social Psychology*, 21, 256–64.

Turner, C. W. and Goldsmith, D. (1976). Effects of toy guns on children's anti-social free play behavior. *Journal of Experimental Child Psychology*, 21, 303–15.

Turner, C. W., Layton, J. P. and Simons, L. S. (1975). Naturalistic studies of aggressive behaviour: Aggessive stimuli, victim visibility, and horn honking. *Journal of Personality and Social Psychology*, 31, 1098–107.

Vasta, R. and Copitch, P. (1981). Simulating conditions of child abuse in the laboratory. *Child Development*, 52, 164–70.

Virkkunen, M. (1986). Insulin secretion during the glucose tolerance test among habitually violent and impulsive offenders. *Aggressive Behavior*, 12, 303–10.

Walker, I. and Mann, L. (1987). Unemployment, relative deprivation, and social protest. *Personality and Social Psychology Bulletin*, 13, 275–83.

Walker, I. and Pettigrew, T. F. (1984). Relative deprivation theory: An overview and conceptual critique. *British Journal of Social Psychology*, 23, 301–10.

Walster, E., Walster, G. W. and Berscheid, E. (1978). *Equity: Theory and Research*. Boston: Allyn & Bacon.

Weidner, G., Sexton, G., McLellarn, R., Connor, S. L. and Matarazzo, J. D. (1987). The role of Type A behavior and hostility in an elevation of plasma lipids in adult women and men. *Psychosomatic Medicine*, 49, 136–45.

Welch, S. and Booth, A. (1975). The effect of crowding on aggression. *Sociological Symposium*, 14, 105–27.

Wheeler, L. and Caggiula, A. R. (1966). The contagion of aggression. *Journal of Experimental Social Psychology*, 2, 1–10.

White, J. W. (1983). Sex and gender issues in aggression research. In R. G. Geen and E. Donnerstein (eds), *Aggression: Theoretical and Empirical*

*Reviews, Vol. 2: Issues in Research.* New York: Academic Press, pp. 1–26.

Whiting, B. and Edwards, C. P. (1973). A cross-cultural analysis of sex differences in the behavior of children aged 3 through 11. *Journal of Social Psychology*, 91, 171–88.

Wicklund, R. A. (1975). Objective self-awareness. In L. Berkowitz (ed.), *Advances in Experimental Social Psychology, Vol. 8.* New York: Academic Press, pp. 233–75.

Williams, R. B., Jr, Haney, T. L., Lee, K. L., Kong, Y., Blumenthal, J. A. and Whalen, R. E. (1980). Type A behavior, hostility, and coronary atherosclerosis. *Psychosomatic Medicine*, 42, 539–49.

Williams, T. M., Zabrack, M. L. and Joy, L. A. (1982). The portrayal of aggression on North American television. *Journal of Applied Social Psychology*, 12, 360–80.

Wilson, L. and Rogers, R. W. (1975). The fire this time: Effects of race of target, insult, and potential retaliation on black aggression. *Journal of Personality and Social Psychology*, 32, 857–64.

Winslow, C. and Brainerd, J. (1950). A comparison of reaction of whites and Negroes to frustration as measured by the Rosenzweig Picture-Frustration Test. *American Psychologist*, 5, 297.

Witkin, H. A., Mednick, S. A., Schulsinger, F., Bakkestrom, E., Christiansen, K. O., Goodenough, D. R., Hirschhorn, K., Lundsteen, C., Owen, D. R., Philip, J., Rubin, D. B. and Stocking, M. (1976). Criminality in XYY and XXY men. *Science*, 193, 547–55.

Wolf, S. and Wolff, H. G. (1951). A summary of experimental evidence relating life stress to the pathogenesis of essential hypertension in man. In E. T. Bell (ed.), *Hypertension.* Minneapolis: University of Minnesota Press.

Wolfgang, M. and Ferracuti, F. (1967). *The Subculture of Violence: Toward an Integrated Theory of Criminality.* London: Tavistock.

Wolfgang, M. and Strohm, R. B. (1956). The relationship between alcohol and criminal homicide. *Quarterly Journal of Studies on Alcohol*, 17, 411–25.

Worchel, S. and Teddlie, C. (1976). The experience of crowding: A two-factor theory. *Journal of Personality and Social Psychology*, 34, 30–40.

Wyer, R. S., Weatherly, D. A. and Terrell, G. (1965). Social role, aggression, and academic achievement. *Journal of Personality and Social Psychology*, 1, 645–9.

Zillmann, D. (1971). Excitation transfer in communication-mediated aggressive behavior. *Journal of Experimental Social Psychology*, 7, 419–34.

Zillmann, D. (1978). Attribution and misattribution of excitatory reactions. In J. H. Harvey, W. J. Ickes and R. F. Kidd (eds), *New Directions in Attribution Research, Vol. 2.* Hillsdale, NJ: Erlbaum, pp. 335–68.

Zillmann, D. (1983). Arousal and aggression. In R. G. Geen and E. Donnerstein (eds), *Aggression: Theoretical and Empirical Reviews, Vol. 1: Theoretical and Methodological Issues.* New York: Academic Press, pp. 75–101.

Zillmann, D., Baron, R. A. and Tamborini, R. (1981). Social costs of smoking: Effects of tobacco smoke on hostile behavior. *Journal of Applied Social Psychology,* 11, 548–61.

Zillmann, D. and Cantor, J. R. (1976). Effect of timing of information about mitigating circumstances on emotional responses to provocation and retaliatory behavior. *Journal of Experimental Social Psychology,* 12, 38–55.

Zillmann, D., Johnson, R. C. and Hanrahan, J. (1973). Pacifying effect of happy ending of communications involving aggression. *Psychological Reports,* 32, 967–70.

Zillmann, D., Katcher, A. H. and Milavsky, B. (1972). Excitation transfer from physical exercise to subsequent aggressive behavior. *Journal of Experimental Social Psychology,* 8, 247–59.

Zimbardo, P. G. (1970). The human choice: Individuation, reason, and order versus deindividuation, impulse and chaos. In W. J. Arnold and D. Levine (eds), *Nebraska Symposium on Motivation.* Lincoln: University of Nebraska Press.

# AUTHOR INDEX

# SUBJECT INDEX